α-23-84

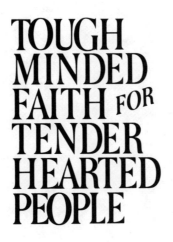

TOUGH
MINDED
FAITH FOR
TENDER
HEARTED
PEOPLE

TOUGH MINDED FAITH FOR TENDER HEARTED PEOPLE

ROBERT H. SCHULLER

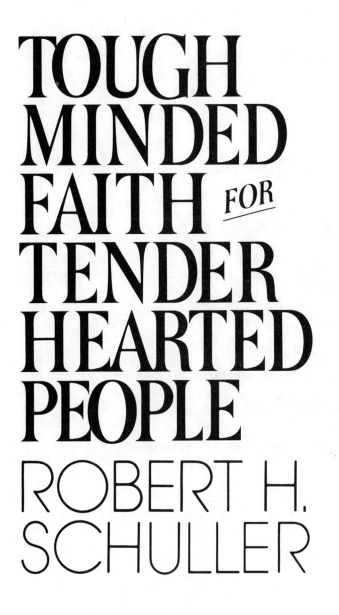

Publishers since 1798

Thomas Nelson Publishers
Nashville • Camden • New York

Scripture quotations in this publication are from THE NEW KING JAMES VER-
SION. Copyright © 1979, 1980, 1982, Thomas Nelson, Inc., Publishers.

Published in Nashville, Tennessee, by Thomas Nelson, Inc. and distributed in
Canada by Lawson Falle, Ltd., Cambridge, Ontario.

Printed in the United States of America.

Library of Congress Cataloging in Publication Data

Schuller, Robert Harold.
   Tough-minded faith for tender-hearted people.

   1. Faith—Meditations.   I. Title.
BV4637.S33   1983   242'.2   83-22144
ISBN 0-8407-5358-6

To

*the thousands of good people
who believe in me enough
to encourage me with
their prayers and support
—even though we may never
have a chance to meet
face to face.*

Acknowledgments

It is with profound gratitude that I acknowledge the editorial help of my wife, Arvella. Somehow she managed to take 2,000 of my written pages and condense them into 366 pages! I cannot count the number of days she arose in the dark of the early morning to tackle this editorial project. Then additional thanks goes to my daughters Sheila Coleman and Jeanne Dunn, both of whom worked so closely and creatively with Mrs. Schuller in improving my work.

This book has been a joyful family project. Both my wife and daughters understand this subject so well. We are one in heart and mind, because we have walked this walk of faith as a successful family for so many years.

Contents

 1. Faith is . . . Trusting the unprovable
 2. Faith is . . . Dreaming God's dream
 3. Faith is . . . Breathing your native air
 4. Faith is . . . Wanting more out of life
 5. Faith is . . . Doubting your doubts
 6. Faith is . . . Surfing on the waves
 7. Faith is . . . Batting all alone
 8. Faith is . . . Sitting in the front row
 9. Faith is . . . Angling for the catch
10. Faith is . . . Knocking down the high bar
11. Faith is . . . Whistling in the dark
12. Faith is . . . Stepping on the scale
13. Faith is . . . Expanding the base
14. Faith is . . . Shooting for the moon
15. Faith is . . . Splicing the gene
16. Faith is . . . Probing for answers
17. Faith is . . . Becoming normal
18. Faith is . . . Integrating yourself
19. Faith is . . . Discovering your natural habitat
20. Faith is . . . Thinking God's thoughts
21. Faith is . . . Praying for guidance
22. Faith is . . . Setting a goal
23. Faith is . . . Charting the course
24. Faith is . . . Believing I will make it
25. Faith is . . . Scanning the horizon
26. Faith is . . . Possibilitizing
27. Faith is . . . Assuming "it is possible"
28. Faith is . . . Viewing success positively
29. Faith is . . . Fearing failure courageously
30. Faith is . . . Risking failure bravely
31. Faith is . . . Defusing the fear of failure
32. Faith is . . . Scoring in the first round!
33. Faith is . . . Expecting to succeed
34. Faith is . . . Drawing mental pictures
35. Faith is . . . Announcing your intentions

36. Faith is . . . Getting excited about succeeding
37. Faith is . . . Allowing for the impossibles
38. Faith is . . . Aiming to achieve the best
39. Faith is . . . Verbalizing victory
40. Faith is . . . Unlocking your positive emotional powers
41. Faith is . . . Plunging before you are positive
42. Faith is . . . Deciding to begin
43. Faith is . . . Entering the contest
44. Faith is . . . Leaving your ruts
45. Faith is . . . Committing to action
46. Faith is . . . Inking the agreement
47. Faith is . . . Imagining the positive possibilities
48. Faith is . . . Initiating positive action
49. Faith is . . . Assuring yourself of success
50. Faith is . . . Arranging to arrive
51. Faith is . . . Desiring to arrive
52. Faith is . . . Complimenting yourself every day
53. Faith is . . . Educating your mind
54. Faith is . . . Auditioning your ambitions
55. Faith is . . . Underscoring your positive thoughts
56. Faith is . . . Adopting an orphan
57. Faith is . . . Tuning into positive thoughts
58. Faith is . . . Filtering the thoughts
59. Faith is . . . Minding the storehouse of the mind
60. Faith is . . . Imprinting the self-conscious mind
61. Faith is . . . Censoring the negatives
62. Faith is . . . Starving your enemies
63. Faith is . . . Washing the windows of the mind
64. Faith is . . . Mining the deeper thoughts
65. Faith is . . . Tolerating your imperfections
66. Faith is . . . Deprogramming your computer
67. Faith is . . . Programming your computer for success
68. Faith is . . . Supposing—positively
69. Faith is . . . Experiencing impossibilities
70. Faith is . . . Rising above depressing situations
71. Faith is . . . Scaling the wall
72. Faith is . . . Dividing to conquer
73. Faith is . . . Challenging the negative judgment
74. Faith is . . . Analyzing inquisitively
75. Faith is . . . Actualizing your positive fantasies
76. Faith is . . . Stretching your imagination
77. Faith is . . . Managing to achieve the impossible
78. Faith is . . . Planning to solve unsolvable problems
79. Faith is . . . Pursuing your objective relentlessly
80. Faith is . . . Splurging in possibilities
81. Faith is . . . Making daring decisions
82. Faith is . . . Snapping the trap
83. Faith is . . . Peeling the orange
84. Faith is . . . Stepping out of line
85. Faith is . . . Flying with an unknown pilot

86. Faith is . . . Adventuring into new territories
87. Faith is . . . Liberating your creative powers
88. Faith is . . . Advancing with boldness
89. Faith is . . . Stimulating positive emotions
90. Faith is . . . Agreeing to advance
91. Faith is . . . Escalating your expectations
92. Faith is . . . Declaring your positive intentions
93. Faith is . . . Talking positive talk
94. Faith is . . . Patting yourself on the back
95. Faith is . . . Exercising enthusiasm always
96. Faith is . . . Exaggerating enthusiastically
97. Faith is . . . Fortifying yourself
98. Faith is . . . Upgrading my standards
99. Faith is . . . Improving yourself constantly
100. Faith is . . . Welcoming a new day
101. Faith is . . . Grabbing the magic moment
102. Faith is . . . Delighting in discovery
103. Faith is . . . Alerting myself to the good in the "now"
104. Faith is . . . Taking a chance on tomorrow
105. Faith is . . . Trusting in tomorrow
106. Faith is . . . Celebrating the unknown
107. Faith is . . . Facing the future unafraid
108. Faith is . . . Timing your move
109. Faith is . . . Rescheduling your timetable
110. Faith is . . . Revising your schedule
111. Faith is . . . Recognizing the reality of miracles
112. Faith is . . . Designing for survival
113. Faith is . . . Feasting on the beautiful
114. Faith is . . . Acquiring an appetite for beauty
115. Faith is . . . Adorning your mind with beauty
116. Faith is . . . Detailing for excellence
117. Faith is . . . Specifying the details
118. Faith is . . . Weaving a beautiful pattern
119. Faith is . . . Cutting the cloth
120. Faith is . . . Mixing the recipe
121. Faith is . . . Smelling the flowers
122. Faith is . . . Plowing the ground
123. Faith is . . . Planting the seed
124. Faith is . . . Watering the tender shoots
125. Faith is . . . Fertilizing the plants
126. Faith is . . . Pruning the trees
127. Faith is . . . Harvesting the crop
128. Faith is . . . Developing progressively
129. Faith is . . . Mapping out the trip
130. Faith is . . . Disciplining yourself to succeed
131. Faith is . . . Energizing your body
132. Faith is . . . Climbing your way up and out
133. Faith is . . . Checking in before anybody else
134. Faith is . . . Prioritizing your possibilities
135. Faith is . . . Chipping away at the block

136. Faith is . . . Chiseling away at the mountain
137. Faith is . . . Positioning yourself in the marketplace
138. Faith is . . . Evolving upward
139. Faith is . . . Pacing your progress
140. Faith is . . . Triple-checking your position
141. Faith is . . . Narrowing the path
142. Faith is . . . Maintaining equilibrium
143. Faith is . . . Comparing the values
144. Faith is . . . Bottom lining
145. Faith is . . . Maneuvering your way skillfully
146. Faith is . . . Buckling your safety belt
147. Faith is . . . Scouting the territory
148. Faith is . . . Creating new products and services
149. Faith is . . . Competing constructively
150. Faith is . . . Tapping the untapped possibilities
151. Faith is . . . Spiraling your way upward
152. Faith is . . . Redoubling the effort
153. Faith is . . . Redoing the job
154. Faith is . . . Staying with it
155. Faith is . . . Forsaking ease and comfort
156. Faith is . . . Paying the high price gladly
157. Faith is . . . Striving for excellence
158. Faith is . . . Stretching the mileage
159. Faith is . . . Phasing in—phasing out—phasing up
160. Faith is . . . Moving ahead step by step
161. Faith is . . . Projecting future growth
162. Faith is . . . Growing with tomorrow's possibilities
163. Faith is . . . Exploring all possible alternatives
164. Faith is . . . Applying old principles to new situations
165. Faith is . . . Negotiating your way forward
166. Faith is . . . Accommodating yourself to others
167. Faith is . . . Sharing the power
168. Faith is . . . Teaming up
169. Faith is . . . Delegating good jobs to others
170. Faith is . . . Assimilating fresh opinions
171. Faith is . . . Hiring smarter people
172. Faith is . . . Listening to wise counsel
173. Faith is . . . Clarifying expectations
174. Faith is . . . Removing growth-restricting obstacles
175. Faith is . . . Following the positive voices
176. Faith is . . . Sorting things out optimistically
177. Faith is . . . Reading the good between the lines
178. Faith is . . . Resolving conflicts creatively
179. Faith is . . . Fixing problems
180. Faith is . . . Inventing solutions
181. Faith is . . . Negotiating your way around obstacles
182. Faith is . . . Catching the blame
183. Faith is . . . Allowing for error
184. Faith is . . . Hearing what your critics say about you
185. Faith is . . . Changing your mind

186. Faith is . . . Learning from past mistakes
187. Faith is . . . Congratulating your competitors
188. Faith is . . . Swallowing your hurts
189. Faith is . . . Sensing success in dark times
190. Faith is . . . Marching on—nevertheless
191. Faith is . . . Insulating against the negatives
192. Faith is . . . Reversing a negative situation
193. Faith is . . . Putting up with the disagreeable
194. Faith is . . . Riding wild horses
195. Faith is . . . Gambling God's way
196. Faith is . . . Encountering opposition positively
197. Faith is . . . Rejecting negative advice
198. Faith is . . . Separating yourself from negative pressures
199. Faith is . . . Utilizing suspicion positively
200. Faith is . . . Reacting positively to a negative situation
201. Faith is . . . Burying old grudges
202. Faith is . . . Coping creatively
203. Faith is . . . Smiling—anyway
204. Faith is . . . Absorbing jolts naturally
205. Faith is . . . Manipulating the rough course
206. Faith is . . . Bearing your cross—constructively
207. Faith is . . . Keeping on—anyway
208. Faith is . . . Thanking God always
209. Faith is . . . Playing it down
210. Faith is . . . Praying it up
211. Faith is . . . Praising God anyway
212. Faith is . . . Biting the bullet
213. Faith is . . . Turning pain into gain
214. Faith is . . . Surviving against all odds
215. Faith is . . . Sublimating your sorrow
216. Faith is . . . Polishing the silver lining
217. Faith is . . . Waiting for a breakthrough
218. Faith is . . . Adding up your assets
219. Faith is . . . Counting your blessings
220. Faith is . . . Coming back after defeat
221. Faith is . . . Reconstructing after ruin
222. Faith is . . . Awaiting your turn—especially after crushing
disappointments
223. Faith is . . . Regrouping after a setback
224. Faith is . . . Redeeming a lost cause
225. Faith is . . . Bouncing back after failure
226. Faith is . . . Saving the broken pieces
227. Faith is . . . Elevating your hopes
228. Faith is . . . Opening yourself to new opportunities
229. Faith is . . . Laminating the life for strength
230. Faith is . . . Filling the tank
231. Faith is . . . Bracing yourself against the storms
232. Faith is . . . Focusing on God's power
233. Faith is . . . Connecting with power sources
234. Faith is . . . Relaxing under pressure

235. Faith is . . . Dissolving anxieties
236. Faith is . . . Replacing worry with hope
237. Faith is . . . Leaning back with casual confidence
238. Faith is . . . Comparing conditions and choices
239. Faith is . . . Framing your awards
240. Faith is . . . Relying on your source
241. Faith is . . . Exposing your colors
242. Faith is . . . Choosing the best option
243. Faith is . . . Opting for the optimum
244. Faith is . . . Harmonizing your inner self
245. Faith is . . . Sacrificing your arrogance
246. Faith is . . . Admitting your inadequacies
247. Faith is . . . Waving at a mystery
248. Faith is . . . Surmising with the soul
249. Faith is . . . Preempting the negatives
250. Faith is . . . Considering all possible resources
251. Faith is . . . Repenting the positive way
252. Faith is . . . Converting to belief in God
253. Faith is . . . Trusting a stranger
254. Faith is . . . Going home after sinning
255. Faith is . . . Returning to my spiritual homeland
256. Faith is . . . Confessing your sins
257. Faith is . . . Asking for forgiveness
258. Faith is . . . Wiping the slate clean
259. Faith is . . . Forgetting your forgiven sins
260. Faith is . . . Yielding yourself to God
261. Faith is . . . Overcoming all fears
262. Faith is . . . Quieting the storm
263. Faith is . . . Bonding a friendship
264. Faith is . . . Ruling out disqualification
265. Faith is . . . Trading off anxiety for peace
266. Faith is . . . Displaying the flag
267. Faith is . . . Going out without looking in a mirror
268. Faith is . . . Sustaining your self-esteem
269. Faith is . . . Broadcasting good news
270. Faith is . . . Forming a partnership
271. Faith is . . . Linking up with winners
272. Faith is . . . Aligning yourself with positive people
273. Faith is . . . Combining contradictions creatively
274. Faith is . . . Drinking from new wells
275. Faith is . . . Perceiving the worlds around you
276. Faith is . . . Adapting yourself to the unfamiliar
277. Faith is . . . Relating respectfully to "foreigners"
278. Faith is . . . Discriminating against prejudices
279. Faith is . . . Disengaging yourself from destructive
              prejudices
280. Faith is . . . Tearing down the walls
281. Faith is . . . Inquiring into scientific reality
282. Faith is . . . Liberating people
283. Faith is . . . Gazing into the eyes of a stranger

284. Faith is . . . Countering the negative with a positive
285. Faith is . . . Bridging the gap
286. Faith is . . . Respecting persons after you know them
287. Faith is . . . Hugging in-laws
288. Faith is . . . Forgiving yourself and others
289. Faith is . . . Questioning respectfully
290. Faith is . . . Anticipating the best
291. Faith is . . . Loving the unlovable
292. Faith is . . . Pleasing God
293. Faith is . . . Centering yourself in God's love
294. Faith is . . . Finding a need and filling it
295. Faith is . . . Channeling Christ's love
296. Faith is . . . Touching someone you don't know
297. Faith is . . . Bailing out a friend
298. Faith is . . . Soliciting help for a great cause
299. Faith is . . . Priming the pump
300. Faith is . . . Filling someone else's cup
301. Faith is . . . Casting your bread upon the waters
302. Faith is . . . Lighting one candle
303. Faith is . . . Applauding the positive projects
304. Faith is . . . Adjusting your attitude toward the community
305. Faith is . . . Winning friends and influencing people
306. Faith is . . . Socializing with a purpose
307. Faith is . . . Mending broken fences
308. Faith is . . . Explaining your position diplomatically
309. Faith is . . . Communicating effectively
310. Faith is . . . Cleaning up our environment
311. Faith is . . . Quilting the scraps
312. Faith is . . . Pyramiding your success
313. Faith is . . . Painting yourself into a corner
314. Faith is . . . Splitting the diamond
315. Faith is . . . Giving before receiving
316. Faith is . . . Pledging support
317. Faith is . . . Tithing your income
318. Faith is . . . Merging to make miracles
319. Faith is . . . Wading into deeper water
320. Faith is . . . Striking water in the desert
321. Faith is . . . Walking on the water
322. Faith is . . . Hypnotizing yourself positively
323. Faith is . . . Transcending the present plane
324. Faith is . . . Swimming upstream
325. Faith is . . . Confessing openly your inner convictions
326. Faith is . . . Teaching someone to think
327. Faith is . . . Seasoning life around you
328. Faith is . . . Inching ahead
329. Faith is . . . Steering a steady course
330. Faith is . . . Soldiering the battle
331. Faith is . . . Undergoing to be an overcomer
332. Faith is . . . Following through—anyway

333. Faith is . . . Laughing up a storm
334. Faith is . . . Compromising on trivialities
335. Faith is . . . Knowing it can be done
336. Faith is . . . Renting with option to buy
337. Faith is . . . Analyzing the obstructions
338. Faith is . . . Daring to fail
339. Faith is . . . Advertising your abilities
340. Faith is . . . Hammering the nails
341. Faith is . . . Standing up to be counted
342. Faith is . . . Embracing God's grace
343. Faith is . . . Glorifying God with great victories
344. Faith is . . . Pressing the wrinkles
345. Faith is . . . Sculpting your spirit
346. Faith is . . . Grandfathering my hopes
347. Faith is . . . Surrendering to love
348. Faith is . . . Singing a new song
349. Faith is . . . Retiring from retirement
350. Faith is . . . Looking forward with hope
351. Faith is . . . Spotting the hidden potential
352. Faith is . . . Living without insurance
353. Faith is . . . Abandoning all fears
354. Faith is . . . Enduring all the way
355. Faith is . . . Compromising before quitting
356. Faith is . . . Bowing out gracefully
357. Faith is . . . Facing death unafraid
358. Faith is . . . Immortalizing yourself—forever
359. Faith is . . . Parting company hopefully
360. Faith is . . . Impressing others
361. Faith is . . . Preparing to live to be one hundred
362. Faith is . . . Renewing your strength
363. Faith is . . . Shielding, fielding, and wielding
364. Faith is . . . Starting and then starting over and over again
365. Faith is . . . Admiring what works
366. Faith is . . . Leaping into the unknown

Introduction

"Of course you can! It's possible! All you do is start and take one step at a time," the guide in the Cologne Cathedral said, encouraging Mrs. Schuller and me to take the challenging climb inside the tower. "It'll be worthwhile—I guarantee you," he promised, continuing, "the thrill of making it to the top is fantastic!" He kept nudging us on: "Come on, it's just one step, then the second, then the third, and before you know it, if you don't quit, you'll have a few hundred behind you, and you will make it! And you will never forget it!"

How right he was. "One step at a time." And we did it! The view was sensational. The ecstasy of achievement still stirs my blood as I recall it. Now, my friend, let me be your guide to super-successful living. My promise? You can climb to the top! My secret? All you have to do is get motivated today—and stay motivated every day until you achieve your God-inspired goal!

How do you do it? Get started! And keep at it one step at a time.

Simply start each day with a positive step up the tower of faith!

Yes, here are 366 steps on a walk of faith designed to build within your personality and soul a mountain-moving, motivational *faith*.

Yes, faith is a noun—but it must become a verb! Action! So I have selected 366 verbs, each designed to reveal a facet of that sparkling diamond we call faith. The self-motivation to get up and get going—that's what faith is all about! Then I have selected 366 faith-generating, human-motivating Bible verses to start off each day. By exercising these verbs and the powerful Bible verses in your daily life, you will release inner emotional powers from their imprisonment. Yes, subconscious emotional restrictions can bind and repress the incredible potential emotional strength that lies dormant within you *right now!* For decades, I have carefully studied the emotional blockages that constrict the forceful flow of emotional strength. I have outlined here 366 days of motivational treatment that will surely, steadily, slowly, but successfully give you emotional freedom! Find yourself free at last! You will reach a point somewhere along this walk of faith where you will feel as if you are power-driven! You will sense that you are upward bound! You will feel tremendous emotional health, energy, and power being released within you! You will finally experience the incredible, powerful truth in this promise of Jesus Christ: "If you have faith as a mustard seed, you will say to this mountain, 'Move . . .'; and nothing will be impossible for you" (Matt. 17:20).

You will have developed in a one-year spiritual fitness program a tough-minded faith that will make it possible for you to go through tough times with surviving power!

What greater gift could I give you? What greater blessing could God bestow upon your life than the gift of a tough-minded faith for a tenderhearted person?

O.K.? Let's take that first step and never stop for the next year.

You'll never be the same again.

ROBERT HAROLD SCHULLER

Trusting the unprovable

"You will seek Me and find Me, when you search for Me with all your heart."—JEREMIAH 29:13

"I would love to be a believer, if I knew it was the truth," an intelligent young Japanese man said to me. "Prove it to me. That's what the unbelieving world is waiting for. We're scientific. We want *proof* before we believe."

1

"But that's a contradiction," I answered. "If there is proof, there no longer is room for belief. For faith believes in that which cannot be proven. Let me sum it up in this sentence:

When proof is possible, faith becomes impossible."

The young man asked, "But if God wants us to be believers, why didn't He prove Himself to us?"

I quoted Hebrews 11:6. "Without faith it is impossible to please [God]."

The same is true in human relationships. When somebody believes in you before you've earned their trust, you have been honored! When they trust you even though you didn't display your credentials, faith is born.

I remember the people who believed in me when I started our ministry. I was unknown. I had no reputation. Yet they believed in me before I could prove myself to them. To this day I have deep affection for and gratitude to those special persons.

God knew what He was doing when He established the belief system. When you strip away all mystery and leave the truth naked and mathematically scientific, something sweet and attractive is lost.

There will always be the unknown. There will always be the unprovable. But faith confronts those frontiers with a thrilling leap. Then life becomes vibrant with adventure!

Dreaming God's dream

"Be renewed in the spirit of your mind."—
EPHESIANS 4:23

2 What's the purpose of life anyway?
Only to eat, drink, work, play, make love?
Or do you have a brain designed to dream dreams?
Is your mind created to be an architect, drawing plans?
Can you imagine beautiful accomplishments?

Think of this:
The human being
is the only creature in the universe
that has the capacity for exercising creative imagination!

This divine quality of *dreaming*
what you want to be,
where you want to go,
what you'd love to do,
projects you hope to achieve,
goals you'd like to reach—
all of this makes you human
and the most unique creature in all of creation!

You really are "made in the image" of the Creator–God!
So you are fulfilling your destiny
as a child of God in human flesh
when you start dreaming the beautiful
dreams God Himself is inspiring in your mind.

A radio is designed to pick up the sounds that are here in this room now!

A television is engineered to pick up the moving pictures that are in the air waves around you now.

Your mind was invented and created by God to pick up the messages and mental pictures He is sending your way.

That's exciting!
Faith is dreaming God's dreams!

FAITH IS . . .
Breathing your native air

"I have come that they may have life, and that they may have it more abundantly."—JOHN 10:10

It's terribly important to understand that a believer is a normal person. Faith is the mark of normality. A persistently negative and cynical attitude is a mark of emotional illness. **3**

Birds were designed to fly. The air under the wings of a bird is the natural habitat of the flying fowl.

Water is the natural habitat of the fish.

> **Faith is the native air to be breathed in and out by human beings.**

It is normal to have faith. It is abnormal to be cynical. Therefore you welcome all stimuli that would encourage you to have faith. Reject all negative forces that would destroy faith and replace it with unbelief.

When you practice positive belief, you are more controlled by positive emotions—love, joy, courage, faith, enthusiasm.

These are the qualities of an emotionally healthy person. Persons who are not breathing the natural air of faith, but are breathing the polluted air of doubt and unbelief, are quickly susceptible to a lower morality. They are quickly consumed by negative emotions—all of which are measured and marked as symptoms of something less than true wholeness and health as a human being.

You were created to be a believer!

Faith is finding your native air.

That's why you feel so great when you're optimistic!

Thank You, Father, for causing me to be a normal, healthy human being by motivating me to walk the walk of faith. Amen.

Wanting more out of life

"Delight yourself also in the Lord,/And He shall
give you the desires of your heart."—PSALM
37:4

4   Faith is a choice, not an argument.
It is a decision, not a debate.
It is a commitment, not a controversy.
Faith fulfills some need in your heart.
It can be defined as wanting more out of life.
Even the superaffluent are attracted to faith; they soon real-
ize that all of their wealth, social standing, and personal power
leave a void in their lives. When you have more money than
you can enjoy what is left?
Saint Augustine said: "Our souls are restless till they rest in
Thee." We suspect that out there, somewhere, there is always
something more. From where does this intuition for "something more" come? It is built into our nature.
The human being has been called an incurably religious animal by instinct and nature.

**Be careful what you want—you'll get it! Wanting is
believing, and believing produces results.**

Strong faith is often the expression of deep desire.
Likewise doubt is the lack of desire. A host of conscious or
subconscious forces can keep you from wanting to believe.
Fears of what God might do *to* your life or *in* your life can
keep you from wanting to believe. Internalized guilt can make
the possibility of God a threatening concept. Deep seated
negative emotions can kill the desire to believe leaving you
with a negative inclination to doubt. Having trouble believing? Why don't you want to believe?
Our Bible verse today contains God's promise of blessings
upon faith. God promises to bless the person who has strong
desires. This is because in God's eyes desire and faith are one
and the same: "He shall give you the desires of your heart."

Doubting your doubts

"God is not the God of the dead, but of the living."—MATTHEW 22:32

"There lives more faith in honest doubt, than in half the creeds," Alfred Lord Tennyson wrote in *In Memoriam*.

5

I find that some people who have serious questions about the existence of God want desperately to believe. Their probing inquiry reflects thoughtful doubt.

Actually, they are far more responsible and serious in their pursuit of a commitment to God than those who blindly recite cold creeds without really daring to explore the tough questions.

Doubt can be a positive force when we learn to doubt our doubts and have faith in our faith!

It is quite apparent that the believer in God and the Bible has as strong a foundation for a rational system of belief as any doubter has for the philosophy of irreligion he has fabricated.

Faith in God will
    increase your moral strength,
        increase your days of joy,
            reduce your days of despair.

I've never seen a person who has been more respected as a leader in the philosophy and faith of religion than Jesus Christ.

Jesus believed in God. He believed in prayer.

He believed in heaven and hell and eternal life.

He believed in salvation.

He believed in every single human being!

He believed in possibility thinking and He believed in faith.

If your doubts collide and clash with the viewpoint of Jesus Christ, it is the better part of wisdom to believe the believer and doubt the doubter. Then you are on your way to a great life.

Surfing on the waves

"The LORD on high is mightier/Than the noise
of many waters,/Than the mighty waves of the
sea."—PSALM 93:4

6 I am one who enjoys the seashore, where the water laps
lazily over the sandy edge. It is there I find tranquility and
creativity. But on occasion, I have watched surfers ride the
wonderful, wild, and wicked waves. They inspire and motivate me!

Quietly, patiently, the surfers lie waiting on their slender,
slippery surfboards, poised and ready to leap to action at any
moment!

Suddenly, there it is! The beginning of a swell in the ocean
foretells the birth of a wave.

The surfer suddenly leaps barefoot on his surfboard, catching the rising crest of the fresh breaking wave. He is lifted high
and carried far by the curling, sweeping, arching, flight of
foam. The ride is on. Bending knees absorb the shocks, swells
and swirls. Arms outstretched slice the wind like eagles
wings. The trusting torso struggles to maintain balance. From
time to time the waves win out as the sportsman is wiped
out—sent off his board and into the sea. But riding or falling
he wins! His challenge to the surf has won him victory over
fear. And so he ends in safe shallows where he turns and pad-
dles out again to catch the next wave.

These same waves that carry the surfer into the shallows
send the timid bather running and squealing, hoping to escape
what threatens to overwhelm him. As the bather turns his
back to escape what he views as a threat, he increases his
chances of being knocked down and sent sputtering into the
foamy surf.

Faith is surfing on the waves of life.

**Faith faces the fears and turns the negative into a posi-
tive. Doubt runs from fear and is overwhelmed by it!**

Dear God, thank You for inspiring me today. I know that
together, You and I can ride out the waves of negativity. Amen.

Batting all alone

"Choose for yourselves this day whom you will serve, . . . But as for me and my house, we will serve the Lord."—JOSHUA 24:15

Faith—we shall see—is sometimes a collective and some-times a very private matter. When a nation unites to defend its peace and freedom against an invading enemy, we see an illustration of collective faith. **7**

But when an institution delegates enormous decision-mak-ing powers to the chief executive officer, the decisions will become painfully private. The presidency of the United States has been described as the loneliest office for that very reason. The buck stops at his desk. He is up to bat. Alone! One man against the world.

Faith, we soon discover, is a very private matter. Our most important decisions cannot be passed off to anyone else. Con-sider the basic decisions. (1) What am I going to do? What career will I pursue? In a free society, *you,* and you alone, must decide! Out in front of you are nine members of another team plus a stand full of spectators watching to see how you will perform! No state bureaucracy will select a profession for you! That's being in the batter's box alone! (2) Who will be my one essential friend? Whom shall I marry? Or shall I remain sin-gle? No government agency, no academic advisory council can make that decision for you. You are in the batter's box—alone! That calls for strong, private faith! (3) What religious choice will I make? I can choose to believe in nothing or I can choose to believe in something. Atheism or theism.

It's your decision. You're up to bat. You can't avoid the mo-ment. Sure, you can run scared, throw the bat to someone else in the dugout—avoid the choice—call yourself an agnostic. But then—face the consequences—you're out of the game!

Choose faith: take a swing at it! Become a believer.

> After all—faith is *the only positive option open to you.* The other alternatives are negative! And nothing positive ever follows negative decisions!

FAITH IS . . .
Sitting in the front row

"O God of our salvation,/You who are the confidence of all the ends of the earth."—PSALM 65:5

8   Why do people rush to get the front seats in a football field, at a baseball game, or in the live theater, while the front seats in the average church are the last to be occupied? The answer seems obvious.

We want to maintain space between ourselves and others who might conceivably intimidate or threaten us. We want to be "in" but remain at a safe distance. Sit in the front row? Never! We might be noticed.

Perhaps you are still struggling with an inferiority complex, so you stand outside the circle or attend only large gatherings where you can hide in the crowd. Why don't you have enough faith to be aggressive? Will you ever have the faith to sell yourself? If not, what doors will remain locked to you forever? What human experiences will never be enjoyed?

Can this fear be overcome? Can such behavioral patterns, probably rooted deep in childhood, be corrected and changed?

Yes! Of course! You and I simply need more faith in ourselves and in God. Decide today to tackle this lifelong pattern of negativity with self-confident aggression.

The best seats in the house are waiting for the people of faith!

Don't miss out on the action! Grab a seat for yourself in the front row now. The same people who dare to sit in the front row are the "go-get-'em" type who are almost always one step ahead of the competition. They're going places!

You'll meet new friends. One of the new friends you'll meet who will change your life will be the new you!

Angling for the catch

"You shall increase my greatness."—PSALM 71:21

My boyhood days of the wide-open spaces of an Iowa farm **9**
were happy times. I had freedom to roam the fields and fish
the streams. I enjoy no memory more than that of the corncob
"dobber," floating on the placid Floyd River. As long as I had a
cane pole, a can of worms, and a pocket full of faith, I was in
heaven.

The largest fish I ever caught were catfish. Imagine how my
eyes grew large when I saw pictures of marlin leaping out of
the water in sports magazines in the barber shop. But that
kind of fishing was reserved for the professional sports fisherman. There was no chance for an Iowa farm boy to go fishing
like that. Right?

Years later, however, I found myself living in California,
only a few hundred miles from where they fish for marlin.
Could I get there? How much would it cost? My next thought
was a negative one, "No, I'm only a cane pole fisherman from
Iowa."

But possibility thinking had already changed my life. I told
myself:

> **"Go for it. Give it a try. You might surprise yourself
> and succeed."**

And I did!

That's the kind of faith you call "angling for the catch." It's
the kind of faith that produces results. Unemployed people
find work. Lonely people find friends.

Today, Lord, You are telling me that I can achieve that long-
held dream if I'll only go for it. I'm going to be superpositive;
I'm going to go fishing for what I really want in life! Thank
You, Lord. Amen.

FAITH IS . . .

Knocking down the high bar

"For the LORD will be your confidence,/And will keep your foot from being caught."—
PROVERBS 3:26

10 Oftentimes faith meets success at the point of failure. For example, the pole vaulter who runs and then vaults over the bar a little higher each time never really knows how high he can jump until he fails to scale the bar.

He succeeds when he fails!

For failure isn't a matter of not reaching your goal!

Failure is failing to give your project all that you've got!

Success is achieving the maximum of your potential in the situation you are in.

When you honestly have attempted your ultimate best, then you have been successful, in spite of failure. The people who are really failures are the people who set their standards so low, keep the bar at such a safe level, that they never run the risk of failure.

Faith is daring to face an embarrassing failure. It's only after the pole vaulter knocks down the bar raised to its highest level that he knows he's jumped as high as he can—today!

Success comes at the point where we can't do any better than we are doing at this moment. The applause doesn't come until you've given all you have to give. Spectators love the winners and they love the losers, as long as both give it their best!

Dear God, thank You for this boost You have given me today. I understand now that I really am not a failure. I am succeeding because I am doing my very best. Thank You for Your confidence in me. I will keep on keeping on! To God be the glory. Amen.

Whistling in the dark

> "If I say 'Surely the darkness shall fall on me,'/
> Even the night shall be light about me;/Indeed,
> the darkness shall not hide from You,/But the
> night shines as the day;/The darkness and the
> light are both alike to You."—PSALM 139:11–12

As a young boy on an Iowa farm, before the days of elec- **11**
tricity, I was often exposed to the threatening mysteries of the
dark. When I was afraid to go out at night to check on my
horse, my father reassured me, "There is nothing to be afraid
of, Bob. And if you are afraid, just whistle!"

Believe it or not, it really worked.

Dad must have sensed that I needed to learn to venture out
in new and potentially threatening situations without the
usual support system.

So one night he refused to go with me to bring the horse in
from the pasture. On my own I ventured forth, whistling in
the dark.

As I entered the darkened stable with my horse, I was
scared nearly out of my wits by the voice of a man! It was my
father, coming to meet me half-way.

Often, I am still called to go out into the darkness, alone.
And I always find that whistling gives me courage.

> **Positive affirmation is like whistling in the dark. It
> gets me there and keeps me going, even at the darkest
> point of the journey.**

We are all called to walk in the unknown darkness.

We are not moving in the area of faith when we walk only in
broad daylight and can see where we are going.

Head out into the unknown today. Whistle in the dark. For
"the darkness and the light are both alike to [God]."

Thank You, Father, that You know where the path is leading. I am trusting You. I am not afraid of the dark anymore.
Thank You, God. Amen.

Stepping on the scale

> " 'I have walked before You in truth and with a
> loyal heart, and have done what is good in Your
> sight.' And the Lord said to Hezekiah, 'I have
> heard your prayer . . . and I will add to your
> days fifteen years.' "—ISAIAH 38:3–5

12   The inch-by-inch principle is building your faith. The little things you do today for someone else will add up to a lifetime of joy!

You can be genuinely optimistic about the prospect of enjoying life.

You have faith today to be able to accomplish the incredible by using the inch-by-inch principle.

Faith is answering the telephone, it is balancing the checkbook, and it is stepping on the scale!

Faith is confronting reality, not running away from it. If a telephone call brings bad news, have the faith to deal with it inch by inch. If finances are depleted—inch by inch, turn the problem around. If the scale says you're overweight, have the faith to tackle your problem slowly and surely—inch by inch!

Faith is not a contradiction of reality, but the courage to face reality with hope.

Recently I prayed for guidance. Gradually—over the past two years—extra pounds crept up on me. "Step on the scale every day." The message was loud and clear! I have been doing that! And writing it down! And I'm succeeding!

Affirmation: Today I shall begin to praise myself by being honest. I am going to stop kidding myself. I'm the last person I want to cheat. And I am cheating myself if I'm not being honest.

Today I shall step on the scale. I shall begin to turn my life around. I am facing up to my reality.

I am not afraid to face any negative situation, for I know that with God all things are possible!

FAITH IS . . .

Expanding the base

"You enlarged my path under me;/So that my
feet did not slip."—PSALM 18:36

When is faith fulfilled? With a wedding? Graduation? Grand
opening day? Victorious election day? When is the dream
fulfilled?

13

"Faith is never fulfilled. It always gives birth to a new
dream," my son, the Reverend Robert Anthony Schuller, observed as he preached his first sermon in his new sanctuary.
And he's right!

The truth is, faith is never fulfilled—it is always upstaged!
At the very moment faith appears to be fulfilled, it is transcended by a new dream. "Now that I'm married we can. . ."
"Now that we are in business, let's. . ." "Now that we have our
new property, we will. . ."

Yes, just when faith seems to be fulfilled, it is upstaged by a
new dream. And it is this new dream, "see what we can do
now," that keeps faith alive. The new dream calls out to faith,
"Come along with me; I need you. After all you got me started
and brought me here. Don't let me down now. I can't get along
without you."

Faith, after all, isn't needed unless there's a gap between the
"is" and the "ought." Faith cannot exist unless there is a
chasm between the "I have it" and the "I want it."

So, when we succeed in our walk of faith, we learn an important life principle.

Unless I am expandable, I am expendable.

Growth is synonymous with life. Keep dreaming, and you
keep growing.

Shooting for the moon

> "Oh, give thanks to the LORD, for He is good!/
> For His mercy endures forever./To Him who
> made great lights . . ./The sun to rule by day
> . . ./the moon and stars to rule by night."—
> PSALM 136:1, 7–9

14 When God created the universe, He did so with an unlimited expenditure of divine creative energy! There are heavens and galaxies that will never be fully explored.

M-31 in the constellation of Andromeda is a galaxy millions of light years away from planet Earth. If NASA can develop a spacecraft that travels at the speed of light (186,000
miles per second) it still would take a few million years just to
reach the edge of that galaxy. It is safe to say we'll never reach
it! In fact, it may be the geographic location of heaven!

Faith is shooting for the moon! Yes, it's planning to reach
heaven someday. To the believer, heaven is the ultimate destination of the road of faith.

But until then, we need to shoot for the moon right here and
now. What do I mean? I mean that a possibility thinker uses
every possible opportunity to be outstanding! Throw yourself
into your work with everything you've got.

**Again and again the person who fails, fails because he
is not willing to shoot for the moon, to give his dream
all that he's got.**

It is that 100 percent effort—some athletes refer to 110 percent effort—that gives a champion the winner's edge. The difference between the number one and the number two spot is
sometimes a matter of fractions of seconds.

Faith is shooting for the moon! It's putting all your eggs in
one basket.

If you really believe in what you're doing, then don't hold
anything back.

Give it your all—go for it!

FAITH IS . . .
Splicing the gene

"I have made you hear new things from this time./Even hidden things,/and you did not know them."—ISAIAH 48:6

Could this incredible Bible verse possibly refer to genetic engineering that is happening today? Did it refer to the splitting of the atom earlier in our century? **15**

I often marvel at how God keeps so many secrets to Himself. Slowly, patiently, He releases new insights and allows each new generation the joy of making its own contributions!

When science is on the verge of a new frontier, there are always negative, fearful eyes that see only the potential dangers. It strikes me as a contradiction when some people who are known as "people of faith" suddenly lose their faith when it comes to moving into uncharted scientific realms. God created the genes, and the potential for life forms to be successfully created through gene splicing. God ultimately holds the final judgment and course of life in His hands.

Christians who walk the walk of faith look positively at the constructive possibilities in scientific discoveries, such as gene splicing. Possibility thinking sees dangers and potential difficulties in every forward move that we might make. But we do not reject an idea of vast positive potential because some incredible dangers might be unleashed. Rather, we take the discovery and try to identify the potential negatives.

We eliminate, isolate, insulate, or sublimate the negative!

That's walking the walk of faith. Faith is splicing the gene! It's welcoming the adventure God reserved for a time like ours!

Probing for answers

"Ah, Lord GOD! Behold, you have made the
heavens and the earth by Your great power and
outstretched arm. There is nothing too hard for
You."—JEREMIAH 32:17

16   I know a chief executive who often calls in his top research
people to ask: "What questions do I need to ask you to get the
answers that will give me the knowledge I need to make the
right decision?"

Faith is probing for answers. Some people are so paralyzed
by their problem that they do not know how to begin to find
the answer.

The search for faith begins with questions.

When you know what questions to ask, you *believe* that
someone, somewhere, sometime, somehow can come up
with the right answer! So, believing is probing!

Faith is a needle:

• It has a sharp point.
• It provokes progress.
• It disturbs the status quo.
• It points to the need for answers.
• It probes until no corner is left unexplored and no pos-
  sibility is left unexamined.

"That was tried, and it failed," the negative thinker may say.
But faith probes deeper into the situation. Perhaps someone
went about it in the wrong way—perhaps it was not possible
yesterday—perhaps with today's new technology and chemis-
try it might be possible!

Like an unsettled sea with a depth that defies measure-
ment, restless faith churns until it finds hidden springs in the
bottom of the ocean floor! There are vast resources that God
wants to give the person who will never give up believing.

Believing is spelled p-r-o-b-i-n-g!

Becoming normal

"And when Jesus went out He saw a great
multitude; and He was moved with compassion
for them, and healed their sick."—MATTHEW
14:14

In the Broadway play, *The Man of La Mancha,* Don Quixote **17**
is near death. He has been mocked and scorned because he is
such a positive thinker! Finally, in a splendid self-defense, he
asks the ultimate question. "Who is crazy? Am I crazy because I see the world as it could become? Or is the world crazy
because it only sees itself as it is?"

Who is normal, the cynic or the believer? The positive
thinker or the negative thinker? The believer in God—or the
atheist? The despairing pessimist or the hopeful optimist?

By now we all know the answer! We must affirm that health
is normal, and sickness is abnormal. That basic value judgment is beyond controversy.

Unbelief is a sickness, and skepticism is damnably dangerous. It gives birth to a multitude of spiritual demons that
can malignantly destroy your mental health and spread an
epidemic of despair wherever you go. As soon as you surrender yourself to negative thoughts, you become host to an
infectious spiritual disease and become the carrier of another
epidemic of gloom and doom.

It is normal for a child to dance and laugh and play. It is not
normal for a child to be downcast, morbid, withdrawn, and
sulking in isolation. It is normal to be a happy believer.

Who is crazy? The realist or the idealist?

The answer is obvious. The Beautiful Dreamer, with His
exalted visions of glorious possibilities, is the Uplifting Force
in society! He comes bringing solutions. He then becomes the
Great Physician, the Healing Source, the Hopeful Friend. We
can follow Him.

His name? Jesus, the Lord. My Savior. My friend.

Integrating yourself

"Let the peace of God rule in your hearts, to
which also you were called in one body; and be
thankful."—COLOSSIANS 3:15

18   In his book *Games People Play,* the psychiatrist Eric Berne
defines three ego states in the human being. There is the *parent* ego state, the *child* ego state, and the *adult* ego state.

By that, he means there is in every human being the *child*
that remains within us. This explains why, as mature persons,
we sometimes act very childishly when we are frustrated. The
child-quality within us never leaves us, nor should it completely. For then we cease to enjoy the childlike quality of
wonder.

There also lives in us, through our memories, the *parent* to
scold or mold us. In unexpected times we recall the stern or
sweet voice of the father or mother, and we find ourselves responding or resisting.

Finally, there is the *adult* ego state. By this Eric Berne
means the real and rugged individual who is today a free individual.

Are you a single person? Or are there several different persons within you? Are they kind? Cruel? Patient? Impatient?
To what extent is your personality fragmented?

The secret of mental health is to achieve a maximum degree of integration until there is an overwhelming magnetic
force at the core of your personality that brings isolated and
fractured elements of your being into a oneness.

The atheist tries to integrate his life around a vacuum—a
belief in nothing.

**The believer becomes integrated around one dominant
overwhelming Magnetic Force that pulls life together.
That Force is Jesus Christ. That power is the power of
belief.**

Thank You, God, that You are the Magnetic Force integrating my life.

Discovering your natural habitat

"We are His workmanship, created in Christ
Jesus for good works."—EPHESIANS 2:10

You are discovering who you are, where you belong, and **19** what a marvelous creature you really are. Once you learn to breathe your native air, you discover that the path of faith is the central corridor, the mainstream, the number one boulevard that runs from one end of the Garden of Eden to the other!

> **The exciting process of discovery is always a mark of authentic living.**

You have already discovered that to live is to grow. And you have made a marvelous growth-producing discovery when you came to know that living by faith is living the healthy and natural way.

You were designed as a human being to be the brains and the body that could execute God's good work on planet Earth. Once your faith has motivated you to a genuine commitment to faith in God, you find your values changing, your priorities reshuffling, and your goals being reviewed. Christ Jesus literally changes your life and retools you to do good work!

In the process of this good work you find joy, self-esteem, and dignity. You have discovered your natural habitat.

- Now you know why you were born.
- Now you understand the divine purpose behind human life.

No other animal has the capacity to be a believer in God. That's your unique heritage.

Thank You, God, for enabling me to make this discovery. Amen.

FAITH IS . . .
Thinking God's thoughts

"For I know the thoughts that I think toward
you, says the LORD, thoughts of peace and not
of evil, to give you a future and a hope."—
JEREMIAH 29:11

20 Each new year is an appointment to become an authentic
optimist.

Each new day is justification for being enthusiastic about
life again.

Each dawning is God's invitation to start over and build a
new life, beginning with the present moment.

Every new week is an opportunity to make new and noble
resolutions! Every Monday morning you have a standing appointment to meet new opportunities!

What does it mean to have faith?

Faith is opening your mind for God's thoughts to flow in.
And when His thoughts flow in, life will change, for you will
have a dream. You will see possibilities in the day—the
week—the month—the year that is waiting to unfold.

Faith moves mountains.

The greatest power in the world is a positive idea.

And the most powerful positive idea is one that comes directly from the God who created the world and broke sunshine through the black of night.

Today I will think God's thoughts. This very moment, I will
open my mind to let God's thoughts enter my brain. I will
listen to the idea that comes from God, and it will turn me
into a new and different person. I feel a freshness and a newness coming over me now as God's thoughts begin to take
control over my consciousness.

I am set free, liberated, by new thoughts that come from
God. Now I know what possibility thinking is—it is the mental activity that happens when I let faith take over.

Thank You, God, that I am being born again. Your Holy
Spirit is filling my mind with your thoughts. I am excited
about today, and I'm excited about my future. Amen.

FAITH IS . . .
Praying for guidance

"Show me Your ways, O Lord;/Teach me your paths./Lead me in your truth and teach me,/For You are the God of my salvation . . ."—PSALM 25:4

The walk of faith is an adventure in a holy partnership. You **21** are a human being with a mortal starting point at birth and a mortal terminal point at death. The span between your birth and death is your earthly life. Your purpose is to fit into a holy scheme, and become a participant with God. He created the world and all of us human beings for the purpose of creatively achieving His holy and happy purposes.

You are walking the walk of faith when you dream God's dreams and seek God's guidance.

Therefore, faith is not merely a super-aggressive activity into which you plunge with a gung-ho attitude, to achieve the first impulse that explodes in your mind. Rather, faith is a steady, stable, and steadfast process of opening your conscious and subconscious mind through prayer to the Holy Spirit. The eternal God will shape your will and direct your way!

God promised He will give you guidance.

In the depth of your heart, you know with an unflinching certainty, and with an invincible awareness, the course of action your life must take. This is God Himself, answering your prayers for guidance. He gives you a strong and powerful will to proceed along the determined pathway. Consider these prayers of affirmation:

I am driven by a divine destiny.

I am praying for guidance now.

I am opening my mind consistently and constantly to God, the way the tip of a branch is unceasingly alert and responsive to the wind!

Setting a goal

"One thing I do, forgetting those things which
are behind and reaching forward to those things
which are ahead, I press toward the goal for . . .
the upward call of God . . ."—PHILIPPIANS 3:13

22 Faith is not merely thinking holy and happy thoughts.

God's thoughts must take the form of good and godly goals.

No act of faith is more dynamic, more constructive, than setting incredible goals!

Have you noticed how negative thinkers avoid setting goals?

"Goals—who needs them? I'll just wing it, thank you. I prefer to roll with the punches."

"I don't want to get trapped by a commitment. Isn't that what happens when you set a goal?"

"I've had enough disappointments. I don't want to be set up only to be let down. Goals? No more failures, thank you."

Failure is not a matter of failing to meet your goal. Failure is not making the most of the possibilities seen and unseen, known and unknown, in your present and in your future!

Use faith to set positive goals, and you'll be sure to rise to the higher plateau. I guarantee that . . .

• when you set a challenging goal, you'll be farther ahead tomorrow than you are today. Even a little can turn out to be a lot!

• you'll be a happier person. Someone stopped me recently and asked, "Why do you always seem to be in such a happy mood?" My answer: "Because I've always got unfulfilled goals, and my goals distract me from my worries!"

• you will feel that your life has value!

If you have goals, you are bound to inspire somebody who is hurting. You will discover your own worth.

Goals—what are they anyway? They are impossible problems awaiting to be solved by someone with this incredible power called faith! So get set to set goals, and move upward!

FAITH IS . . .
Charting the course

"Let us run with endurance the race that is set before us."—HEBREWS 12:1

You are walking the walk of faith, thinking God's thoughts, **23** seeking God's guidance, and setting good and godly goals.

Now, how can you possibly succeed when your goals are beyond your grasp? Did you go overboard? Are you thinking too big? Should you scale down your dreams? How can you possibly pull off what seems to be an impossibility?

What you must do is think, plan, and chart your course through the uncharted waters before you.

You cannot expect God's ideas to automatically evolve as actualized achievements. You must assume responsibility to make success happen. You must develop a strategy and a scheme that will allow you to succeed.

If you fail to plan, you plan to fail.

Now exercise your faith by affirming . . .

I am trusting God to give me wisdom to chart my course as carefully as a captain who looks at a map, chooses his route, and calculates the time and resources needed to finish the journey.

I want to reach the destination and see God's dream for my life accomplished. I am planning to make it possible.

I am excited. I am ready to begin! I am going to fulfill my divine destiny.

I am confident that
• if there's a will, there's a way.
• if it's God's will, He will show the way.
• if I keep the faith, He will show me how!

Thank You, God, for giving me the motivation to run the race. Thank You for the wisdom to chart the course that fulfills Your successful plan for my life!

FAITH IS . . .
Believing I will make it

"He [God] who has begun a good work in you
will complete it . . ."—PHILIPPIANS 1:6

24 Deliberately exercise your faith by repeating these positive
affirmatives:

I am thanking God—today—that He has a plan for my life.
I am motivated to seek and serve God's will.
I am trusting that God has inspired me to begin—surely He
will guide me to succeed.
I am walking the walk of faith.
I am thinking God's thoughts.
I am setting goals.
I am charting a course.
I am believing that I will succeed.
I am disciplining my mind to weed out negative thoughts.
I am rejecting all thoughts of discouragement.
I am visualizing myself making steady progress.
I am basing my ultimate success on the character of God.
God never starts a project and abandons it!
God is no quitter. He is a finisher!

**God gave me a dream; motivated me to set a goal; and
He will keep stimulating me to succeed.**

I will keep on believing in success, for I know that success
is inevitable as long as I focus my belief on eventual success.
I will make my life an exclamation mark! Surely God
wants me to be successful. He certainly does not dream up
plans for people to fail at! Because I am responsible for my life,
I will decide to succeed. I am believing I will make it.

God, who has begun a good work in me, will complete it!

Scanning the horizon

"Set your mind on things above, not on things on the earth."—COLOSSIANS 3:3

We define *horizon* as the place where heaven meets earth. But it is also where today's state-of-the-art ends and tomorrow's new developments move in.

Faith refuses to surrender control to negative doubts of yesterday. Doubt adds up all of the bungled debts, fruitless research, foiled efforts, and shattered dreams.

Doubt finds its life by digging in the cemeteries of buried hopes.

Faith finds its life by scanning the horizon, knowing there will be a sunrise tomorrow.

Today is the beginning of a new age. What medical breakthroughs will be made before the sun sets today? What new technological achievements will be possible by the end of this year, or this decade?

Faith is belief in the future. It is scanning the horizon for new ships that will sail into view, carrying treasured cargo of new discoveries. Faith expects and predicts headlines of new cures and breakthroughs that will be announced in the next 365 days.

Affirmation: Today I will cultivate a mental attitude that expects progress. I will steadfastly scan the heavens!

Through positive prayer, I look forward, expectantly and excitedly! Thank You, Father, for what You are planning to do in my future. Amen.

Possibilitizing

"For a dream comes through much activity."—
ECCLESIASTES 5:3

26   Today, I want to introduce you to a new word—*possibilitizing*. It means coming up with solutions where none were apparent; creating a way when there has been no path. This involves the process of research and development, which leads to new inventions.

Are you faced with a seemingly unsolvable problem? Then possibilitize! Play "the possibility thinking game." It's an incredibly practical and extremely valuable technique for solving rugged problems.

Make a list of one to ten on a sheet of clean white paper. Now open your mind to God in prayer. Then *list every possible way* of accomplishing the impossible problem, no matter how wild, how far out, or how preposterous it seems—until all ten lines are filled.

Begin right now by listing here the first thoughts that come to your mind:

_____

_____

A few decades ago, the idea of taking a healthy heart out of a dead body and transplanting it into the chest of a living person with a decaying heart would have been unthinkable.

As long as they are not immoral or unethical, list your ideas. You'll be surprised at how God operates! As you write your ideas down on paper, if one has come from Him, it will grab you. You'll not be able to shake it. It will become a part of the answer!

Possibilitizing—it moves mountains!

FAITH IS . . .
Assuming "it is possible"

> ". . . but with God all things are possible."—
> MATTHEW 19:26

Faith is the process of *acting upon glorious assumptions.*   **27**
If you attempt to achieve an objective that is easily reached, then you are not moving within the circle of faith.

Faith is not necessary unless your projects are humanly impossible.

Unless there is strong reason to doubt, you are not living in the higher altitude of real faith.

You must commit yourself to projects where there is a possibility of failure before you can claim to be walking the walk of faith.

How does faith move us forward when success is uncertain? Faith moves us onward by giving us the courage to act upon positive assumptions. We assume that:

With the help of God, the impossible can be possible.

There will never be progress until someone acts upon a grand assumption. Surely, you have the right to assume that God, who made your dream, will also make it possible for you to succeed.

Keep moving forward, steadily, assuming that when you reach the door it will swing open! Even Moses moved toward the Red Sea, assuming that a way would clear for him to cross it!

O God, with Your help today, I believe the impossible can be possible. I assume that my problems are solvable; that help will be forthcoming; that new breakthroughs will come my way; and that positive and exciting new healings will flow into me. I believe that today's assumptions will become tomorrow's grand accomplishments! Thank You, God. Amen.

Viewing success positively

"You shall also be a crown of glory/In the hand
of the Lord,/And a royal diadem/In the hand of
your God."—ISAIAH 62:3

28 Is it possible that some people are more afraid of success
than failure? Can it be that they are unsure what success will
do to their lifestyle? Will they lose some of their old friends?
What new pressures and temptations will come into their
lives?

I am constantly surprised to find Christians who are afraid
of success. Many suffer from the hang-up that success contra-
dicts the Christian virtue of humility. They associate success
with pride; therefore, they refuse to consider it. Faith views
success positively. Don't be afraid of success!

**God can do great things through successful people
who are dedicated to Him!**

The cynic cannot save the world. The doubter cannot share
faith, hope, and love. God's work needs all the success it can
get!

Faith welcomes success and then uses it positively.

How does faith deal with success positively?
- Faith does not *fear* success.
- Faith does not *fight* success.
- Faith *accepts* success as *noble.*
- Faith *pursues* success with enthusiasm.
- Faith *welcomes* success with gratitude.
- Faith *shares* success.
- Faith *uses* success to solve the problems of the world.

I'm so grateful, Lord, I know that it's no sin to succeed? I'll
not be afraid of winning. Amen.

Fearing failure courageously

"Come, . . . I will teach you the fear of the
LORD. . . . who desires life? . . . do good;/Seek
peace and pursue it."—PSALM 34:11–14

A successful black multimillionaire and entrepreneur told
on a national television interview how, fifteen years earlier, he
had plunged into a business opportunity that came his way.

29

When no bank would take a chance on him, he sold his idea
to friends and relatives, convincing them that they should
loan him one hundred dollars here and five hundred dollars
there.

He was asked by the interviewer: "How do you explain such
an unusually high record of sales that first year?"

He spoke up swiftly and sincerely: "The fear of failure! I
couldn't possibly contemplate failure. I was so afraid I might
fail that I just worked and worked and worked!"

> **The possibility thinker is turned on by the fear of
> failure; an impossibility thinker is turned away from
> ever trying!**

Fear of failure *can* be a positive force! It not only keeps us
going but *pushes* us to produce more than we ever thought we
could!

What that black entrepreneur didn't know is this: with his
drive, determination, and positive mental attitude, he was already a success. He succeeded before he even knew it! Even if
his business had ultimately failed, he would have learned
enough to tackle any opportunity that came his way.

It is true—*the fear of failure can be the insurance policy of
success.*

Lord, give me the drive, the determination, and the positive
mental attitude today to succeed. With Your leading, I can't
possibly contemplate failure. Amen.

Risking failure bravely

"The Lord is my light and my salvation,/Whom shall I fear?/The Lord is the strength of my life,/Of whom shall I be afraid?"—PSALM 27:1

30   You are really making progress in your walk of faith. When you made the decision that you dare to fail, you conquered an enormous obstacle that stops 90 percent of the people from experiencing mountain-moving faith.

Now you can move ahead to pray specifically, engage contracts, make forward-moving commitments, reaffirm original goals, and set forth immediate goals that shall mark progress in your walk.

Faith is impossible without risk.

Unless you're running the risk of failure, you're not totally living within the parameters of faith.

Unless there is the possibility that you can experience a rejection, or a defeat in your project; then you're obviously playing it so safe you can't lose. This means you are not even on the playing field of faith.

God does not promise to bless the coward. However, His promises are packed full of reassurance for those who are brave in heart. Are you in the playing field of faith? Ask yourself these questions:

What goals would I set for myself today if I knew I could not fail? _____

What announcements would I make to the world if I knew I could succeed? _____

Affirmation: Today I'll make my decision based on the good that can be accomplished if I succeed, not on the pain I would experience if I suffered failure! Then truly I can know that I'm being controlled by possibilities instead of problems!

Glorious achievements happen when you and I decide to dare to run the risk of failure!

Defusing the fear of failure

"He shall set me high upon a rock./And now
my head shall be lifted up above my
enemies."—PSALM 27:5–6

You have taken a giant step forward on the walk of faith. **31**
You dare to fail! You *will* risk failure bravely.

Today you will defuse the fear of failure once and for all.
The fear of failure is the explosive bomb that can blow you
out of the water and devastate your destiny. How can you defuse this fear, once and for all? By analyzing intelligently what
the fear of failure really is.

Ask yourself this key question: Why does the fear of failure
frighten me? _____

_____

The fear of failure is really a fear of rejection, of embarrassment. (What will my friends say? What will my loved ones
think of me?) The fear of embarrassment is the fear of the loss
of respect of people who support me emotionally.

And the fear of rejection is really a fear of a loss of self-
worth, self-esteem, and self-respect. I can live without much
money, and I can live with just a few friends, but I can never
live with myself if I hate myself! And I'm really afraid I'll hate
myself if I try—and don't succeed.

How do you defuse this fear? It's simple! Tell yourself that
there is no shame in trying to do something great and failing.
It is much more an embarrassment if I am a coward, lacking
the courage to *try* to do something wonderful and worthwhile.

**There is more self-esteem generated in honest and no-
ble failure than there is in cowardly retreat from great
opportunity!**

"So I'd rather attempt to do something great and fail, than
attempt to do nothing and succeed!"

Scoring in the first round!

"Wait on the Lord,/Be of good courage,/And He shall strengthen your heart,/Wait, I say, on the Lord!"—PSALM 27:14

32 Once you dare to risk failure and defuse the fear of failure, you have scored in round one.

From now on you will dare to try.

Once you have attempted to do something great, it is impossible to be a total failure.

At least you have succeeded in conquering cowardice.

You have dared to step into the ring.

Round one in the fight of life is daring to try even though you know you might fail.

To make a commitment to attempt something great, despite the very real possibility of failure, marks you not as a reckless fool, but as a daring person of great faith.

Most people lose the battle of life by never conquering the fear of failure *enough* to attempt to climb the biggest challenges God puts before them. They've never even stepped into the ring! They were knocked out before the first round!

Until you have enough nerve to set some "gutsy" goals, you run the far greater risk of becoming a total failure!

Affirmation for today: I'll never be a total failure, for at least I can conquer the problem that stops most people. I have looked the fear of failure in the face and I've stared the enemy down!

I'm trying—therefore, I am a success!

Every competitor is a winner! The losers never tried. Every contestant is a winner! The losers never made it to the contest.

Here I go!

No matter how it turns out, I'm getting one award—the badge of courage! Thank You, Lord!

Expecting to succeed

"In all your ways acknowledge Him [God]/And
He shall direct your paths."—PROVERBS 3:6

Can faith really move mountains? Can faith really release **33**
hidden healing powers in dying people? Can faith attract divine and human powers to transform your life? Can you expect your prayers to be answered if you believe?

Of course! For by believing, we exercise the mental practice
of dreaming God's dreams and seeking God's goals.

**And God deeply desires that His plan for your life will
be fulfilled.**

The question is, how can you move your faith from low
gear to high gear? By practicing the mental habit of *expecting
positive results*. In this practice of mental expectation you
strengthen your faith!

You wish you had a tougher faith? Then put your faith on a
vigorous fitness program.

To begin with, give your faith a good diet of spiritual miner-
als and vitamins. Withhold all negative consumptions that
would make your faith "sick."

To maintain the health and the vigor of your faith, it must
be exercised regularly! How?

Ask yourself these questions: Am I really expecting to succeed? Am I mentally keen on achieving my desired goal? Am I
genuinely enthusiastic about the prospects of success?

Faith that passes the fitness test must register high in expecting to succeed. Stretch your faith today by increasing your
expectations!

Affirmation for today: I affirm that my goals are definitely
going to be realized. I am a lot farther today than I was when I
was merely daydreaming. I am committing myself 100 percent to making my dreams come true.

I am expecting to succeed!

I can feel my faith getting stronger already!

Drawing mental pictures

"Where there is no vision, the people perish."—
PROVERBS 29:18 KJV

34 If I asked you to draw a picture, how would you go about it?
You'd probably reach for a blank piece of paper and some pencils or crayons. Or you'd reach for a canvas, with oil paints and brushes.

I am no artist, but I can teach you how to draw pictures in the mind. Your mind is the canvas. Your willpower is the brush. Your thoughts are the oils and colors. Within your mind is an incredible assortment of colors; every idea is a potential color! Begin to "see" ideas in "color." Ideas that are happy can be colored red, yellow. Depressing thoughts? Color them gray. Angry thoughts? Color them black. Loving thoughts? Color them blue. Forward moving, growth ideas? Color them green!

Today choose to become an artist with ideas. No training is necessary. God gives gifts of imagination—your thoughts. Now use your creative power to draw the mental image of the dream *accomplished.* See the finished project in the mind.

The me I see is the me I'll be. If I cannot see it, I will never be it. Until I believe it, I will never achieve it!

It may be helpful to you to actually take out a blank piece of paper and draw a picture of what you want to accomplish. Sketches on paper plant an image on the brain. The subconscious, like a roll of undeveloped film, picks up the image and the picture is drawn. And at this very moment faith moves into a motivational phase. Energy and enthusiasm begin to be released.

Have fun! Become an artist with ideas.

O God, give me a vision, a mental picture of the person you want me to be, the project you want me to pursue, the objectives you want me to manage toward actualization. I open my mind like a screen to the Holy Spirit. I will paint the pictures within my imagination now. Thank You, God. Amen.

Announcing your intentions

"O Lord, open my lips,/And my mouth will
show forth Your praise."—PSALM 51:15

Look at the upward steps that the walk of faith is taking. **35**
Faith takes the first step in dreaming. It climbs higher
through drawing mental pictures, and it takes a giant step upward through the public announcement of your goals!

I suppose this is one of the most frightening steps that you
can take in the walk of faith. As long as you keep your mental
picture to yourself and secretly harbor your unspoken desires,
then the dreaming is relatively safe. But once you open your
mouth and tell the world what you intend to do, then you
place your integrity on the line. You place your reputation as a
believable person on the line once you announce your intentions. Now you must either produce or be proven unreliable at
best and a phony at worst.

The public declaration of commitment intensifies the risk.
You can immediately expect opposition and criticism to come
out of the woodwork. Negative thinkers will leap forward—
"It can't be done," "It won't work," "Somebody else tried it
and failed." Or they'll attack your motives. "What kind of an
ego trip are you on?"

> **Take the leap of faith upward today. Tell the world
> what you're going to accomplish.**

Don't be afraid of criticism. Just as criticism and opposition
will come, so support will come from unknown and unexpected sources. The power of a positive idea is greater than the
power of a negative idea.

O Lord, open my lips, and my mouth shall show forth Your
praises. I shall tell the world of the dream You have given me
and what You and I will attempt to accomplish for Your glory.
Amen.

Getting excited about succeeding

> "For who is God, except the LORD?/And who is
> a rock, except our God? It is God who arms me
> with strength,/And makes my way perfect."—
> PSALM 18:31–32

36 Now that you've drawn the mental picture and announced your intention, you are getting excited about the idea of success.

You can pass the course.

You will succeed in the examination.

You are going to get married and make it work.

You are going to set physical-fitness goals, and will succeed.

You are going to establish a new career, open a new business, take a challenging trip.

It's all going to happen! How can you get so excited about succeeding? Because God is your Rock, your Refuge, your Fortress. He called you! He installed you! His power and His vision enthrall you!

Read Psalm 18:31–33. Here the psalmist tells us what we can expect from God . . .

It is God who arms me with strength.

It is God who makes my way perfect before me.

He makes my feet like the feet of a deer . . .

swift and skillful in maneuvering, sometimes slow down rocky pathways and sometimes swift in the race on the meadow, sometimes powerful for the plunge across the canyon or the leap across the stream or the bounding lunge to the upper rock!

There God sets your feet on the high places! And you, from your vaulted vantage point of spiritual height catch a vision of success so bright!

Thank You, Father, that You have given me the dream—and now the gleam—of success. I need that today! Amen.

FAITH IS . . .
Allowing for the impossibles

"As you do not know what is the way of the
wind,/Or how the bones grow in the womb of
her who is with child,/So you do not know the
works of God who makes all things."—
ECCLESIASTES 11:5

Is it possible for the sun to rise in the west? At first thought, **37**
the answer is, "No, it is impossible." But—

Faith allows impossibilities to become possibilities.

There are several ways impossibilities can become possibilities.

There may be supernatural laws that override natural laws.
Or there are probably natural laws known only to God.

Recently, when I was in Europe for a religious conference, I
was asked to make a fast trip to Washington, D.C., for an important appointment. The only way I could reach my destination in time was to fly via the Concorde—the supersonic
transport plane that hits speeds of over fifteen hundred miles
an hour. Our plane was to leave the Paris airport in time to
watch the sunset. Unfortunately, a problem arose and the
plane was delayed. Consequently it was nine o'clock and dark
before we took off.

"We missed the sunset," I lamented. And then it happened. I
watched a replay of the sunset! I saw the sun rise in the west!
Because our plane was traveling faster than the speed of the
rotation of the earth, we literally caught up with the sunset. I
watched the sun rise from the western horizon to a position of
four o'clock in the afternoon as we landed in the sunshine in
Washington!

Faith is allowing for the apparent impossibilities to be realities.

O God, give me the humility to make allowance for the
possibilities that I am tempted to reject as totally unrealistic!
Help me to see that I cannot grow as a person until I am willing to be a believer. Amen.

Aiming to achieve the best

"[God] is able to do exceedingly abundantly
above all that we ask or think, according to the
power that works within us."—EPHESIANS 3:20

38 Have you noticed that people who do not walk the walk of
faith are also the people who have no clear-cut aim in life?
These people "wing it" without any plan. They fail to set
achievable goals. They often take refuge behind the pious
phrase: "God knows what's best for me and He will provide
it."

If you aim at nothing—you're sure to hit it!

The truth is, the person who sets low goals achieves little.
*The size of the dream will determine the size of the person
you will become.*

There are no great people in this world; there are only ordi-
nary people. The only difference is that some people set
higher goals, dream bigger dreams, and settle for nothing less
than the best!

Excellence is the motto of great people. All-out effort is the
hallmark of their character. They focus on goals and aim carefully at a measurable, manageable target the way a crack rifle-
man sights the target, takes aim, and fires! All the while they
confidently trust God to give them a victory.

Today, are there problems that transcend your ability to
solve them? Are your dreams beyond your reach? Then stop
leaning on your abilities and start trusting God's abilities. He
is able!—"to do exceedingly abundantly above all that we ask
or think . . ." (Eph. 3:20). You just aren't able to think big
enough to match God's abilities!

Affirmation: I know that I can never dream big enough to
match God's dreams! He's always ahead of me and beyond
me!

Verbalizing victory

"For whatever is born of God overcomes the
world. And this is the victory that has
overcome the world—our faith."—1 JOHN 5:4

Do you remember the marvelous and true story of Babe **39**
Ruth? The bases were loaded, and there were two strikes
against him. It was a crucial inning. Suddenly, Babe Ruth
stepped out of the batter's box, lifted his bat, and pointed it at
the stands off in center field, indicating to the crowd that he
was going to hit the ball out of the park. The pitch came
across the plate. He swung. And the ball sailed exactly to
where he had pointed!

> **When you dare to predict your own success, you at-
> tract support and you produce the pressures that will
> ensure your success.**

I've never been good at the game of pool so I marvel at the
pool player who can point to his goal and say, "Number six in
the corner pocket," then shoot, and make it! He verbalizes
victory—beforehand!

It takes a lot of faith to announce your grandiose intentions!
"What if I fail after I made the announcement?" Be proud that
you had the courage to try!

Today, ask yourself this question: Do you believe in God
enough to announce what the two of you are going to do together? It's your responsibility to demonstrate that much
faith. It's God's responsibility to make it happen.

When you verbalize victory you give yourself a new injec-
tion of enthusiasm. People will say that you talked your way
into success. That's only partially true. You acted out your
faith. In the process you put the ball back in God's court. Isn't
it marvelous how God planned for life to be such a challenging game of faith?

Unlocking your positive emotional powers

"You are my hope, O Lord GOD;/You are my
trust from my youth./By You I have been
upheld from my birth;/You are He who took
me out of my mother's womb./My praise shall
be continually of You."—PSALM 71:5,6

40 Tremendous power is released when you begin to thank God for making you the way you are.

I know of no one who doesn't wish to change something about his or her appearance.

Even winners of beauty contests see some imperfection in their physical makeup. Some say, "I wish my nose were shaped a bit differently." Others say: "Don't you think my chin protrudes a little?"

And what about you? How satisfied are you with your physical appearance? Have you accepted yourself as you are? Tremendous power will flow into your life once you do.

I did not choose my race, my skin color, my ethnic origin, or the time of history in which I was born.

There was a destiny that predetermined the basics of my life. I call that Destiny *God.*

> **I will unlock the emotional powers within myself by believing that God knew what He was doing when He created me the way I am.**

Affirmation: Today I shall praise God for the positive people He used to mold my life—a teacher, a parent, a relative, a minister, a friend.

Thank You, God for those moments when You give me the opportunity to lift my sights and improve myself! Thank You, Father, that You created me with wisdom and beauty in mind. I thank You that I have been led to take this walk of faith. My faith is unlocking positive emotional power within me now! Thank You, God. Amen.

Plunging before you are positive

"Do you not know that those who run in a race all run, but one receives the prize? Run in such a way that you may obtain it."—1 CORINTHIANS 9:24

An exciting illustration of faith is portrayed in the running of a race. The runner jumps at the starting gun, even though he cannot be sure he will win. But one thing is certain.

The person who does not start can never win!

This means that another truth becomes markedly evident: Every starter is a winner. The losers are those who never tried. If you need to be sure that you will win, if you need to be confident of success *before* you make a commitment, *then you are not even walking the walk of faith!*

It is the element of uncertainty that adds excitement to life. The predictable always produces boredom. The element of the unpredictable always generates the interest and involvement of spectator and participant alike.

So the person who walks the walk of faith is alive and is keeping others alive, speculating on his success. He is news, because he has entered the race before he is positive that he can win.

God's promises are not offered to the "play-it-safe" spectator in the stands, but to the "let's-take-a-chance" player in the middle of the game!

Take this positive plunge: Today I'm going to double-check my life. Have I plunged ahead with the new opportunities that came to my mind only a day or two ago? If not, then today I will step on the starting line, I'll put both hands to the ground. I'll step up on tiptoe. I'll look ahead at the course. Here I go! I'm running the race. This time, I'm not a spectator in the stands, but a *contestant* and *participant!*

41

Deciding to begin

"In the beginning God created the heavens and the earth."—GENESIS 1:1

42 God has given you a dream. Now you must prepare to make brave decisions.

Faith is not daydreaming, it is decision making!

Even God's ideas aren't worth anything—until a believer acts upon them! We exercise our faith when we make the toughest decision—the decision to get started.

Procrastination is an exercise of doubt.

Postponing tough decisions is, more often than not, the result of a lack of faith.

God does not promise to bless us, until we make a commitment to live and walk by faith.

We cannot expect God to bless our profession of faith until we stop doing nothing and start doing something.

Faith is deciding to begin. Affirm with me:

Today I shall tackle my biggest enemy—inertia.

I will walk.
I will run.
I will talk.
I will write.
I will launch the project.
I will tell people what I am starting.

And I will trust God to enable me to keep moving once I demonstrate enough faith to get going! I really am walking the walk of faith. I am going to start today.

**In deciding to begin, I have solved my biggest problem.
I'm going to succeed, for beginning is half done!**

Entering the contest

"Commit your way to the LORD./Trust also in
Him,/And He shall bring it to pass."—PSALM
37:5

As a young child I never entered contests because I never **43**
wanted to lose. I did not want to compete because I always
wanted to win. Looking back, I realize how preposterous the
whole negative-thinking process was. Obviously, if I never entered the contest, I never would win!

There is more to winning than never losing! In the walk of
faith

**The person who enters the contest has already won a
battle. He has overcome the fear of failure!**

What contest are you preparing to enter?
What competitions should you engage in?
You can at least compete with your own best record!
Why don't you enter the contest of "generosity champion"?
Wouldn't it be wonderful to be known as one of the most gen-
erous persons who ever lived?
Why don't you enter the "encouragement contest," and win
the gold medal for doing more than anybody else to encourage
the discouraged?
Why don't you enter the "honesty contest"? In the final
judgment honesty pays off. What company would knowingly
hire a dishonest person?
Why don't you, in the name of Christ, compete against
negativity, sin, evil, and greed?
Almighty God, there is a race I should run,
    a contest I should enter,
        a competition I have to get involved in.
Show me the way, and I will follow. Win or lose—I'll know
I've kept the faith! Thank You, Father. Amen.

Leaving your ruts

"Your word is a lamp to my feet/And a light to
my path."—PSALM 119:105

44 It takes the power of God to release us from negative,
locked-in thinking. It takes guts to leave the ruts.

Is it possible you are in a negative-thinking rut?

If aeronautical engineers in the 1920s said it was impossible
to fly faster than the speed of sound, is it possible you might
be placing your faith on some negative precept? What ideas
are limiting your growth? What opinions are restricting you?

Ruts have a way of becoming security blankets in your second childhood. Most little children have their favorite
blanket. Many of your negative, deeply ingrained opinions
and well-entrenched conclusions become emotional security
blankets, holding you back

—from daring to go out in business for yourself,

—or daring to go back to college,

—or daring to tackle a physical fitness program,

—or daring to learn another language.

It takes a lot of courage to make a major career change in
midlife!

It takes a lot of faith to pack up and move to a new city,
state, or country.

What ruts are you in? You're free to leave that rut. A rut,
you know, is a grave—with the ends knocked out.

Come alive. Climb out of it. Tackle some exciting new possibilities today! Just make sure you are guided by God Almighty and His holy Word. Be certain you are not jumping out
of the frying pan into the fire. God's "word is a lamp to my
feet/And a light to my path"! Follow it. Get started today by
accepting His challenge.

FAITH IS . . .
Committing to action!

"Go your way; and as you have believed, so let
it be done for you."—MATTHEW 8:13

Miracles never happen just through meditation—but with
mighty action! Read carefully in the Gospels the words of
Jesus and notice the verbs. *Follow, go, seek, ask, knock.* The
walk of faith is not merely the serene, silent, spiritual, un-
speaking stroll of a holy man in the stillness of the sunrise or
the secret silence of the sunset.

**Faith is the mental activity that draws God into our
mind and imagination until a passion begins to in-
flame our wills, motivating us to action!**

It is then that the commitment is made. And what is a
commitment? It is entering into an honorable contract, pledging oneself before the problems are solved. Every commitment generates a new set of problems. And if we waited until
we saw solutions to problems before we made the commitment, we would obviously not be walking the walk of faith! It
is for that reason that commitment—
    in marriage,
        in religion,
            in interpersonal relationships,
                in devotion and dedication to your career goal
                or the fulfillment of a project
becomes self-inspiring.
Walk the walk of faith today. Make a fresh commitment to
God, saying prayerfully and sincerely:
"God, I'm ready to take the plunge. Give me the push that I
need, and I'm trusting that with Your help we'll tackle every
problem at every turn of the road with a positive mental attitude! And together we'll succeed joyously!"

45

Inking the agreement

"For behold, I have made you this day/A fortified city and an iron pillar,/And bronze walls against the whole land."—JEREMIAH 1:18

46   Until I'm solidly committed to an appointment, I write it in pencil. But then comes the time when it needs either to be erased or written in ink! That's the point of commitment.

Faith is inking the agreement. It's pouring the concrete! It's breaking the mold and throwing the pieces away.

On the grounds of our Crystal Cathedral is a beautiful bronze statue of Christ surrounded by sheep, sculpted by Henry Van Wolf. When we purchased the Good Shepherd statue and were completely satisfied with the finished bronze piece, the sculptor asked that the mold be destroyed, thereby protecting the uniqueness of the work that would stand on our property. I had no choice in the matter. It was a directive of the sculptor. He didn't want copies made.

> **Irrevocable commitments that offer no loopholes, no bail-out provisions, and no parachute clauses will extract incredible productivity and performance.**

One of the reasons my marriage has been so successful is because there isn't a single ounce of doubt in our minds that it has to be, it must be, and, therefore, it will be, a happy relationship until the end! We really meant it when we promised to love each other "for better, for worse; for richer, for poorer; in sickness and in health, till death us do part."

Inking an agreement is making a commitment to continuity. Try it. Believe me, that kind of faith moves mountains!

FAITH IS . . .
Imagining the positive possibilities

"But those who seek the LORD shall not lack
any good thing."—PSALM 34:10

List on a piece of paper all the resources you need to achieve **47**
your desired goal. Overlook nothing. Do you need more time
or money,
education or tools,
books or credit,
property,
consultants or friends,
specialized technicians,
or marketing plans?
Make sure you've included everything. Have you included
on the list your own positive imagination, your faith?

Now, look down the entire list and number the items according to their importance. What, in your list, will prove to
be the single most important factor to your success?

That's right—your own faith, your own power of imagination!

**What you imagine is what will transpire. What you
believe is what you will achieve.**

When you imagine positive possibilities, you release enthusiasm. You are driven with a strong desire to succeed. Nothing
is more important on that entire list than your own faith and
imagination!

You have the power to control pictures that are put into
your mind. Do not allow yourself the destructive luxury of
imagining all the negative possibilities.

Imagine the positive possibilities actually happening. You
will get so excited that the best people in the world will be
attracted to your side.

Everybody wants to associate with a winner!

Think success, and you'll achieve it.

FAITH IS . . .
Initiating positive action

"I will go in the strength of the Lord GOD."—
PSALM 71:16

48   By now you have observed that faith is not a plateau, it's a pyramid. It's not a sidewalk, it's a ladder. Faith is wading in the shallow water and moving on to the depths.

Wanting more out of life is the incentive to get going. Mountain-moving faith requires that you and I be initiators!

Be prime movers, leaders! A leader is the first person who stands up out of his chair and says, "O.K., gang, let's go!"

Our world today needs positive leaders of faith. Good things don't just happen. You have to make them happen!

People frequently comment on the success of our church. "Things seem to be going great for the ministry of the Crystal Cathedral."

My answer almost always is, "Yes, because people pray, prepare, plan, and promote these achievements. We initiate our own success. It doesn't just fall into our lap."

Where do you get the courage to be an initiator; a self-starter; a motivated individual? Draw motivation from faith.

I have been motivated for years by a phrase that is printed on the masthead of my little hometown paper in Alton, Iowa. I read it all of my childhood days: "The saddest words of tongue or pen are these: it might have been."

Become a "do it now" person. The world is out there waiting to follow those who have the faith to move ahead. Be the *initiator* of good and the *imitator* of God Himself!

I believe it will work, if I work it!

Assuring yourself of success

"There is not a word on my tongue,/But behold, O Lord,/You know it altogether./You have hedged me behind it and before,/And laid Your hand upon me."—PSALM 139:4–5

Faith is not folly. It's a responsible confidence rooted in the assurance that a wiser providence maneuvers your life. Confidence is not human arrogance. Rather, possibility thinking and self-assurance are the reflection of an abiding trust in the Lord who knows us perfectly. He has only our best interest in mind.

Our relationship with God allows us to be affirmative. Exercise your growing faith now with these declarations:

"I'm on the right road. I am walking the walk of faith. I have made the decision to follow the Lord."

"I have given my life to God and He is in control of it."

"The God who has command over my life is protecting me from hidden shoals that could sink the ship of my soul and spirit."

"God is opening doors that will surprise me with new opportunities."

"God is closing doors that I want to go through because He knows they will lead to my failure and destruction."

Thank You, Father, for assuring me of success on my walk of faith. I know I'm on the right road. I thank You, Lord, for opening and closing doors, thereby guiding me on my daily walk. I sense my faith growing stronger as I declare my faith and affirm You as Lord of my life. Thank You, O God.

49

FAITH IS . . .
Arranging to arrive

"Your eyes saw my substance,/being yet
unformed./And in Your book they all were
written,/The days fashioned for me,/When as
yet there were none of them."—PSALM 139:16

50   **It's terribly important that in the walk of faith you maintain your sense of responsibility.**

Faith seeks positive action through
• careful calculation
• wise planning, and
• clever arranging.
The greatest example of this is God Himself, the Divine Arranger, the Master Organizer!

Any scientist, chemist, or physicist will tell you how neatly and brilliantly every cell, genetic chain, and piece of matter is wondrously made and organized.

The way in which two microscopic elements meet in the womb to create a human being is wondrous. How beautifully today's Bible verse records it: God's eyes saw your substance before you were formed; He arranged your days before you were born. There is a divine plan for your life on earth.

God challenges you to so arrange the elements of your life that you might fulfill His plan. He assigns you the responsibility to consider all of the resources, time, energy, money, and relationships, and then arrange them to keep on target.

It is essential to put your life in good order. This is especially true of the health of your eternal soul and its relationship with the heavenly Father. Make sure that your life is so carefully arranged that when your calling comes to make the transition into eternity, you will arrive at heaven's gate without fear. You can do that now by committing your life to the God who made you.

Be sure of this—God will never turn one of His friends away!

Desiring to arrive

". . . when the desire comes, it is a tree of life."—PROVERBS 13:12

More than anything else, faith is an all-consuming desire to succeed!

51

Faith without passion is soda water without the sparkle.

"You don't lack faith," I said to a young man who had just complained of that problem. "Your faith lacks drive." Somehow a strong desire must be injected into the project of living, or faith will fizzle out and failure will overtake you.

Open a can of cola or soda water and let it stand for a few hours—and the fizz will all be gone. What the sparkle is to soda water, is what an inner passion to succeed is to mountain-moving faith. If you've lost your desire, if the fizz is gone, and the beverage is flat, then you need a new birth of divine desire!

How do you get it?

1. Perhaps you need to take a complete break, a holiday, a vacation.
2. Double-check your motives. Are you too self-serving?
3. Draw close to a hurting person. Feel his anxiety, loneliness, and emptiness. Know that, through your success, you can put a smile on his face and a sparkle in his eye; the passion will return.
4. Invite God to totally control your moods and your mind! For God Himself is the holy passion of helpful, appealing love which will override all other inclinations!
5. Calculate—who will be helped if I hang in—and succeed? And who will hurt—if I quit and fail?

Complimenting yourself every day

"Do not cast away your confidence, which has a great reward. For you have need of endurance. . . ."—HEBREWS 10:35

52 Practice all the faith you can by complimenting yourself, honestly, genuinely, and fluently! Be effervescent in complimenting yourself today.

As Christians we sometimes become so programmed to humility, coupled with the awareness that we can accomplish nothing without the grace of God and the goodness of our Lord, that we fail to give ourselves adequate credit.

God knows you and I need a pat on the back. There are nobler dreams that God wants us to pursue; there are bigger battles to be fought. The need to endure to the end compels us to give ourselves all the motivation possible.

Self-congratulatory remarks—in the privacy of your prayer time with God—are in order!

> **In the presence of God, in the privacy of prayer, take time to applaud the great human being that you really are!**

You are a redeemed child of God! Let your light shine!

Try complimenting yourself every morning when you begin the day by praying.

Thank You, Father, for giving me enough faith in myself, and in Your goodness to me, to give myself these compliments! I thank You that I have been created with a mind capable of dreaming dreams! I thank You that I have a heart through which the love of Jesus Christ can flow to human beings around me. I thank You that I do have talents, abilities, and gifts that You can use. I thank You, God, that my life is definitely on the right road. Stay with me, Father, all the way. Amen.

FAITH IS . . .
Educating your mind

"When wisdom enters your heart,/And knowledge is pleasant to your soul,/Discretion will preserve you;/Understanding will keep you."—PROVERBS 2:10–11

There is only one *now*—I'm going to make the most of today. There is only one *me*—I'll make the most of myself. **53**

People who have a lot of faith believe in themselves and their potential enough to invest everything to make the most of the one life they have.

How?

If you believe in yourself, you'll educate yourself.

You'll pay the price to become informed. Perhaps you need to go back to school, or aim for another degree.

Do you need to be brought up to date on new technology? Today more than ever before, a neglected intelligence is folly. "A mind is a terrible thing to waste" is the slogan of the United Negro College Fund.

Faith means being good stewards of the treasures God has put at our disposal, the opportunities He puts before us, the gifts He has given us, and the resources He has entrusted to our care.

Is any treasure more valuable than your ability to think? Remember, faith and intellect are not opponents. The smarter you become, the stronger your faith can grow. Be wise. Seek the counsel of the smartest people. Go to the person you would like to work for and ask what you need to do to qualify for the job you would like.

Keep this formula in mind today.

> **Inspiration + preparation + self-motivation = successful faith**

Prepare yourself to become a leader. You can do it—you are a possibility thinker.

Auditioning your ambitions

"For out of the abundance of the heart his
mouth speaks."—LUKE 6:45

54 Now that you have educated your mind don't assume that a
degree will automatically unlock any door. Education merely
entitles you to go out and sell yourself with integrity! Your
credentials only give you the right to audition your ambitions
in the market place.

There was an advertisement: "Help wanted: office boy."
One positive-thinking youngster rushed to answer the ad,
only to find a long line of boys ahead of him waiting to be
interviewed. He was afraid that by the time he got to the door,
a selection would have been made.

So he wrote this note: "To the boss: My name is Johnnie.
I'm number thirteen in the line. Don't hire anybody until
you've interviewed me!"

He handed the note to the secretary, who brought it into the
office. A moment later she came out, approached young Johnnie, and said, "The boss would like to see you." It was no surprise that he got the job!

**If you don't believe in yourself, who will? You owe
yourself every possible chance!**

Faith is auditioning your ambitions. Jesus said, "Let your
light so shine before men, that they may see your good works"
(Matt. 5:16). And He cautioned us not to "light a lamp and put
it under a basket, but on a lampstand" (Matt. 5:15).

Don't be afraid of boasting. You are only witnessing honestly to the talents God has given you! Remaining a silent,
shrinking violet can be a sin of ingratitude to God for the position and privilege He has bestowed upon you.

Are you arrogant? Lacking in humility when you step forward? I think not. Rather I suspect you are a dynamic possibility thinker! You're good—by the goodness of God and
both of you know it! Go for it!

FAITH IS . . .
Underscoring your positive thoughts

"You have put gladness in my heart."—PSALM
4:7

Today let's underline the positive thoughts. Let's honor creative ideas. Let's take the constructive ideas and crown them with a leadership role in our life. **55**

Look at a person who's moving forward, making commitments in faith, and you'll see somebody whose actions underscore his positive thoughts. Observe the person who is setting goals and going for them with all his might and you'll see somebody who has turned the leadership of his life over to a dynamic faith.

Stop and think of the most creative thoughts you've had in the past twenty-four hours. What have you done with those ideas?

Now go back and underline the most exciting ideas you've had in the last year. What have you done with them?

Life becomes what you make of it, and what you make of life depends entirely on how you manage the ideas that come to your brain.

> **Wisdom is the gift of spotting a positive idea and underscoring it by letting it become incarnated into action.**

Here's a positive thought that you can underscore right now:

God is alive.

He is there even if you do not feel His presence.

He is guiding your life by directing positive thoughts into your mind to keep you on the pathway of faith.

This is proof of God's existence and His goodness.

What a tremendous thought!

Adopting an orphan

"God has dealt to each one a measure of
faith."—ROMANS 12:3

56 Many positive ideas come into your mind like orphans.
They don't seem to be your own. But be prepared to adopt
them, especially when they are loaded with possibilities.

Faith is adopting an orphan; it's buying without a warranty; it's paying in advance; it's ordering from a foreign menu; it's traveling away from home without reservations.

Our wedding took place in a little country church in Iowa.
After the reception, we rushed to the car under a shower of
rice and headed off for a weekend honeymoon. As we drove
toward the direction of the state border, my wife asked,
"Where are we spending the night?" I looked at her dumbfounded. In all of the excitement of the wedding, I completely
forgot to make reservations!

"I thought we'd probably stay in a hotel somewhere in Minnesota," I said.

"You mean you didn't make reservations?" she asked.

We still laugh about that today, over thirty years later! As it
turned out we had a wonderful room, and a wonderful night.

In the first years of our marriage we supplied our house
with used utensils and appliances that were auctioned off by
moving companies. It was fun to watch unopened barrels
wheeled onto the platform and auctioned off. Nobody had any
idea what they were buying. They could be filled with old
clothes or, possibly, fine crystal and silver.

A positive idea sometimes comes across your mind like a
sealed box at an auction. Who knows what great possibilities
are waiting in that orphan idea? Adopt it!

This is your chance! Grab it.

FAITH IS . . .
Tuning into positive thoughts

"Make a joyful shout to the LORD . . ./Serve the LORD with gladness;/Come before His presence with singing."—PSALM 100:1–2

Faith is tuning into positive thoughts. When an uninvited and unwelcomed negative thought comes into your mind, tune it out by tuning in a good idea.

When my children were growing up, they often had childish sibling quarrels. They usually ended up pouting and sulking. Then I would take my finger and brush it lightly across the forehead from one side to the other saying, "Your mind is like a radio. And right here is the dial." Then I playfully switched the ear on the right and then the one on the left and said, "These are the little turning knobs. Why don't you turn the dial and pick up a happier channel?"

On more than one occasion when this little exercise didn't seem to achieve the immediate desired objectives, we joined as a family at the table and sang a happy song. Even though none of us were celebrating a birthday, we sang the happiest song we could think of. We knew "dear someone" would be glad we remembered his or her birthday!"

You and I have the power to choose the wave lengths we will tune into—wave lengths that will generate harmony or disharmony within your mind.

Imagine that the positive emotions are radio stations waiting for you to tune in and get turned on. Here are some positive wave lengths for you to select:

L–O–V–E
H–O–P–E
J–O–Y
P–E–A–C–E
C–O–U–R–A–G–E
C–H–E–E–R

If you really want to—you can find sources—like radio stations—sending out these signals. Tune them in, and you'll *come alive!*

Filtering the thoughts

"Whatever things are true, whatever things are noble, whatever things are just, whatever things are pure, whatever things are lovely, whatever things are of good report . . . meditate on these things."—PHILIPPIANS 4:8

58 A faith that is committed to success in the pursuit of an excellent and noble idea will require fine tuning. Fine tuning happens as you develop the practice of filtering the thoughts that come through your mind. Gradually your conscious level will rise as it relates in sensitivity to
what is positive and what is negative,
what is good and what is evil,
what is productive and what is counter-productive,
what is constructive and what is destructive,
what is healthy and what is unhealthy.

Your faith will be strengthened or insulted on a daily basis by the thoughts that enter your mind.

You can choose many of your thoughts by selecting the reading material, the television programs, and the deliberate exposures that you choose to encounter.

Still, there are the thousands of unsolicited stimuli that hit the average brain from a variety of unpredictable sources in the course of a single day. Consequently, a filtering system must be built into your mind that screens out the negative while allowing the positive to pass through. The Bible verse of today gives you the blueprint for establishing a six-layer mental filtering system.

1. Is it true?
2. Is it noble?
3. Is it just?
4. Is it pure?
5. Is it lovely?
6. Is it positive?

Now meditate on these things!

Minding the storehouse of the mind

" 'Therefore give to Your servant an
understanding heart to judge Your people, that I
may discern between good and evil.' " (The
prayer of Solomon)—1 KINGS 3:9

No wise builder builds a house until he knows the mate- **59**
rials available to him. Likewise, anyone who walks the walk
of faith requires constant spiritual nourishment. You must
have an adequate supply of positive beliefs for emergency use
in the battle against negative and destructive forces that can
conquer you.

I remember a young man, a member of my church, who
suddenly became uninterested in his faith and went into a
period of depression. He finally asked me for help. I asked him
the basic questions. "What have you been reading lately?"
"Have you been reading your Bible?" "Inspirational literature?" "Have you been listening to positive-thinking people?"
He admitted he had allowed himself to be exposed to much
negative thinking.

I shared with him the old computer programmer slogan,
GIGO—Garbage-in-garbage-out. If you program garbage into
the computer, garbage will come out of the computer.

A psychologist friend of mine, who was counseling a client
suffering from depression, put on a dramatic demonstration.
He filled a glass with water, then added some dust to it. He
reached in the ash tray for a cigarette butt and dropped it in.
He reached underneath a chair and, finding a dried piece of
gum, added it to the glass of water. Now he mixed the polluted mixture thoroughly and proceeded to pour it into a nice
clean cup. As he did, he said, "You will only pour out what
you have put in."

**At least once a week hear a positive-thinking message
from some positive-thinking church. Add to that positive Bible readings and positive prayer, and then your
faith will remain vital and alive.**

Imprinting the self-conscious mind

"For You are great, and do wondrous things;/
You alone are God./Teach me Your way, O
Lord;/I will walk in Your truth."—PSALM
86:10,11

60 It's important to understand how faith works, from the scientific and psychological perspective as well as from the theological and scriptural perspective.

We have already studied previously that the subconscious mind is like
- a film in a movie camera
- the tape in a tape recorder
- a chip in a computer

Knowledge is stored permanently.

We now know that the human being never forgets anything. Every experience we ever have had is indelibly recorded within us.

We may lose the powers of conscious recall. But under deep psychoanalysis we can usually recollect experiences that have long been forgotten in the depths of our memories.

When you exercise positive faith by imagining, visualizing, or picturing in your brain the expectant achievement, you are in effect making a cybernetic imprint. Your strongly held beliefs leave an indelible stamp on your subconscious, almost like a tattoo on the skin. As you evaluate the thoughts that you allow into your conscious mind, remember this:

> **Each thought becomes a tattoo on the skin of your memory either for good or ill.**

Therefore, it is vitally important to your mental muscles that you control what you will allow to be imprinted on your eternal memory.

Thank You, Father, for teaching me the power of faith. I am going to succeed because I am imprinting my conscious now with this affirmation and declaration of faith.

You, alone, are God!

I will walk in Your truth.

I'm going to make it! Amen.

FAITH IS . . .

Censoring the negatives

"Behold, I stand at the door and knock. If
anyone hears My voice and opens the door, I
will come in."—REVELATION 3:20

Possibility thinking includes the process of positive censoring. It involves sifting out the good from the bad.

61

Faith asks the question: Does this idea deserve my attention or the trademark of my name? Maintaining a constructive critical overview is a constant process.

Faith is not afraid to censor. It stands guard at the portals of your mind, checking the ethical and moral credentials of the ideas that could disrupt, disturb, and possibly destroy your attitude of faith.

So firm up your willpower.

Assign responsibility to the spiritual laws that manage your thoughts. Without guidelines, controls, and censorship, life is like an airplane with a drunken pilot. A crash landing is always looming.

I have made several trips into Egypt to study ancient Egyptology. Pharaohs often are portrayed with a cobra poised over their heads. King Tut not only is pictured with a head gear featuring a cobra—but also a vulture. The cobra was to attack the poisonous ideas before they entered his head. The vulture was to consume the rotten ideas.

You need Jesus Christ to help control your thinking. He stands at the door of your mind and heart waiting to come in.

Lord Jesus Christ, my mind was designed to be a mansion with many rooms. Will You come and be the Doorkeeper at the main entrance? Admit only those guests who would bring honor to the household. Dismiss the unworthy from my doorstep. Welcome those honorable visitors that would flood my mind with hope and health and happiness.

Lord, will You come to be the Guest of Honor? Amen.

Starving your enemies

"Do not be overcome by evil, but overcome evil with good."—ROMANS 12:21

62 Do positive-thinking people deny the reality of evil? Not at all. We recognize that there is an opposite to everything; when we declare our faith in positive thinking we automatically acknowledge the alternative—negative thinking.

So we can expect to encounter enemies as we walk the path of faith. Possibility thinking is a threat to impossibility thinkers. Positive thinking is a judgment on negative thinking.

Faith is a positive attack on doubt.

What enemies have you encountered, so far, on the walk of faith?

In the walk of faith we describe an enemy as anybody who diminishes your faith in yourself, in your neighbors, and in almighty God!

Therefore, our strongest enemies are the negative thoughts that come into our minds.

Who then is your greatest enemy? You may lament the fact that those closest to you do not give the encouragement you think they should. But nobody puts you down more than you do yourself. Nobody has rejected more of your best ideas than you have!

How many good ideas have come into your mind only to be discarded by you?

So how will you handle an enemy? If you can't convert him, starve him. Whatever you do, don't feed your negative thoughts! Starve your negative thoughts by ignoring them.

Feed your positive thoughts with faith. Fill your mind with beautiful affirmations and powerful promises that are abundant throughout the Bible.

My promise to you is this: Your walk of faith will be productive, prosperous, and worthwhile!

FAITH IS . . .
Washing the windows of the mind

"The path of the just is like the shining sun,/
That shines ever brighter unto the perfect
day."—PROVERBS 4:18

If you tune in positive thoughts and censor out negative **63**
ones, will these dynamic exercises of a daily, disciplined faith
keep the windows of your soul sparkling continually? No, not
completely.

• Accidents can dent a new car.
• Spills can stain clean clothes.
• Upsets can frustrate a good person.
• Storms can litter the clean year.

Recently I attended a religious conference in Amsterdam.
Each morning we saw Dutch people washing their windows,
even if there was no dirt on them, no rainfall to stain the glass,
no heavy dew that would dry and leave a misty film.

That's a good practice for us also.

Faith is washing the windows of the mind, every morning
beginning the new day, bright with God's love, and each night
washing away the film of negativity.

Have you noticed how quickly windows that were clean
can lose their sparkle? From somewhere a film comes, cloud-
ing the reflection of the sun.

Are the twinkle and the sparkle of faith gone from the win-
dowpanes of your soul? Is the reflection of God's love no
longer mirrored brightly in your life as it used to be?

**Ask the Holy Spirit to come in each morning and
again in the evening to wash the skylights of your soul.
Visualize the Lord, living within your mind like a
bright light of love and faith!**

Lord, make my life a window for your light to shine
through, and a mirror to reflect your love to all I meet. Amen.

Mining the deeper thoughts

"O LORD, You have searched and known me./
You know my sitting down and rising up;/You
understand my thought afar off."—PSALM
139:1–2

64 I have long marveled at the courage of the miners who dare
to dig deep shafts in the heart of the trembling earth, in search
of diamonds, gold, or precious ore.

**A vibrant and shining faith comes from mining deeper
thoughts, exploring deeper and darker regions of your
soul.**

Joshua Lightman tells of a colleague, a professed atheist.
The young Jewish man, undergoing depth analysis to understand his subconscious feelings, recalled a long-forgotten experience. His mother had enrolled him, at the age of five, in a
synagogue school to "learn about his heavenly Father." This
little boy's earthly father was cruel; therefore, he believed all
fathers were cruel. In a negative emotional reaction he made a
decision *not* to meet "another father"—God. When he discovered that his atheism was rooted in negative emotional-
ism, not healthy intellectualism, he was liberated and became
a believer!

Are there blockades that need to be blasted out of the way
before you can discover the wealth within your grasp? Delve
into your conscious and subconsciousness—mine the depths
of your faith. God has searched you and knows you. He *understands* your thoughts afar off.

O Lord, my Father, You know every experience I have ever
encountered. Heal me of deep obsessions, of negative experiences that would prevent me from believing with joy. Then
may my faith sparkle like a diamond! Thank You, Lord.
Amen.

Tolerating your imperfections

"Do you not know that you are the temple of
God and that the Spirit of God dwells in
you?"—1 CORINTHIANS 3:16

How's your self-image today? Having trouble accepting **65**
yourself after goofing, bungling, or sinning?

Are you pulled down by a painful awareness of your shortcomings and your frailties?

Then today is the time to reprogram your mental attitude,
remodel your self-image, and give your self-esteem a "faith-
lift."

• Remember that even though you are imperfect, you still
are a child of God.

• Decide to join the human race. Nobody's perfect; no one
is sinless! Who do you think you are? Why are you so rough
on yourself?

• The power of God within you can compensate for your
imperfections and inability.

• Tolerate your imperfections, and keep striving for excellence!

• But never tolerate your own negative thinking!

• Do separate yourself from negative thinkers who put you
down! You need to be built up.

• Gravitate to positive people who give you a lift!

• Choose—willfully and deliberately—to be a "bigger" believer! Yes, you are designed to be a positive thinker.

God is within you now, living in the best thoughts you are
thinking.

Affirmation: I shall tolerate my weakness and shortcomings by shifting my focus to the mighty power of God.

**God is able to do great things through imperfect
people!**

Thank You, God, for living in me. Knowing this, I claim
Your power, Your holiness, Your ability, and Your wisdom,
that my weakness may be made perfect in Your sight. Amen.

Deprogramming your computer

"Let us know, let us pursue the knowledge of the LORD. His going forth is established as the morning; He will come to us like the rain, like the latter and former rain to the earth."— HOSEA 6:3

66 The mind is like a computer. Think of yourself as a multi-track, supersophisticated recording device. From the moment you are born, this complex, four-track tape recorder starts running and never stops!

On one track you record in the memory and subconscious every sound you ever hear.

On another track a video camera starts filming everything your eyes see from the moment they open and begin to focus.

On still another track your subconscious begins to record sensual experiences—pain and pleasure. The entire psychological system of Pavlovian behavioral modification takes off on this track.

On still another track, another subconscious recording starts the moment you are born. This channel will record every emotional experience you ever encounter.

God created your memory to record the audio, video, sensual, and emotional trips you'll take in life.

We have all experienced *deja-vu*, that experience whereby something we see, hear, or smell touches the replay button of our subconscious recorder and we immediately experience a visual or emotional flashback. We are suddenly caught up in a mood—pleasant or unpleasant. We cannot explain why. A long forgotten experience from the distant past is trying to surface in the memory. The vague recollection hazily lingering in the subconscious memory only succeeds in "filtering through" as an unclear mystifying mood.

So you realize how important it is to limit the negative input in your life. Every time you repeat a negative word or phrase, you contribute to the collective underground pollution of your mind.

Deprogram, then *reprogram yourself with positive words, positive affirmations, and positive prayers.*

This is mountain-moving faith at work!

Programming your computer for success

"The fruit of the Spirit is love, joy, peace, longsuffering, kindness, goodness, faithfulness, gentleness, self-control."—GALATIANS 5:22

Knowing that the mind is a complex recording system, you **67** choose to either program it for failure, or for success. Today, program these positive thoughts:

Faith puts positive thoughts into my mind, knowing they will flash back on the digital screen of my conscious mind at the press of a button.

- I am programming my mind to see the good in bad situations.
- I am programming my computer to react positively to negative situations.
- I am programming my computer to create a subconscious mental picture of my success already achieved.
- I am affirming only positive expectations.

I marvel that God gives me the freedom to program my computer any way I choose. If I fill it with inaccurate data, that's exactly what will come out; so I am treating my subconscious mind seriously. I cannot be frivolous in playing mental games. I cannot take a lighthearted attitude toward negative fantasies that flash through my mind.

God gives me the freedom to choose what my life and destiny will be. I shall prove responsible to this awesome responsibility. I know that success is certain if I program positive thoughts for great possibilities.

Thank You, God, for all the positive encouragement You send my way. Your blessings are so many I cannot count them all—love, joy, peace, kindness, goodness. . . . What a rich reservoir I can tap when I program Your power into my life. Thank You, Lord. Amen.

Supposing —positively

"Surely His salvation is near to those who fear Him."—PSALM 85:9

68 Life proceeds on the basis of many unproven assumptions. Faith moves ahead, acting on suppositions that may or may not be verifiable. A negative-thinking person assumes the worst will happen, and then wonders why his negative expectations are always fulfilled. But a positive-thinking person assumes that the best will happen and sees positive results!

Faith is *supposing—positively.* A negative thinker says, "But suppose it won't work." A positive thinker says, "Suppose it *will* work!" The negative thinker says, "But suppose it can't be done." A positive thinker says, "Suppose it *can* be done! I don't want to pass up this opportunity!"

Faith practices the art of creating positive alternatives to negative assumptions! Here's how supposing positively works: An idea comes to mind, an opportunity presents itself, a problem confronts us. Now watch the "supposing positive" mind at work: "*Suppose* this idea came from God?" "It sounds impossible, but *suppose* I give it a try?" "*Suppose* I announce my plans?" "Then *suppose* some people believe that it's a great idea and come to my support!" "*Suppose* I pray about this and believe it is the right thing to do." "Is there reason for me to *suppose* that God will bless me?"

There is no *supposing* when it comes to the faithfulness of God! The word in the Scriptures is *surely!* "*Surely* His salvation is near to those who fear Him." "*Surely* goodness and mercy shall follow me/All the days of my life;/And I will dwell in the house of the LORD/Forever" (Ps. 85:9; 23:6 italics added).

God's promise is that He will replace our positive *supposing* with His *absolute surety.*

FAITH IS . . .
Experiencing impossibilities

"Your sun shall no longer go down,/Nor shall your moon withdraw itself;/for the LORD will be your everlasting light."—ISAIAH 60:20

Is it possible to live where the sun never sets? Yes, northern **69** Sweden is the land of the "midnight sun." Some years ago when I was on a preaching mission in Sweden, we traveled to the northernmost point of the earth, which is reachable by commercial floating vessels. On the third day of the cruise, at 11:00 P.M., there was only blue sky around us.

We watched the sun drop until it was low in the sky and looked as though it would disappear. But then it began to move to the right, parallel with the horizon. At midnight, still as bright as day, the sun moved across the horizon without setting. It was a great experience to witness one of those days when the sun never sets.

When you experience something that you always assumed was an impossibility you can be sure you've been believing!

Faith is the practice which allows for the possibility of apparent impossibilities to become actual scientific realities.

Walking the walk of faith is the attitude of keeping your mind open to new possibilities that only God knows about!

"God is the sum total of the vast unknown," said my friend Dr. Arnold Beckman, founder of Beckman Instruments. This explains why some of the greatest scientists alive in the world today are believers in God.

The next time you face a problem or a challenge that appears to defy solutions, keep an open mind to the impossibility. . . . It might be possible after all!

Today, O God, I am going to keep an open mind to experience some new surprises of spiritual growth. Today, I am going to believe that the impossible really is possible! Amen.

Rising above depressing situations

"To whom then will you liken Me . . . ?/Lift
up your eyes on high,/And see who has created
these things. . . ."—ISAIAH 40:25–26

70 What do you do when the analysis of your condition leads
to a depressing diagnosis?

What do you do when your doctor tells you that you have
an incurable fatal disease?

How do you keep an open mind to the possibility of a cure
when there is no known cure?

You practice faith! You rise above the depressing attitudes
and situations.

Think of the locks that enable a boat to rise and proceed up
a stream that otherwise would be impossible to navigate.
When ships travel upstream they are "locked" into an en-
closed area which is then filled with water. Ships weighing
tens of thousands of tons, are lifted easily through the floata-
tion power of water. The lock system enables ships to sail on
and on through higher bodies of water.

What do you do when you are trapped with a negative analysis that appears to block your way through life?

> **Lock in your mental attitude with positive thinking
> and allow your mind to float upward by the invisible,
> silent, escalating flow of the spirit of faith which only
> the eternal God can give.**

Suddenly you are moving forward again!

You are rising above the shoals that would have grounded
you.

O God, today I feel Your enormous power streaming into
my life, flooding my soul. I am rising like a giant ship, lifted
by water. I am floating above the negative predictions because
I know my condition is never hopeless! My faith is escalating!
Thank You, God. Amen.

FAITH IS . . .
Scaling the wall

"For by You I can run against a troop;/By my
God I can leap over a wall."—2 SAMUEL 22:30

You have heard about those incredible incidents where an **71**
average human being exhibits almost superhuman strength in
an emergency situation. It's a frequently recurring phenomenon.

Two people are working on an automobile. One is underneath the car. The jack collapses. The car falls. The companion
finds himself picking up the car and rescuing his companion
from certain, crushing death. Where did the strength of a giant
come from?

Do you know how strong you are? Do you know how high
you can jump? We really don't know! For every single human
being, without exception, has the potential to tap into physical power that far transcends normality. We just don't know
the how, the why, and the wherefore.

What that means to you today is that you can scale that
wall! The "impossible" obstruction! You can leap over that
fence of frustration! Suddenly you can surmount that obstacle
as your spirit soars!

Any person becomes a bigger person when he becomes ob-
sessed by a "giant complex"! You can be a giant, too. You are
as big as you think you are!

Think "leaping over" thoughts and you will scale that wall!

> **The "will" is more important than the "skill" when it
> comes to scaling a wall.**

You will not fail to scale the wall. "By my God I can leap
over a wall." Break wide open with big-thinking belief and—
away you go!

Dividing to conquer

"Look, the LORD your God has set the land
before you; go up and possess it, as the LORD
God . . . has spoken to you; do not fear or be
discouraged."—DEUTERONOMY 1:21

72　　One day president of McDonnell Douglas Corporation, Walter Burke, received a telephone call from President John F. Kennedy. "Mr. Burke, we need a rocket with enough booster power to put a man on the moon. I have already been told all the reasons why it can't be done. Now you go ahead and solve the problems to get the job accomplished!"

"How did you ever begin to tackle such an impossible assignment?" I asked Walter Burke.

"I learned many years ago that one large problem is really a collection of many little problems," Mr. Burke said. He explained:

> **"The way to tackle an impossible problem is to break it down and solve the several little problems one at a time."**

You tackle each one until only one stubborn problem remains. Now all attention is focused on this remaining obstacle and the breakthrough happens! You have divided and conquered the total problem one chunk at a time.

It worked for Walter Burke and it will work for you. When you face a seemingly insurmountable problem—divide it.

Part of the problem is a decision you need to make.

Part of the problem is your lack of patience.

Part of the problem is your negative attitude.

Part of the problem is your preoccupation with yourself. You can handle all of these parts of the problems. Right?

You will succeed in conquering the insolvable problems! What a great feeling of success you'll experience!

Challenging the negative judgment

"There are many who say,/'Who will show us
any good? LORD, lift up the light of Your
countenance upon us.'"—PSALM 4:6

Many problems continue to remain unsolved because **73**
negative-thinking experts say, "It can't be done." Remember Walter Burke? One day I asked him, "How did you ever
manage to believe that it was possible to develop a rocket
big enough to put a man on the moon?"

He answered, "I was a student in aeronautical engineering
in St. Louis, Missouri, in the 1920s. At that time, we were
taught as a matter of scientific truth that the speed of sound
was the absolute, ultimate limit we would ever be able to
travel. The reasons made sense: (1) the weight of such a machine, because of the amount of fuel needed, would render
it unflyable; (2) we believed an object crossing the sound
barrier would disintegrate."

"And how did we ever break through such locked-in
thinking?" I asked Dr. Burke.

"Well, the Second World War came along," Dr. Burke explained. "And in the emergency, farmers from Iowa and
Nebraska were drafted. We put them in a cockpit and in a
matter of days taught them to fly an airplane. We never
bothered to teach them aeronautical engineering. With a
few victories, they were promoted to officers. Well, these
uneducated officers got together and decided we ought to
focus our energies on developing a jet engine that could fly
faster than sound. They did it. *Because they didn't know it
couldn't be done!"*

The next time somebody tells you, "It is impossible!" "It
can't be done!" "It's hopeless!" "It's terminal!" challenge the
negative assumption.

God doesn't know the meaning of *impossible*.

That's what faith is all about.

Analyzing inquisitively

"Understanding is a wellspring of life to him who has it."—PROVERBS 16:22

74 Stop and analyze the creative people who have been responsible for big breakthroughs and have made distinctive contributions in the world of science, art, humanity, and religion. You will find that each has an inquisitive nature.

After all, thousands, even millions of people must have sat under a tree and had an apple hit them on the head, but all they did was complain! According to legend, Newton looked up and ask, "Why did the apple fall *down?*"

If you are having problems with your faith, perhaps you need to be more inquisitive. Do not fear that your faith in God can ever be shaken by an increased intelligence. Make sure the sources of your newly acquired knowledge are persons who are not prejudiced and who are not proclaiming as fact assumptions that are rooted in negativity.

Can you see how widely the poison of negative thinking has penetrated our culture? How often have you and I been heard saying, "Curiosity killed the cat"? In fact, curiosity has been responsible for many scientific achievements and medical breakthroughs!

The inquisitive nature of the human being is a God-implanted impulse, designed to entice us down the road of faith toward exciting progress!

Analyze God Himself. You'll be surprised how this can be the beginning of new growth into a maturing religious consciousness. The possibility thinker who pursues his inquisitive nature is the one who will find the buried treasure!

Thank You, God, for the faith to analyze Your Word today. I will no longer be afraid in Your presence. My finite mind cannot begin to understand the vastness of Your infinite knowledge. Walk with me today and teach me a new truth about Yourself. Amen.

Actualizing your positive fantasies

"Your old men shall dream dreams, your young
men shall see visions."—JOEL 2:28

I once did a study of those great people we call "geniuses." I **75** observed a recurring quality in them—the amazing quality of positive, childlike fantasizing. Great people are intuitive and imaginative. They have the capacity to let their minds fly into wild and wonderful flights of fantasy. It was said of Walt Disney that he never stopped being a little boy.

Faith is actualizing *positive* fantasies. Obviously, negative fantasizing that leads to antisocial behavior must be restrained. Faith tests your fantasies. Are they positive? Will they help society? Will they bring happiness? Dare to dream the most wonderful dreams in the world!

Now make your fantasies come true by believing they *can* come true, even though they appear to be totally and completely impossible! Your fantasies will attract attention if you dare to talk about them! At first you may not be taken seriously, but your fantasies will soon become realities as you take the first strong steps forward.

> **Positive people will intuitively respond to your positive dreams. Encouragement will come from places and people you least expect. Believe in your positive fantasies and you will begin to actualize them.**

I speak from experience. An all-glass church? A Crystal Cathedral? A fantasy? Yes—and today, it is a fantastic reality!

Positive fantasies become positive realities when by faith you start to do something about them. Make them happen. They will become tomorrow's talked-about achievement.

FAITH IS . . .

Stretching your imagination

"Enlarge the place of your tent,/ . . . Lengthen
your cords,/And strengthen your stakes./For you
shall expand to the right and to the left."—
ISAIAH 54:2–3

76 The word *imagination* comes from the root word meaning
"to image." Every person has the ability to imagine. It is the
mark of the image of God within us. The trick is to stretch
that imagination! Expand it higher, wider, longer, and deeper.
Think bigger thoughts, and bigger results will come your way.

Measure a person by the stretch of his imagination.

You can tell where he is going by how expansive his powers
of imagination are.

It was said of Joseph Stalin that he kept a world globe on his
desk. He used it as a device to help him think bigger! The
conquest of the world was his goal.

Today the tentacles of Communism have effectively
reached around the world! It has become, along with Christianity and Islam, one of the three leading ideologies, in terms
of worldwide power and following.

Now consider Jesus Christ. He, too, had a vision of world
conquest. A simple, untutored, uneducated Carpenter left this
challenge with twelve of His followers: "You shall be wit-
nesses to Me in Jerusalem, and in Judea and Samaria, and *to
the end of the earth*" (Acts 1:8). The results?

Today, more people claim to follow Christianity than any of
the other major world philosophies.

Christ needs you to expand His ministry around the world.
Can you stretch your imagination that far? Nobody—except
yourself—can tell you how big you can think!

You have the freedom to dream as big, beautifully, and
bountifully as you want!

*Since it doesn't cost a dime to dream you'll never short-
change yourself when you stretch your imagination!*

Managing to achieve the impossible

"Through wisdom a house is built,/And by understanding it is established. By knowledge the rooms are filled/With all precious and pleasant riches."—PROVERBS 24:3–4

Can you say—   **77**
  • I've taken the plunge?
  • I'm pushing myself to the limit?
  • I believe in success and I will manage until I succeed?

> **The impossible can become possible through wise management.**

Management is taking control of a situation in which you will be held accountable for the results.

Think of this: Responsibility means that you will be held accountable for your successes or failures. If you have to answer for your performance then you are ipso facto in a management role. Then you must have freedom to control.

The word *control* implies the exercise of leadership. Leadership is the force that sets the goals. It is the force that analyzes problems that make certain situations *appear impossible.* Leadership is the managerial power that sets goals to solve problems, clear the way, remove obstacles, invent solutions, hire experts, until what once seemed impossible now becomes possible.

Leadership takes control of a situation to reshape, rearrange, reorganize, and retool the operation until the project turns around! Be patient. It takes time to stop a freight train. It will take time to turn impossibilities into possibilities, but you will make it!

Perhaps you have to learn to manage by setting definite goals. *Your situation isn't impossible—you simply have to exercise leadership!* Don't confuse indecision for problems!

What is one of the first arts of a good manager? It's making hard decisions!

Planning to solve unsolvable problems

"Ask, and it shall be given to you; seek, and you will find; knock, and it will be opened to you."—MATTHEW 7:7

78 The walk of faith inevitably leads you into a position where you face problems. On first sight, these problems may appear unsolvable! The fact is

We are not operating in the arena of faith unless we are dealing with problems that at the present moment appear unsolvable.

Is your walk taking you to the brink of a possible failure? If not, you may be living so safely that your faith can be called into question.

Your faith moves from the infantile stage to the adult stage when you face seemingly impossible situations. At that point, your faith is no longer mental fantasizing, but active planning.

How do you put your faith in action? Simply count to ten, pause, and pray. Then listen to every wonderful, wild, and wacky idea that enters your mind and which might conceivably whittle away or chip off a corner of your enormous problem. Write the ideas down. Before you know it, you will have listed ten ways to solve your unsolvable problem. This is the process of planning solutions to your problems through possibility thinking! This is faith on the adult level.

So set goals. Today! Make them impossible enough to get God involved! You—and God—will come up with a plan to make them happen!

Let my prayer and yours today be these words of an old hymn:

> O for a faith that will not shrink
> Though pressed by every foe
> That will not tremble at the brink
> Of any earthly woe!

FAITH IS . . .
Pursuing your objective relentlessly

". . . be strong in the Lord and in the power of
His might."—EPHESIANS 6:10

Human behavior can be dissected and divided into three
sections:

(1) Intellectual—when you walk the walk of faith you use
your head. Be smart about it.

(2) Emotional—be inwardly secure enough that you do not
fear the mysterious and marvelous geysering of positive emotions. Enthusiasm is a mark of health—not illness. However,
it's not enough to merely "experience a religious feeling." In
fact, many people with a strong faith never do have an emotional conversion experience. It's possible to be "born again"
and not know the exact hour or time.

(3) Volitional—faith must be applied to daily life. The word
volitional comes from the root, *velle* which means expressing
tremendous proven internalized energy that becomes exter-
nalized energy in the pursuit of an all-consuming objective!

Faith moves from emotional and intellectual stages to a volitional stage when you are determined and disciplined. All
great athletes who have won medals or earned crowns have
done so because of tremendous faith. They believed they
could win! And *then* they exploded with an inner volition.

Have you discovered this capacity in yourself? It's there. If
you have experienced it, you know what I mean. But if you
haven't, you've got to believe that there is a lot more within
you than you ever experienced.

**It begins when faith becomes an act of the will; when
belief is translated into dynamic willpower.**

O God, help me to discover the power that comes from
within me when I make up my mind wholeheartedly to pursue my objective relentlessly. Amen.

Splurging in possibilities

> "Then Mary took a pound of very costly oil . . .
> and anointed the feet of Jesus."—JOHN 12:2

80 "It may help you," I explained to a new Christian who asked about his new-found faith, "to think of the walk of faith which you have just started as a symphony in four movements."

The first movement of faith is the *urge*—deep within yourself there was a voice that said, "There is something more." Intuitively you suspected that you were missing out on something. An inner urge nudged you to open up your mind to the possibility of a religious reality that until now you had avoided. There was a hunger deep within yourself that nothing seemed to really satisfy in spite of your successes and achievements.

The second movement of faith is known as the *surge*. What started as a gentle thought—*It would be wonderful if . . .*—grew into a passion: *I want it! I need it!*

The third movement of faith is known as the *purge*. Negative thoughts rushed in to destroy your desire and torpedo your dream with negative forces. This movement was filled with discordant notes and contradictions.

All of the destructive thoughts *must* be purged. Abort all negative thoughts before they can take an embryonic fix in your mind.

The fourth and final movement is the *splurge*—you made the leap. You went all out for it. You put everything on the line. You held nothing back. It is the splurging of your dream that will make it come true!

> **Like that beautiful woman who opened the flask and poured all of the costly perfume over the feet of Jesus in a display of extravagance, I'm going to give my dream my all-out effort; for I am a believer!**

Making daring decisions

"I have set before you life and death, blessing and cursing; therefore choose life, that . . . you . . . may live."—DEUTERONOMY 30:19

Success never happens until you make it happen. And you **81** make good things happen when you make decisions that cause a movement to begin. You can be sure that you are walking the walk of faith so long as you make those decisions.

How can you make a decision when there is risk involved? How can you make a decision when dangers may follow?

The answer, of course, is this:

Life, by its very nature, rejects protectionism.

Do you refuse to make decisions because problems and perils might result? Do you want to play it safe? That's one of life's rare impossibilities! When you play it safe, you can be sure you will face the dangers that inevitably come: boredom; lack of growth; stagnation; emotional death! The zest that comes from decisions will be gone. What is left is a shriveling and shrinking spirit with false promises of security.

Of all the cruel illusions there is none more insidious or disastrous than the alluring call of safety and shelter when you retreat from taking a risk!

The truth is, if you continue to make daring decisions, you will succeed—at least you will succeed in filling each day with excitement!

The promise from the God of life, abundant and eternal, is only offered to those who dare to walk the walk of faith.

Keep walking that path by daring to make the decision you have already postponed too long!

Success is no accident. Success is a commitment—not a coincidence! Decide today where you want to be five, ten, twenty years from today.

FAITH IS . . .
Snapping the trap

"*. . . that we may know the things that have been freely given to us by God.*"—1
CORINTHIANS 2:12

82   I grew up out in the country, on a farm at the end of a road. I discovered early in life that I did not appreciate living at the dead end of a road.

There wasn't much excitement there! The only cars that ever came down that road were those of relatives, friends, or someone who was lost. Whenever a lost traveler realized that he was on a dead-end road, he would turn around in a cloud of agitated dust and retreat over his fresh path clearly marked in the dirt, racing faster to make up for lost time.

I learned this lesson early in life: *Dead-end roads never go anywhere.*

Dead-end roads are traps. As a young man I never allowed myself to be trapped by conditions that weren't leading me upward, outward, and onward.

I quickly made this youthful observation: I could walk away from dead-end roads! Yes, I could get out and walk when I couldn't drive any farther. But I would never stop and sit in a parked car spending my life on a dead-end road.

Are you trapped today in a job that has no future? Is your life bogged down at a dead end with nothing exciting in your future path? Even God cannot steer a stalled car. Get out and move. It takes guts to leave the ruts.

Analyze your obstruction. Who, or what, is blocking you? Chances are, you are your own greatest obstacle.

Faith is snapping the trap!

So set new goals.

Chart a new course.

Consider a midflight correction and a midlife change.

You are free to go anywhere from where you are!

FAITH IS . . .
Peeling the orange

"Behold, now is the accepted time; Behold, now is the day of salvation."—2 CORINTHIANS 6:2

At the core of faith, there is that innermost, indivisible cell called commitment. Faith always commands some decisive action. More often than not, it represents an irreversible decision. **83**

Faith is peeling the orange. It's cracking the egg. It's opening the can of Coke! Faith is delivering the ice. Now you either consume it, or throw it away.

Faith is serving the soufflé hot from the oven! You must eat it, or watch it deflate. What's left cannot be saved or stored.

Our family always remembers one night when we had a family party. Our favorite dessert, a baked soufflé, was just taken out of the oven and put on the table when there was a knock at the door. It was a police officer, commanding, "Come out quickly! There are armed robbers who have escaped from the police. They are believed to be in the grove behind your house. There will be shooting so we need to evacuate you now!"

Two hours later we returned. The robbers were captured, and the soufflé was a deflated, miserable sight. But we were alive and safe. There are those tides and times in the affairs of human life when we must take action—now! There can be no procrastination! To delay is fatal!

Dear God, what decisions are before me now that require firm action on my part?

> **Give me the faith to make the move at the right time in the right way. Protect me from the false security that indecision foolishly promises me. Today I shall move from faith. I shall not be mesmerized by fear.**

Thank You, God, for giving me the faith to make decisions courageously. Amen.

Stepping out of line

"And do not be conformed to this world, but be transformed by the renewing of your mind. . . ."—ROMANS 12:2

84   Do you dare to be a maverick? A maverick is a spunky, spirited calf that doesn't run with the herd but ventures out into the beckoning canyons.

Mavericks are essential to the survival of the herd. A herd with no mavericks huddles together with backs to the wind, heads down, shoulders together, seeking to survive the storm. More than one herd of cattle has frozen to death that way. Where is the one who can break out of the group, put his head to the wind, and venture out to find shelter from the storm or discover new grazing ground?

Early in my ministry I was labeled a maverick by a rigid institutionalist in my denomination. My first reaction, I confess, was negative. I was offended. But when I checked on the definition, I admitted that I was indeed a maverick and proud of it. For being a maverick is a characteristic of people who walk by faith. When you start looking at what everybody else is doing before you make a move, you surrender leadership to your social group.

Dare to be a wise but wonderful nonconformist.

Look at the leaders of the world! They all step forward and upward and onward. And that's beyond the line of conformity—always.

Let God have command over your life. When the Holy Spirit of the living God guides and leads in your life, you will be "transformed by the renewing of your mind." You will break out of the mold and be unique!

O Lord, give me enough faith to step out of line and move ahead with courage toward the dream You have given me. I shall dare to be a maverick today. Thank You, God.

Flying with an unknown pilot

"Examine yourselves as to whether you are in the faith. Prove yourselves."—2 CORINTHIANS 13:5

Today I'm going to give you a checkup on your walk of faith. **85** How shall I grade you? Are you passing the course? The good news I have is that you, indeed, are passing with higher marks than you expected. The fact that you have continued this far on the walk of faith shows that you really are a believer.

Even on the days when you wonder about the very existence of God and were tempted to doubt His presence and power—even on those days your faith gets a passing grade!

Why? You are a believer even when you do not feel it.

The walk of faith is like traveling on an airplane. You never see the pilot at the controls. You've probably never met him face to face. His credentials are not hanging on the wall of the plane. Yet you step into the plane, believing he is there and that he can handle the flight.

There isn't a day that you can't assume there is a God in charge of this incredible flying vehicle called planet Earth. That's *faith!*

> **We ride this spacecraft called Earth, traveling at an incredible speed, and we assume there is a pilot at the controls! That's *faith!***

The world would soon turn to madness if there was no heavenly Pilot in control, no God at all! Our hearts tell us there is a Pilot even when we have never met Him face to face. We may not know Him, but we trust Him! That's *faith!*

Yet, by faith we know Him!

By faith we believe in Him!

When we become acquainted with Jesus Christ, the unseen Pilot comes out of the cabin and we meet Him, in person.

When we do know Him, that's *faith!*

Thank You, Lord, that I really do believe in You. I assume You are there all the time—and You are! I have a stronger faith than I realize.

FAITH IS . . .
Adventuring into new territories

> "Where can I go from Your Spirit?/Or where
> can I flee from Your presence? . . . If I take the
> wings of the morning,/And dwell in the
> uttermost parts of the sea,/Even there Your
> hand shall lead me."—PSALM 139:7–10

86   When we trust the Pilot at the controls of our lives, then we are ready to venture into new territories.

Is anything quite as exciting as an adventure? Can you imagine how dull life would be if all risk were removed; if you knew exactly how everything would turn out before you plunged; if the outcome were certain when you made the commitment?

I recall a positive-thinking friend who received the news she had cancer. She needed surgery and then chemotherapy. The prognosis was grim, and the outlook was grave.

Yet when I came to call at her bedside, I saw an excited sparkle in her eye. "I've never taken this kind of trip before!" she said. "I think it's going to be quite an adventure—enlightening, and potentially life-enriching, if not lifesaving." And she really meant it. That's faith!

When a member of my church knew that she was at death's door and was soon to make the transition from earth to heaven, she was genuinely excited. As she patted her Bible affectionately, she said, "My suitcase is packed. My bills are all paid. My passport is in order. I've been looking forward to this trip all of my life."

Faith—it's seeking adventure into new territories!

Are you starting a new business? Are you unemployed? Did you get laid off? Maybe you need to move to a new locality, learn a new trade, or be reeducated. Maybe you need to take a trip you've never taken before!

Look upon each new day as a new adventure into new territories! With God as your guide you need not be afraid. We cannot travel beyond His care and keeping.

FAITH IS . . .
Liberating your creative powers

"For you shall go out with joy, and . . . peace;
the mountains and the hills shall break forth
into singing . . . and all the trees of the field
shall clap their hands."—ISAIAH 55:12

When we begin to breathe the breath of faith we discover we **87**
are becoming creative persons. How exciting!

When we become believers and walk the walk of faith, we
find salvation from life's tensions—sin, fear, anxiety. When
we walk the walk of faith, we become whole and healthy normal persons. In the process our stress level is drastically re-
duced. Tensions that attack us are noticeably eliminated, and
the peace of mind that naturally results sets the stage for
creativity.

Have you noticed? In the quiet hours of the early morning
you get your brightest ideas. That's because those are the
times when you are protected from the possibility of un-
welcome, pressure-producing interruptions that stimulate
tension. Deep relaxation allows creativity to happen.

In a garden we are creative, for

The sounds and sights of nature relax the soul.

We find it natural to believe in God when we behold the
starry heavens from the mountaintop.

There is a reasonable explanation for the greater prevalence
of religious belief in the rural countryside. The farmer is
closer to nature. He is in his natural habitat. The person who
is surrounded by the tension-producing sounds of engines and
sirens finds that his eyes and ears, designed to be channels of
tranquility, have become blocked from the flow of creativity.

Faith in God liberates the creative powers, for faith gives me
peace of mind! Tranquility is conditioning for creativity.

Thank You, Father, for creating me to be a partner in the
creative work in this world. I open my mind to Your ideas. I
believe that Your ideas can be translated into constructive creative activity. Thank You, Lord. Amen.

FAITH IS . . .

Advancing with boldness

> "The kingdom of heaven is like treasure hidden in a field, which a man found and hid; and for the joy over it, he goes and sells all that he has and buys that field."—MATTHEW 13:44

88   It's easy to see why some people fail. They are under the lordship of an unholy trinity—acidity, frigidity, timidity.

Some fail because of *acidity*. Their personalities are bitter. They are poisoned with negative thinking. There is acid in their souls.

Others fail because of *frigidity*. They're cold. They lack the warmth of affection to attract good people. Love is missing in their lives.

Still others fail because of *timidity*. They demand guarantees of safety before they move. They need all the problems solved before they make a commitment.

Successful people are controlled by a faith that dissolves acidity with sweet thoughts, thaws out frigidity with an enthusiastic attitude of kindness, and replaces timidity with boldness.

Today, move forward with faith. Take at least one step forward in some area of your life.

Where should you advance? To what degree? Pause now to pray that God will show you where you are holding back and where you ought to be moving forward. God knows you better than you know yourself. One thing is certain:

You'll never get ahead until you start advancing.

In our Bible verse a person is walking across property with a "for sale" sign on it, stumbles on hidden treasure, hides it, then what? He moves fast! Sells everything—and buys it!

You are walking across opportunities today! Spot them, grab them—fast.

FAITH IS . . .
Stimulating positive emotions

"We also should walk in newness of life."—
ROMANS 6:4

Living the faith stimulates positive emotions. In the same **89**
way, doubt constantly feeds negative emotions. Doubt is an
anesthetic. Skepticism drains the spirit. Unbelief makes us
drowsy. Negative thinking turns us into dreary people, fearful
of our fears and worried about our worry. What a despairing
cycle!

But you are out of the rut! You walk the path of faith. Stimulate positive emotions today: Jesus Christ has freely saved
me from all doubt! *My faith stimulates my hope.* Like a bird
awakening the others with a song, until all are singing a happy
chorus, so one positive thought alerts and awakens others until I am moving on a higher energy plane.

My faith stimulates positive thinking, and positive thinking stimulates me to see all of the possibilities.

> **I have made commitments.**
> **I am involved.**
> **I'm pursuing a project.**
> **I am out of the ruts.**
> **I'm on the way.**
> **The adventure's begun.**
> **The countdown has started.**
> **Blast-off is inevitable.**
> **I'm now swept up into dynamic action**

God is encouraging me. The Lord is nudging me forward.

Thank You, Father, for drawing me into this circle of excitement. Thank You, for saving me from the sad cycle of deadly
skepticism and fatiguing boredom. Humor has returned to my
life. Joy has stepped into my morning. I hear the birds sing
again. I'm overwhelmed by an abundance of blessings. Thank
You, Lord. Amen.

Agreeing to advance

"For you shall go out with joy,/And be led forth with peace;/The mountains and the hills/Shall break forth into singing before you,/And all the trees of the field shall clap their hands."— ISAIAH 55:12

90 You are moving upward, forward, and onward!
- You are deprogramming yourself of negative input.
- You are reprogramming yourself positively.
- You are transcending human distractions and inadequacies.
- And you agree today to advance in your walk of faith until you give God complete lordship over your life.

Faith is the process of agreeing to allow positive forces to control you. Your inadequacies help you recognize that you need to be led by somone smarter than yourself.

Agree to advance and turn the leadership of your life over to God!

> **When you turn leadership of your life over to God, then you agree to advance, even though you do not know where God will lead. Remember, faith is moving beyond the realm of the sure into the realm of the uncertain.**

Faith means you enter an agreement before all the questions can be answered!

Affirmation: Of one thing I am sure: As long as Christ is the leader of my life, I'm in the best of company! I shall be advancing. And that's all-important!

O Lord, I'm putting everything I am into my belief in You. Deep within in my heart I feel right about this move, even though I don't know where You will lead me. Thank You, Lord. Amen.

FAITH IS . . .
Escalating your expectations

"For as the heavens are higher than the earth,/
So are My ways higher than your ways,/And
My thoughts than your thoughts."—ISAIAH 55:9

Now that you're on the move, stretch your faith until it is **91** big enough to unfold the plan God has for you!

Make your thinking big enough for God to fit in!
Let the size of your faith set the size of your goals!
Match your expectations to God's abilities!

Visualize a scale in your mind—one of those old-fashioned scales with two trays balanced against each other. In one tray place your beliefs about God—His goodness; His might; His wisdom; His connections with sources and resources, financial, intellectual, emotional, and organizational. The God that you believe in is on one scale.

Now on the other side, place your expectations—how far you want to go, how high you wish to climb, how rich you'd like to become. (Remember, it's not a sin to be wealthy; it is a sin not to be generous!)

By now you are in the process of escalating your expectations. You think bigger than when you first started. You increase the size of the goal you eventually expect to reach. That's great! That means your faith is growing. That means you are under the influence of God and not evil.

You are an optimist, not a pessimist.

You are a possibility thinker, not an impossibility thinker. Browning said, "A man's reach must exceed his grasp, or what's a heaven for?"

Reach for heaven today.

Reach for God's way.

Reach for His thoughts.

Faith is escalating your expectations!

Declaring your positive intentions

"Let the words of my mouth . . ./Be acceptable
in Your sight,/O LORD!"—PSALM 19:14

92 God will lead you out of the wilderness of complacency and despondency once you have enough faith to declare your positive intentions. Enormous power is released once you make a public announcement of what you are going to accomplish. You put your integrity on the line. When you declare your intentions publicly and positively, the pressure is on to produce! Publicly announcing a project is one of the most successful, yet most painful, ways I have utilized to accomplish my goals.

Be careful to declare your intentions only to positive people! You will need all the help you can get.

Even so, be prepared for negative reactions from those who will resist or resent your goals. To some people, you will appear to be a threat, to others, a wild-eyed idealist. Still others will simply laugh at your plans. After all, they're impossible, aren't they?

But,

Once the idea becomes a word, it will come to life.

There is incredible creative power in the spoken word. It was with a spoken word that God created the world. Christ, who is called the Incarnation of God, is referred to as the Word "made flesh" (John 1:14 KJV).

Do you really want to succeed? Then practice faith. Declare your intentions positively and publicly with enthusiasm and integrity! And you cannot fail, unless you give up on your dream.

Talking positive talk

"Anxiety in the heart . . . causes depression,/But a good word makes it glad."—PROVERBS 12:25

Faith is more than positive thinking. It's positive talking. **93**
- Fantasizing becomes incarnate in verbalizing.
- Ideas take the form of the spoken word.
- Believing becomes speaking.
- There is incredible emotional power released through the spoken word.

By the word of God the heavens and the earth were created. God spoke—and it happened!

Read the Bible and underline the words *say, speaks, spoke, word.*

Until persons speak, they remain a mystery. Christ was God exposing Himself in a language people could understand. He is God speaking to us by lip and by life. Once a dream is articulated in a public announcement, you are committed. Once you program your mind with positive language and positive words you are programmed for action.

Faith must rise to the level of affirmation.
- Declare you are the person you want to be.
- Tell yourself you have already accomplished what you hope to accomplish.

When you are in a downward mood, never verbalize a negative emotion. Rather, declare positively, "I feel great!" You are expressing incredible faith and belief that God will hear and answer your prayer in an instant.

The kind of faith you need now is to affirm that you are succeeding. You are making progress even if you can't see it, or feel it! You know you are because God is on your side. Trust Him and talk positive talk.

Patting yourself on the back

"For You have made him [us] a little lower than the angels,/And You have crowned him [us] with glory and honor."—PSALM 8:5

94 Take time today to applaud yourself. For in congratulating yourself you are glorifying God by recognizing the goodness of His grace.

- I am a truly remarkable creation!
- There isn't another human being just like me.
- I believe in myself.
- I congratulate myself for the person I am and the person I am in the process of becoming!
- I have survived a great deal.
- I have been given incredible endurance.
- There is nothing I cannot accomplish once I set my mind to it. I have proven that more than once.

By the grace of God, I am somebody marvelous!

- I am praising and applauding God for the good work He has done within me.
- God loves me so much that He would stop at nothing to save my soul! The cross of Jesus Christ is proof of that!
- I am proud to be known as a believer.
- God's love is flowing through my life.
- I am a channel of His joy.
- I am doing a lot of good through my positive attitudes.
- I am building up others around me through my faith.
- I am really a wonderful person.
- God is crowning me with glory and honor.
- I am still a Christian in the process of maturing. I am improving.
- I am growing spiritually.
- I'm pressing on the upward way; new heights I'm gaining every day.

Exercising enthusiasm always

"Rejoice in the Lord always. Again I will say,
rejoice!"—PHILIPPIANS 4:4

One thing will become apparent as you walk this walk of **95**
faith. Faith is a walk. That means exercise!

People who never walk, jog, or move around soon become
flabby and weak. It doesn't take long for human muscles to
lose their resiliency.

**Faith is exercised when we exercise enthusiasm. En-
thusiasm is the emotion that feeds faith and keeps it
alive.**

Faith drinks of the cup of enthusiasm and takes off with
youthful energy.

To walk the walk of faith can be perceived as the constant
revitalization of our innate inclination to be enthusiastic, for
enthusiasm is the mark of an emotionally healthy person.

By contrast, lack of enthusiasm is evidence of something
less than peak mental and spiritual health. Tragically some
educators see youthful enthusiasm as something to eliminate.
Enthusiasm is often viewed as an emotional weakness;
whereas cold, calculating rationality is viewed as the epitome
of mental alertness.

Not so! You are a healthy person when you are enthusiastic.
Enthusiasm is a mark of youth. It is the fountain of energy.

Exercise enthusiasm today. Begin by counting your blessings. Begin with God! He is alive! You can be enthusiastic
about His love for you!

Now express enthusiasm about faith—itself! The late Dr.
Daniel Poling had a positive addiction. Each morning he
would turn his face toward the new light and repeat aloud—
very loud—several times, two words: "I believe!" "I believe!"
"I believe!" "I believe!"

Try it! It will really give you faith! Energy! Life!

Exaggerating enthusiastically

"My soul shall make its boast in the LORD."—
PSALM 34:2

96   What is exaggeration? (a) A sad symptom of an inferiority complex? Sometimes. (b) A deliberate deception to con someone? Sometimes. (c) A positive attempt to convey a true impression? Yes! Sometimes exaggeration is just that.

Consider the artist who exaggerates the size of a human hand. He is giving the honest impression of strength.

Consider the musician or the actor who exaggerates the soft and loud tones, thereby giving an honest expression of the dynamic range.

Consider the reporter who exaggerates the attendance. He is giving an honest impression of a big crowd.

Consider the pastor of a fast-growing church who reports membership as "nearly one thousand" after the roll call has passed six hundred. He is conveying an honest impression of great growth.

"My soul shall make its boast in the LORD." There is such a thing as honest exaggeration.

Exaggeration is honest when it is really an "advance announcement"—when your overstated numbers will be "right on" by the time people hear the news.

Exaggeration is honest when it is the expression of an "inner vision seen" in the mind of a positive believer!

It is an audacious and daring act of faith to declare that you have already achieved what you prayed and believed you would achieve.

Yes, it's dangerous! For now, you either have to produce the predicted results or be labeled a braggart and a liar and lose credibility. But this risk can be used as a powerful, positive pressure to produce.

Yes, the powerful practice of making "advance" announcements will release incredible, positive forces.

Positive exaggerations generate great expectations that stimulate enormous enthusiasm.

Fortifying yourself

"The LORD is my rock and my fortress and my deliverer."—PSALM 18:2

The walk of faith does not guarantee that we are completely **97** protected against the disintegrating forces that are always around us. Like termites in a wooden beam or dry rot in the timbers, moral decay can set in subtly and insidiously.

Where did your enthusiasm go? What happened to your drive? You thought that you had your act together, and now you seem to be coming apart.

Enthusiasm and confidence are not welded to your spirit— they're glued. The bonding can lose its adhesive quality quickly if you allow disintegrating forces to come into your thinking or action.

Faith is fortifying yourself; building an invisible shield of faith around you.

Walk out into the new day imagining that there is an invisible barrier of impenetrable and indestructible material that surrounds you like a fracture-proof bubble.

> **Deflect the poisonous darts of negative thoughts with holy stubbornness.**
> **Your mind is fortified by faith!**
> **Through persistent positive thinking develop an immunity that instinctively, intuitively, fights off the would-be invaders of negativity.**
> **Positive projects provide built-in prevention.**

Because you are walking in faith, negativity, pessimism, cynicism, unbelief, like invading germs, drop dead before they ever reach you.

Thank You, Father, that I have a faith that fortifies me against the destructive spiritual forces loose in our world. I have the ultimate security, for You are beside me. Thank You, Lord. Amen.

Upgrading my standards

"For You have formed my inward parts;/You have covered me in my mother's womb./I will praise You, for I am fearfully and wonderfully made;/Marvelous are Your works,/And that my soul knows very well."—PSALM 139:13–14

98 It's amazing how an actor will perform at his peak when he knows an important person is in his audience.

More than one athlete has knocked himself out because he knows that his dad is in the grandstand! The story is told of a boy who always had to settle for second-string position. Yet his father never missed a game. After his father's death, the son, with tears in his eyes, said, "Coach, please let me start tonight. I want to play for Dad."

The coach, knowing that the boy's dad had never missed a game, agreed. The young man's performance on the field astounded the coach. When asked to explain his phenomenal level of achievement, he said, "Coach, I played that one for Dad. My father never missed a game, but he never saw me play—until tonight! You see, Coach, my father was blind."

How much better could you be doing in the game of life?

God is in a front-row seat watching your performance on the stage of life today. He is applauding the moment you move into the scene. What previously untapped levels of energy and creativity and accomplishment will you reveal?

You can do more than you have done.
You can go further than you have.
The Lord deserves the best of whatever you can be.
Today, upgrade your standards!
Raise that goal!
Set your sights on higher targets.
Our Lord is watching you—now!
He'll applaud you.
So will I.

FAITH IS . . .
Improving yourself constantly

"Add to your faith virtue, to virtue knowledge,
to knowledge self-control, to self-control
perseverance, to perseverance Godliness, to
Godliness brotherly kindness, and to brotherly
kindness love."—2 PETER 1:5–8

Does this verse show where the path of faith leads? Will we **99** never reach a point where we've got it made? Does this mean we will constantly have to improve ourselves?

Absolutely! That's what spares us from death. For plateaus are boring. Nothing is as dull as yesterday's race when it is over! Who cares to look at the bumper stickers of last year's political campaign?

We must always be living in today—and tomorrow!

What is exciting to know is that the real stimulation of life never needs to diminish with age. Real excitement comes as you make constant commitments to new projects that hold creative challenge.

You can continue to feel young as long as you live, because a youthful attitude is basically a commitment to progress. You can have that no matter how old you are! You never need to grow too old to escape the opportunity for self-improvement. The walk of faith calls you to improve yourself constantly, consistently, and continually!

Affirmation: I shall choose one of these elements within today's Bible verse and focus on improving myself. It may be
faith,
virtue,
knowledge,
self-control,
godliness,
kindness, or
love.
Then my life will remain fruitful no matter how old I am! Thank You, God, for this glorious promise.

Welcoming a new day

"This is the day which the Lord has made;/We will rejoice and be glad in it."—PSALM 118:24

100 How do you welcome a new day? I invite you to join me in this positive meditation:

What surprises do You have planned for me today, Lord?

I am excited about the abilities that I have at my disposal.

I am able to see, and think, and hear!

I am able to read.

I have the ability to plan.

I am excited about the hours and minutes that this day holds.

I am suddenly conscious, heavenly Father, that You give to all human beings the same number of minutes and hours in every day.

And I am well aware of the fact that the most important resource I possess is not money but time!

For time is life.

With the gift of time I have the opportunity to laugh! to love! to talk! to think! to pray! to give of myself to people whose paths will cross mine. Surely, my dreams will come true because I am blessed! I am alive! I am being given the priceless gift of another day to live! I take the time to carry my dreams out. Today I can move them forward!

My problems can be solved for I am walking the walk of faith! For I am filled with genuine thanksgiving. I will use the gift of this day wisely. I will do something about my life's opportunities and obstacles, its dreams and disappointments.

O God, thank You for treating me fairly!

You have given me a fresh day with freedom to do something constructive!

This faith gives me hope.

Thank You, Father. Amen.

Grabbing the magic moment

"Then you shall see and become radiant,/And
your heart shall swell with joy."—ISAIAH 60:5

There are magical moments of life that come unexpectedly, **101**
and then, suddenly, they are gone!

There is that magical moment when the darkness of the
night disappears and the sky becomes light. The first bird
awakens and throws its head back to announce the new day.
His early song awakens the others, who join in a heavenly
chorus.

To capture that magical moment, you must learn that the
birds do not wait for you. The beautiful but very brief symphony will not be delayed until you finish your domestic
chores. So bow to the birds! Have faith that other activities
can wait.

It is the same with the sunrise. There is that magical moment just before the sun rises above the horizon when the
orange sky becomes brilliant with color. And just as quickly
as it appears, the resplendent glory of the sunrise fades. The
high point has passed. The exquisite elegance is no longer
there.

**The brilliant moments of magic never last long. Plan,
accommodate, and adjust your schedule so you will
not miss the magic when it comes. Faith is carefully
planning to capture the highest, happiest, and holiest
moments in life.**

Moments of inspiration do come. The soul seems to soar for
a brief moment when we sense God's presence.

Drop everything when this moment surprises you, for the
beauty of the fast fleeting moment will not wait for you. Grab
it! It is God's special gift to you.

Delighting in discovery

"Behold what manner of love the Father has
bestowed on us, that we should be called
children of God!"—1 JOHN 3:1

102   People with faith to explore make grand discoveries. Like a
father who leaves wrapped gifts hidden where his children
will find them, so God waits behind doors left ajar, where He
watches His children venture in.

What delight He takes in watching us discover and then
open the carefully planned surprises.

God delights in our delights.

He may or may not open the door far enough to expose His
generous Self. We may not even know where the gifts have
come from. To Him it does not really matter. But how His
heart leaps when He hears us say, "Father did it. Isn't He wonderful!"

As God's children we may never see His face or hear His
voice, but we sense a goodness and love that planned something good and beautiful for us!

One morning, as I opened God's gift to me of a new day, I
hummed the familiar tune, "Morning Has Broken." Then
these words came to me:

> Dawn is awakening, bright with a new light,
> calling our hearts to love while we pray.
> Thank God for living.
> Thank God for breathing.
> God's recreating new life today.

Father, the doorway of a new day is opening. Who is turning
the knob? Who is opening the door? Who will show His smiling face? It is joy opening the door to release the new day to
my life. God is alive. He is blessing me. Alleluia.

Alerting myself to the good in the "now"

"Every day I will bless You."—PSALM 145:2

Faith gives one of the most beautiful invitations that any **103** person can covet! Have you ever envied someone for being invited to an affair where your name was not on the list?

Well, every person is invited by faith to come into "today"! Step into the joy of the present moment.

- **Today there are flowers blooming. You are invited to notice them.**
- **Today there are birds singing. You are invited to listen to them.**
- **Today there are people who are crying for help. You are honored with the invitation to comfort them.**

Imagine being invited by God to a special showing in a beautiful theater to witness a premiere event never seen by any human being before! You step into the theater. You have a prize seat. The stage is before you. You sense that something is happening on stage. You are unable to experience it because the curtains of yesterday and tomorrow remain closed—your preoccupation with the past and your anxiety about tomorrow can cause you to miss today's premiere showing.

Now the curtains begin to separate. The stage is wide open. You experience the music, the dance, the drama—the living and the loving, the laughing and the crying, the dreaming and the despairing, the struggling and the succeeding—all happening this very moment! It's exciting. It's life! You must not miss it.

Today is the tomorrow you dreamed about yesterday! It has arrived. You are in the center of God's love. Praise your God!

Taking a chance on tomorrow

"Tomorrow the LORD will do wonders among you."—JOSHUA 3:5

104   The true stories of amazing accomplishments experienced by possibility thinkers who act on faith make unbelievable reading.

For instance, a friend of mine, Christy Wilson, was a missionary in Afghanistan. He missed the comforts of life in America, not the least of which was his favorite food—Long Island duckling. He proceeded to order fertilized duck eggs! He assumed that they could be transported by air and arrive in Kabul, the capital of Afghanistan, before they were spoiled. That's faith!

When the shipment finally arrived, after long delays, there were fewer than two dozen eggs left. Only two hatched out! Would you believe that one was a male and the other a female?

Of course, that was all he needed. They reproduced and soon Christy had a very successful enterprise.

Meanwhile, an epidemic was becoming a near national disaster: the sheep in the country were being killed by a tiny parasite.

Then it was discovered that the parasite was spread by snails. Ducks love to eat snails. So Christy Wilson's ducks spared the country from an agricultural and, consequently, human tragedy.

One day a member of the royal family heard the story.

Christy Wilson was summoned to the king's residence. The whole story came to light and the missionary was finally recognized and given credit for importing the ducks and saving the sheep. He received royal honors! That is a historical recorded fact!

Believe in tomorrow! Who can count the apples in one seed?

FAITH IS . . .
Trusting in tomorrow

"Surely goodness and mercy shall follow me/All the days of my life."—PSALM 23:6

You sense a new enthusiasm flowing through your life at this moment, for you are walking the walk of faith. Today your faith will become stronger as you learn to trust in tomorrow.

Your course, however well it is charted, may require adjustments. But, if you keep your eyes fixed firmly on the goal, then your future is your friend. You need never be discouraged, because God is walking beside you in this walk of faith.

God plans your today and all of your tomorrows. Trust Him! The storms may rage. The plan may fail to unfold as rapidly or efficiently as you had hoped. But every tomorrow is a new opportunity to take a fresh grip on your goal and catch a strong hold on your commitment!

Tomorrow will not fail you unless you choose to throw it away.

Yes, you may make mistakes but you are not stupid. For God gave you intelligence and common sense. Use it now! God is reminding you through His Holy Spirit that something good will happen tomorrow.

So, trust in tomorrow! For trust releases incredible power, which sustains energy and releases enthusiasm within you!

Believe that tomorrow will give you time to move your projects forward.

Believe that tomorrow will give you the opportunity to take positive action that will prove beneficial.

Thank You, God, for this power that is coming from You now! Thank You that there will always be a tomorrow. And You are creating it. I know that there is bound to be a lot of good, waiting behind the next sunrise. Amen.

Celebrating the unknown

"Oh, satisfy us early with Your mercy,/That we may rejoice and be glad all our days."—PSALM 90:14

106   Enjoy the present moment. You know your past mistakes are forgiven, your pathway for tomorrow is planned. You do not know what the future holds, but you know who holds the future.

- So celebrate the blessings that are waiting for you!
- Praise God for the blessings He is planning for your life.
- Celebrate the unknown!

That's living in faith.

It is the unknown that provides the magnets to draw you into tomorrow.

If the future could be predicted, the excitement of uncertainty would be replaced by the boredom of the predictable.

Today I welcomed my fifth grandchild. My heart took a happy leap as the news reached me by long-distance telephone. I offered thanks to God for new life.

Then, in prayer, I talked to that invisible little grandchild only a few hours old: "Scott Anthony Coleman, welcome aboard! Today is the first day of the rest of your life. You have stepped into a fantastic world, filled with opportunities to love!

"What does your future hold, young man?

"Where are you going in life?

"I am so happy I don't know.

"It gives me the freedom to imagine the most wonderful life possible for you! Your father and your mother share with you their most precious gift, God's gift of faith."

The unknown is our great cause for celebration, for God is there!

FAITH IS . . .

Facing the future unafraid

"And the LORD, He is the one who goes before
you. He will be with you, He will not leave you
nor forsake you; do not fear nor be
dismayed."—DEUTERONOMY 31:8

I have given two daughters away in marriage. Both times **107**
they were beautiful brides in long white gowns with their
arms circled through mine, walking with nervous excitement
down the aisle to meet their grooms and make their lifetime
commitments in faith! Believe me, they really held onto my
arm!

In the same way, God leads you down the aisle to be married
to a great cause and a great project that awaits you today!

Loop your arm through God's and you will face your future
unafraid! "The LORD, He is the one who goes before you. He
will be with you, He will not leave you nor forsake you; do
not fear nor be dismayed."

Affirmation: I have no fear of the future because I am completely convinced that the situations I have been thrust in are
providential!

• I am doing God's work.
• I am walking in the center of His will.
• He is leading me.
• I am following Him.
• He is guiding me.
• I am making His chosen decisions.

He only asks me to believe—that He may relieve!

He relieves me of responsibility when it's beyond me, and
He knows when and where that is. So I sing with hope in my
heart:

> Be not dismayed, whatever betide
> God will take care of you.
> Beneath His wings of love abide
> God will take care of you.

Timing your move

"... come before winter."—2 TIMOTHY 4:21

108   Is it possible that some people have an intuitive gift of timing? Is it a special gift of God? Surely it must be His Holy Spirit at work in the lives of His people, for timing is everything.

"He who hestitates is lost" . . . "Time waits for no one" . . . "Haste makes waste" . . . "Make hay while the sun shines" . . . "Come before winter." The age-old proverbs and classic clichés sometimes seem confusing and contradicting. You need the wisdom of God to know how to schedule the calendar of life and when to make the moves.

One thing is certain. It is most important to announce the schedule when you make a commitment. Put a time frame around your plans. Once your goals are established, then fit them into a calendar.

Motivation loses steam quickly if you cannot see progress. Consequently, you must schedule some goals to be accomplished today.

In your timing, plan for emergencies. When I was growing up we were never late for church or community events because my mother always insisted that we "leave enough time for a flat tire." We never had a flat tire, so we were always the first ones at church.

Set your goals. Then plan to achieve them by timing your moves.

Finally, be prepared to adjust your calendar to God's calendar. "Come before winter."

> **Time waits for no one. Give your goal and dream all you've got! Let go—and let God make it happen in His way.**

Rescheduling your timetable

"The LORD knows the days of the upright,/And their inheritance shall be forever."—PSALM 37:18

It's often possible to take a positive mental attitude toward what appears to be an impossible situation—*if you have enough time.*

109

In all the promises God has made, never does He surrender control over the schedule. He promises that we can move mountains and achieve the impossible if we will keep on believing. But He doesn't say *when* or *how long* it will take.

Give God time, and He will perform the miracle.

When a human condition appears to be totally impossible, don't check out; ask for an extension of time. The hotel sign reads, "Check-out time is 12:00 noon." Don't believe it if you run into a predicament! Ask and believe. They will extend the check-out time.

Just don't be locked into an ironclad schedule. Don't surrender leadership to a clock or a calendar. Of course you set time-dated goals. Of course you generate energy by creating urgency. But be prepared to *revise your timetable before you bury your dream!*

Every passing hour of every passing day and every new month increase the possibility that things will turn around.

What you may need is not more faith, but more patience. The impossible may become possible when you take the long look.

As we walk the walk of faith, we must become more God-like. And one quality about God is His immeasurable long-suffering and patient attitude.

What great impossible deeds could you accomplish if you had a forty-year goal?

If you are tempted to abandon your dream—don't!

Help me, my God and Father, I pray. Amen.

Revising your schedule

"My times are in Your hand."—PSALM 31:15

110 Faith is a constant process of reviewing the calendar against your accomplishments. Just because it's impossible today doesn't mean it will be impossible tomorrow.

When you set goals, put a time limit on them. Without it you are normally and naturally lazy and lethargic more often than you want to admit. It's amazing how much you can accomplish in a short period of time if the pressure is on.

What do you do when you have not succeeded in meeting your time limit, and it becomes apparent that the project will take longer than you expected?

You keep walking the walk of faith. You revise your timetable:

"It's not impossible; it just takes a little longer." Suddenly seemingly unachievable projects become very realistic!

What can you accomplish if you take ten years? You might be able to get a new degree. Perhaps you can acquire a much larger financial base. You might even be able to overcome that handicap.

Keep walking the walk of faith. Don't give up believing: just revise the timetable!

God has never promised to deliver an answer to prayer according to our timetables.

Dear Lord, if I fail to meet some of the goals that I have set, don't let me quit. Give me the ability to stretch the project out over a longer period of time. I'll wait for the rain to fall. I'll expect it, and I'll hang in there, knowing my times are in Your hand. Thank You, Father. Amen.

FAITH IS . . .

Recognizing the reality of miracles

"Everyone who is called by My name,/Whom I have created for My glory;/I have formed him,/ yes, I have made him."—ISAIAH 43:7

How would you respond if someone challenged your faith with: "Show me a miracle—and I'll believe in it!" You could answer: "Take a look at me—I'm one! Then take a look in the mirror. You'll see another one!"

The fact that you are alive today is nothing short of a miracle! Your life is the continuation of an unbroken genetic string reaching back all the way to the first parents. Look back at your family tree and see how many times the cord came close to being severed. Was it in the Civil War? Was it in a plague epidemic? Was it on a slave ship crossing the waters from Africa to America?

You are a survivor of survivors of survivors! How often you yourself have survived near-death experiences, you will never know!

Your life has a special purpose. There is a reason why you are alive today. You are a walking miracle! Whatever your racial origin, ethnic identification, educational level, or economic bracket, *you are special! You are a winner! You are alive!*

So give your life totally today to the God who brought you here. Let Jesus Christ—the Ultimate Survivor, who rose from the dead on Easter morning—be your best Friend, and share His wonderful love with the people you come into contact with today. That, at least, is your reason for being here.

> **God must have believed that you'd be a good person to spread His love around in the world today! God has not let you down. You won't let Him down either. You have every reason to be supergrateful. Think of it: Saved for such a high and holy purpose.**

111

FAITH IS . . .
Designing for survival

"You are my hiding place and my shield;/I hope in Your word."—PSALM 119:114

112   The walk of faith is a day-by-day, week-by-week, month-by-month, year-by-year process of building a solid fortress reinforcing the human spirit against assaults of the enemy of doubt. This daily motivational guide is building such a wall of faith.

Each day we add one brick upon another, until we have developed a philosophy of possibility thinking that is designed to save the human spirit from being broken and crushed in the worst of times.

Richard Neutra, the famed architect with whom I worked in designing our Tower of Hope, wrote a book entitled *Survival Through Design.* Neutra believes that architecture should be designed to envelop the human emotions in healthy, positive surroundings. "Some structures and houses really are haunted," he once told me. "By that I mean that some structures are designed in such a way that the sun never shines in. You never feel the play of light. The ceilings are so low, they come down on you. You feel oppressed, instead of liberated and surrounded by light. The corners are gloomy. Hence the structures produce the moods that will haunt the human spirit with depression and gloom."

Even as great architecture attempts to design for emotional survival, you are designing a faith that will allow you to survive the emotional storms of life.

Dear God, help me to keep praying and believing day by day, week by week, to develop such an impenetrable shield of faith that the fiery darts of doubt will be deflected in the worst times of life. Amen.

Feasting on the beautiful

"Man shall not live by bread alone, but by
every word that proceeds from the mouth of
God."—MATTHEW 4:4

I'm driven by the awareness that through Jesus Christ any **113** person can be transformed into a beautiful person. I have watched a cold eye become misty with the warmth nourished and fed by a spiritual love of God. That is a fantastic experience! I feast on beauty! "We shall not live by bread alone."

Allow me to quote Richard Neutra again. Often he reminds me, "Beauty is practical, too!" Then he tells how his clients would object to his designs and wanted to replace the reflection pools, lawns, and fountains with practical asphalt and cement. He would wisely reply, "But the human being was designed to live in a garden. He needs beauty to sustain his soul and his spirit. Put him in a concrete jungle, and he'll become a concrete beast. He'll lose his sensitivity to beauty. And when that happens he'll cease to see the potential of beauty in human beings around him. Then he will begin to treat them abusively and violence will be the result."

Beauty is not an option—it's a nonnegotiable necessity!

Beauty is what keeps the human family human. And that's the first step toward becoming Godlike, which is our heavenly Father's plan. The next time you hear somebody criticizing a work of art or architecture as "a waste of money in a hungry world," remember this: What good is it to sustain human life if the human beings are not really human? This is why I am so incurably attracted to Jesus Christ. Everything I know about Him leads me to see Him as the most beautiful human being who ever walked on planet Earth.

Jesus, come into my life and fill me with Your beauty. May my life be beautiful, too. I can be a beautiful creature if Your love will shine through my eyes. Thank You. Amen.

Acquiring an appetite for beauty

"Consider the lilies, how they grow . . . even Solomon in all his glory was not arrayed like one of these."—LUKE 12:27

114 When a person acquires a sense of beauty, you can be sure he or she is walking the walk of faith. For beauty is spiritual value that is the result of a belief system.

If you want to succeed in the walk of faith, you must acquire a sense of beauty.

Once addicted with an insatiable appetite for beauty, you'll never be able to surrender your dreams to the tempting offers of lesser values.

People often ask me: "Where did you get the strength to take the idea of the Crystal Cathedral and see it through to its debt-free completion at such an enormous cost?"

My answer is simple. "Somewhere along the line I acquired an uncompromising and insatiable appetite for beauty." I saw the Crystal Cathedral as a work of art that would inspire persons for centuries to come. And that hunger for beauty kept my commitment to the pursuit of the project fueled and sustained!

A commitment to excellence demands an enormous amount of effort. One can quickly become fatigued at fighting the majority of persons and forces that gladly want to compromise quality on the altar of mediocrity.

What keeps you from burning out before you have finished the project? How can you conquer that tough, unyielding, recurring weakness in your personal behavior?

The answer is obvious: Get the kind of faith that will not surrender to anything less than the best. It's a tough faith that will not compromise in its loyalty to beauty.

Beauty is bread, too! It feeds the soul!

FAITH IS . . .
Adorning your mind with beauty

"And the desert shall rejoice and blossom as the rose; it shall blossom abundantly and rejoice."—ISAIAH 35:1–2

It is not accidental that the Christian religion has produced **115** the richest outpouring of great art in paintings, sculpture, and architecture. That's because God is the Source and Creator of beauty. He makes the desert "blossom as the rose."

If God can make a dry, barren desert come alive with a garden of flowers, then He can certainly turn us into beautiful personalities. He can redesign, restyle, remodel, and redecorate our minds with beautiful thoughts. When that happens, our eyes reflect the difference. The lines around our mouth change the shape of our lips, and smiles come naturally. When God becomes the source of our thinking, the mind that was dull with boredom begins to blossom with beautiful ideas and dreams.

God adorns your mind with beautiful ideas, and suddenly your life becomes amazingly fruitful!

God's promise is that even the most barren life can be turned into a garden.

A friend recently told this story: "I have a little house on the beach. I love watering the sand!" Laughingly, she continued, "I know it sounds funny, but it relaxes me." Suddenly her eyes flashed. "And you'll never believe what has happened! Grass has started to grow!" she said, excitedly. "Honestly! The beach turned into a front lawn where I watered it. Everyone was astonished. So was I. Apparently there are all kinds of miniature seeds mixed up in all of that sand."

Thank You, God, for being the Source and Creator of beauty! I know now that I can be beautiful, too—through Your thoughts. Redesign and redecorate my mind today so that I may bloom where I am planted.

Detailing for excellence

"And let the beauty of the LORD our God be upon us,/And establish the work of our hands for us."—PSALM 90:17

116 "God is in the details" is a favorite quotation of the late famed architect, Mies van der Rohe. When Mies van der Rohe taught architecture at the University of Illinois, he required his students to draw in every single brick in an entire wall! "It will force the stone masons to put in the precise number of bricks," he said. "Only then can you be sure that the fine detailing at the edges will come out the way you want them to come out."

Many students complained. They simply wanted to draw a few bricks in a small section with the instructions: "Follow this form for the entire wall." But of course, when that pattern was followed, some bricklayers became a bit generous with the cement and the mortar. The building didn't end up with exactly the number of bricks that would have given the most beautiful impression.

God is in the details.

Beauty comes through the final refinement. The exquisite and elegant emerge when the white dot glistens in the eye of the subject on the canvas. A room can be well appointed, but put a garbage pail in the middle, and the charm and beauty are spoiled. It takes a lot of faith to resist the temptation to overlook or overdo.

Affirmation: Today I shall examine the details of my life. Do I yield carelessly to shortcuts and forget the details?

Faith focuses on the final product, the ultimate accomplishment, the completed act.

Faith knows success is in the details, for God is in the details.

Specifying the details

"But the very hairs of your head are all
numbered."—MATTHEW 10:30

The walk of faith, then, focuses on the finishing touch, the **117**
final dab of the artist's brush, the fine tuning of the tightened
string.

The compulsion to excellence assures excitement! And
that's where the road of faith really leads the committed person. If one instrument is slightly off tune, the orchestra is
noticeably less than its best.

Through nearly twenty-five years of collaborating with two
of the world's most esteemed architects of the century,
Richard Neutra and Philip Johnson, I have learned this principle of success:

> **Greatness comes through the toughness of being very
> specific even in the details!**

So, how do we achieve success in life? We cannot assume
that others will adequately carry out the details unless we
specify them carefully.

Apply this principle now to your private life, your prayer
life, to your Christian walk with God.

Apply this principle to your own professional pursuit.

Building a reputation, a character, or a life achievement in
personality development demands a devotion to the details.

What causes you to behave your worst? Be specific!

What are your shortcomings and sins? Be specific!

Specify in detail what you need to accomplish before you
achieve your desired objectives.

Dear God, thank you for specifying the details of my life
when even the hairs of my head are numbered. How great You
are! Teach me today to be concerned about the fine details
that make me a more effective believer. Thank You, God.

Weaving a beautiful pattern

"In all things showing yourself to be a pattern of good works."—TITUS 2:7

118 Faith looks upon life's projects as commitments to

- start
- develop
- *complete!*

A beautiful piece of embroidery doesn't happen except for the patient, persistent commitment to a completed work of art. That *first stitch* is an act of faith.

I've watched my wife and daughters do beautiful embroidery, and I've seen remarkable weavers at work, particularly in mainland China. There I saw weavers working on a carpet that had been in progress for over twenty-two years. It was estimated that it would take another fifteen or twenty years before it would be completed.

Your attitude toward this walk of faith is one of lifetime commitment. You are *developing* a pattern of living! A new life pattern will steadily, slowly, and beautifully emerge as you keep making decisions, spotting opportunities, solving problems, and shuttling the colorful threads through the loom of your life. With the passing of years, your personality unfolds, and your reputation is established as a beautiful creation by faith under the influence of an inspiring Creator—God!

> **Sow a thought, and you reap an act.**
> **Sow an act, and you reap a habit.**
> **Sow a habit, and you reap character.**
> **Sow character, and you reap destiny!**

Even the dark experiences of life can add character to the pattern if you weave them in with a positive attitude.

Cutting the cloth

"She makes linen garments/and sells them/. . .
Strength and honor are her clothing;/She shall
rejoice in time to come."—PROVERBS 31:24–25

You bought just the right amount of yardage. After all, the **119**
material was very expensive.

But this is a very special project.

You laid the pattern on the cloth, and it's going to work out
perfectly.

There will be no leftover scraps.

There will be no waste.

There is no room for error on this job.

An old Russian tailor's proverb is "Measure three times but
cut only once!"

Now the scissors are in your hand.

You put the sharp edges to the cloth and apply the pressure.
You have cut the cloth.

You have made an irreversible commitment! You have exercised faith!

> **Making an irreversible move which runs the risk of
> permanently wasting a resource, gambling that the
> outcome will work, is cutting the cloth!**

I remember seeing a beautiful piece of pure silk yardage on
the shelf of my mother's closet. This gift of exclusive Chinese
cloth had been brought to her by her brother, a missionary to
China. Often she would talk about what she might do with it.
She wanted to make sure she used it for the right thing, but
she was always afraid to ruin the special material. The sad
thing was that, when she died at the age of nearly eighty, it
was still there on the shelf.

She never did make anything out of it. We unfolded it to
find that it had faded on the edges.

It was good for nothing!

What patterns must I lay out today, O God? Give me the
courage to make the right choices and to cut the cloth! Amen.

Mixing the recipe

"Oh, taste and see that the LORD is good."—
PSALM 34:8

120   A childhood memory will always live within me. It is a picture of my mother baking apple pies, kneading the dough for homemade bread, or mixing up one of her fabulous desserts. The remarkable thing about Mom was that she never used a recipe. She had it all in her head. She would catch a little flour in her hand and sprinkle it in. She would take the salt shaker and give a few shakes. She'd take a cap off a bottle of vanilla and pour some into the mixture. I always became a little uneasy. "Mom, are you sure you are putting in the right amount of ingredients?"

She would always smile confidently and say, "Oh, don't you worry. It will come out right!"

Faith is mixing the ingredients before you can be positive that the outcome will be satisfying. That's the dynamic success principle that is before us today.

As you expose your mind to new truths from other disciplines, can you be sure that your philosophy of life can accommodate and absorb new truths?

Essentially, when we live by faith, we are declaring that we have enough confidence in God and in ourselves that we can mix ingredients together into a harmonious and productive service. It may be a faculty in school; the work force in the company; the membership of the local church. It may be something as commonplace and beautiful as a family.

Life ceases to be stale when we dare to come up with a new recipe.

Dare to invest time, energy, food, thought, or other treasured resources in a new experiment. In the process you'll grow spiritually, intellectually, or emotionally.

FAITH IS . . .
Smelling the flowers

"For lo, the winter is past,/The rain is over and gone./The flowers appear on the earth;/The time of singing has come."—SONG OF SOLOMON 2:11–12

I see a flower blooming today! As I reach for it, I breathe deeply of its fragrance. A natural high lifts me as I breathe the breath of God coming from it. **121**

Faith is smelling the flowers; it's enjoying the sweet fragrances of faith, hope, and love that blossom in the Garden of Belief.

A friend of mine, Bill Camp, is nearing one hundred years of age. Historians credit him for importing the first cotton to California from the Deep South.

Shortly after his move west, Bill's wife died. He set about hiring a housekeeper, who came and stayed for over forty years until she died. Bill said, "I asked three things of her: (1) Cook a delicious meal, (2) keep a clean kitchen, and (3) *keep a fresh flower on my table every day.*"

Try to find the means to place a blooming flower on your table. A beautiful blossom resembles a circle of positive-thinking people who bring color to brighten the day. When they leave, it is as if the perfume of joy lingers behind.

Can I be a blossom like that, spreading joy to brighten someone's day?

I will bloom where I am planted today!

I must develop the habit of nurturing each positive thought, for that's like smelling the flowers along the way.

Thank You, Father, for the gift of flowers, for the fragrance and beauty You've created in each blossom. Thank You that the most beautiful flowers are the positive thoughts that come from You. They're free! As I smell the flowers now, I feel nearer to You, O God. Thank You. Amen.

Plowing the ground

"No one, having put his hand to the plow, and looking back, is fit for the kingdom of God."—
LUKE 9:62

122 Who are the great possibility thinkers of all time?

Would you name the space scientists who put a man on the moon? Certainly they qualify.

But throughout the ages, I contend that the greatest possibility thinkers are the farmers.

I recall my father's plowing the ground in Iowa. Plowing was a great commitment. Once the ground was broken and prepared, the precious seed was planted.

I remember my grandfather's telling me how virgin prairies were originally broken into cultivated farmland in the midwestern states of America. The pioneer tied a red handkerchief to a long stake and hammered it in the ground. Then he retraced his steps, put his hands to the plow, and with his eyes firmly fixed on the red flag, he commanded his oxen or his horses to pull! Never once did he look back; otherwise he would plow a crooked row.

Can you imagine the faith it took for that farmer to keep looking ahead without turning for a moment to see how well he was doing?

People who reach their goal are the ones who keep pressing forward until they reach a point when God allows them to pause long enough to see how the Lord has blessed them! It all begins to add up, doesn't it? Faith works because it keeps your eye firmly fixed on your goal.

Keep the faith . . . keep looking ahead!

How would you like to make the Possibility Thinkers Hall of Fame? You can! Start plowing and never look back!

Planting the seed

"In the morning sow your seed, and in the
evening do not withhold your hand; for you do
not know which will prosper . . . or whether
both alike will be good."—ECCLESIASTES 11:6

Every spring we planted seeds on my father's farm.

123

Ask any farmer what faith is and he will tell you it is planting seeds. In an act of faith a farmer throws seed away in the
hope that they will come back multiplied!

Most of us today are not farmers of the field; but we can
become farmers of ideas when, as possibility thinkers, we
treat ideas as seeds.

**Any fool can count the seeds in an apple, but only God
can count the apples in one seed.**

Take an idea and treat it like a newborn child. Feed it, nourish it, protect it, and clothe it, for that seed might sprout and
become a full-fledged project for the good of our human family and for the glory of God.

The farmer runs the risk that the seed may rot in the soil.
We run the risk that our ideas may never materialize as we
hoped.

But the person who is unconditionally committed to a lifetime pilgrimage on the path of faith will inevitably come out
far ahead of the person who chooses to surrender to doubt and
despair.

Got an idea?

Plant it!

Nothing happens until you do something to start to make
something happen!

Plant the seed of faith today in your home, your place of
work, your community. Speak a positive word—only a sentence—about your faith in God to someone.

Watering the tender shoots

"See how the farmer waits for the precious fruit
of the earth, waiting patiently for it until it
receives the early and the latter rain. You also
be patient."—JAMES 5:7–8

124   At no point is the farmer's faith tested more than when he
searches the sky in the dry season looking for a cloud that
might hold the promise of moisture. Once the young seeds are
sprouted, the short, tender roots can quickly dry out and die
for want of drink. The Iowa farmer depends entirely upon natural rainfall. Without it his crop could be a disaster.

The California farmer, quite by contrast to the Iowa farmer,
cannot expect enough natural rainfall. Consequently, he in-
vests enormous sums of money in irrigation systems. He buys
the water long before there is any guarantee that a harvest will
be gained. That's faith.

Parents exhibit a similar faith when they invest everything
they can in their child without any assurance that this investment will really bear fruit.

Watering the tender shoots? That's faith!

It is payment in advance.

It is knocking yourself out for a good grade long before the
final exam.

It's putting out your best effort on the job before the
paycheck is extended.

When my son graduated from high school, he wanted to
take his prom date to a fancy restaurant. To make sure he
could afford it, he visited the place a week ahead of time, pre-
ordered the entire menu, and paid everything up front. "Gosh,
I just hope the place doesn't burn down before prom night," he
said. We laughed. He believed!

**The walk of faith demands effort before the outcome
can be assured.**

It's an exciting way to live, isn't it!?

FAITH IS . . .
Fertilizing the plants

"He who tills his land will be satisfied with bread."—PROVERBS 12:11

It would be so much simpler if life were all a matter of cash **125** on delivery.

Or would it?

The farmer puts investment on top of investment, effort on top of effort, output on top of output, before he is assured that it will pay off as he waters and fertilizes the plants. He does it simply because he has faith in the tender growing shoots.

Some people fail because they don't have enough faith to plow the ground.

Others fail because they don't have enough faith to plant the seed.

Still others find that their supply of faith runs out at the stage when they have to start fertilizing the plants. They ask, "How much must I invest before I can expect a return? How do I know that I'm not putting too much into this project?"

These are fundamental questions that everybody is going to ask somewhere along the walk of faith, so it is time to remember that everything nice has its price.

Prosperity demands payment in advance—and as you go along—as well as a final payment on delivery!

It is part of God's design to keep us depending upon Him at every step in life's walk.

There is no phase in faith when we can "go it on our own."

God, help me to believe in my dream enough to keep giving it my best effort today! Forgive me if I have been neglecting it! I'm going to give it a shot of nourishment now with new effort. Amen.

Pruning the trees

"I am the true vine. . . . Every branch in Me that . . . bears fruit [the Father] prunes, that it may bear more fruit."—JOHN 15:1–2

126 It has always shocked me to watch an expert pruning trees or shrubs. It appears to be such a violent act.

When I watched my father trim fruit trees, I was shocked that he would cut off the very branches from which I had just picked fruit the previous season.

I pleaded with him, "Dad, not those branches—they're the ones that bore the most fruit!"

But my father would patiently reply, "The new growth will come out in the spring—*that's* what bears the best fruit."

My father was correct in his prediction, but it took tremendous faith to cut off the branches that bore the best fruit, trusting in new branches yet unborn.

In the Bible passage beginning with John 15, verse 1, we see how important success is in the mind and teaching of our Lord. Success can be defined as bearing fruit (being productive) and fulfilling God's plan for our lives.

We also see that the pruning of dead branches is essential to success.

Do you need to prune an obsolete product from your inventory?

Do you need to retool, restyle, or update your efforts?

Do you need to reeducate yourself in future technology?

Keep growing—or start dying. Faith requires tough pruning. Believe in the knife like the surgeon believes in the scalpel.

O God, give me the courage to say good-by to the old that needs to be buried with dignity before I can say hello to the new that waits with youthful vigor to step in as my new friend.

Harvesting the crop

"... whose hope is the LORD. ... shall be like a
tree planted by the waters, which spreads out
its roots by the river ... nor will cease from
yielding fruit."—JEREMIAH 17:7–8

We can all understand that it takes a lot of faith to plow the **127** ground, to plant the seed, to water, fertilize, and even prune the growth. But to harvest the crop? How is that an act of faith? Isn't harvest time a time for thanksgiving? Now is the time for relaxation. Right? Wrong!

Harvesting requires its own walk of faith, for the farmer who harvests believes that his crop will find a buyer in the marketplace.

Likewise, when I finally have a sermon prepared, I deliver it in the faith and belief that it will be helpful to others.

When you complete your college education with the degree tucked away in your pocket, you'll need a new level of faith. To make the most of your education, you have to tackle the job market.

And once you've achieved a financial base and have acquired some savings, can you relax? Hardly. As a crop rots in the field if it isn't harvested, so a financial fortune quickly dwindles away unless it is invested wisely. Inflation alone will reduce it rapidly.

Success can tempt you to take it easy. If the joy of the harvest, plus the high price paid to achieve it, tempts you to retire and retreat from future expansion and growth, then you're in real trouble! Even while my father harvested the crop he was planning a new crop for the following year.

How wise are the words of Viktor Frankl:

"The *is* must never catch up with the *ought.*"

Not having a new goal is to be feared more than not reaching a goal.

O God, give me faith strong enough to harvest the crop!

Developing progressively

"When you walk, your steps will not be hindered,/And when you run, you will not stumble."—PROVERBS 4:12

128   The high-flying trip of success doesn't usually happen swiftly and spontaneously. American success stories are of people who developed their businesses progressively. Faith progresses step by step. Each step is an exercise in possibility thinking.

Step 1 is *setting.* This is the stage similar to the chicken's waiting for the egg to hatch. You think things through. You do some raw market research. You do not leap forward impulsively. There is a lot of faith and possibility thinking in this first step.

Step 2 is *fretting.* Once you have an idea, begin to imagine the real obstacles you have to overcome. It's unrealistic not to prepare for this overcoming step in developing your project. Hopefully, you have been well prepared in this walk of faith to survive this stage—and the next one, too.

Step 3 is *getting.* Now it's time to get out and crack each problem one at a time. Refuse to surrender leadership to frustrations or forces that surround you.

Step 4 is *sweating.* You may have second thoughts. You may even ask yourself, "Is this what I really want?" Remember that it's usually darkest just before the dawn. God is setting things up for a miracle.

Step 5 is *netting!* You netted your catch! You reached your goal. Now what? Now you can find time to be alone and creative. You are not the same person you were when you took that first step. In this walk of faith, step by step, you have developed and progressed along with your dream.

A dream developed never leaves you where it found you. It makes you the person God wants you to be.

Mapping out the trip

"He who walks with integrity walks
securely."—PROVERBS 10:9

A great deal of faith is required when mapping out a trip **129**
before you hit the road. The same is true of the walk of faith.
For faith is a commitment to your highest values and noblest
calling. Begin by asking the questions:
Where will this road lead?
What if this becomes a habit?
What if others imitate me?
What if my children follow in my footsteps?
What if the whole world lived this way?
Occasionally our family vacations in Hawaii. We enjoy eating breakfast at the beautiful Kahala Hilton hotel dining room
overlooking the beach. Nearby is a private walkway leading
through a tunnel of trees. There is a sign posted which reads
"private."
One day our family visited a condominium near the hotel.
From the condominium we walked back through a wooded
area and came out to the same spot where the sign was. There
we found ourselves in front of the hotel's breakfast room. My
little daughter said, "Oh, that's where the road leads!"

**Map out your trip. Make sure you know where the
road leads. Know where you want to go.**

Today, check out your private life. Are your personal relationships healthy? Are your associates positive—or negative?
Take a long look at your goals. If you keep following the
path you're on, where will you end up?
Will you be pleased and proud once you get there? Will your
children be proud of you once you're gone?
Today, Lord, I'm going to walk the walk of faith. I'm going to
map out the path of my life carefully to make sure that I'm
walking in faith. Thank You, God. Amen.

Disciplining yourself to succeed

"I discipline my body and bring it into
subjection, lest I myself become disqualified."—
1 CORINTHIANS 9:27

130   Faith is focusing all of your conscious and subconscious
thought and your natural and supernatural powers to create a
spiritual cable more powerful than any steel cable.

**Faith, through this cable, moves mountains. This ca-
ble is *discipline!***

The words *discipline* and *disciple* come from the same root.
Early Christians were called disciples. That means they became persons so totally and completely committed to the
Christian cause that they were willing to die for it. That, essentially, is the spirit that makes up the word *discipline.*

The person who disciplines his body practices faith,
whether it's through controlling appetite for food or drink, or
any other natural physical appetite.

There are mysterious, intricate, and complex connections
of body, brain, and soul. Persons who discipline their eating,
drinking, and sexual appetites, often experience a mysterious
upsurge of creative powers and a rebirth of spirituality. In contrast, the undisciplined person who "lets himself go" and
doesn't care about proper exercise, physical fitness, or dietary
disciplines finds his faith becoming "flabby." *Undisciplined* is
another word for *disqualified.*

Affirmation: Today I am determined that I am going to
qualify as a disciple of Jesus Christ.

I will be disciplined in the control of my eyes, my ears, my
mouth, my stomach, my hands, and my sexual desires.

I shall bring my body under control.

I shall become a spiritual athlete!

Help me, O God, to succeed in this colossal challenge. Let
my life give evidence, O Lord, of being a disciplined disciple!
Amen.

FAITH IS . . .
Energizing your body

"The zeal of the LORD of hosts shall do this."—
2 KINGS 19:31

You have drawn the mental picture of your dream. You an- **131** nounced your intentions. You're excited about succeeding; now your faith must continue to release enthusiasm so you can perform at your best.

The word *enthusiasm* comes from two Greek words, *en-theos*, literally translated "in-God."

Enthusiasm is the force of God Himself energizing your body.

So, the zeal of the Lord, the enthusiasm that comes from our God-inspired faith, gives us peak performance power!

Most fatigue is the result of lack of faith. Negative emotions such as worry, frustration, anxiety, fear, indecision, guilt, and depression are weights causing tremendous fatigue of the human spirit. Make room for Jesus Christ. He saves you from all of these negative emotions—and inspires you to set great goals. With Christ, positive emotions replace negative emotions. *Weights become wings!* When our Lord gives us exciting dreams and reassures us of success, we become so energetic that the aging process is transcended by our strength-inducing faith.

Yes, look at some older people move fast, think fast, act fast when they are excited about life's possibilities!

In contrast, young people who have no goals and are not caught up in a consuming project act old. They move in slow motion and are tempted to draw upon chemicals for an unnatural high!

Our Lord comes and calls you to love Him and be His minister of mercy in a suffering and morbid world.

Suddenly you've got exciting goals! You're enthusiastic. His strength flows through you. Your faith is your energy.

Thank You, Father. Amen.

Climbing your way up and out

"For the body without the spirit is dead, so
faith without works is dead also."—JAMES 2:26

132 We have all seen people who profess to have dynamic faith.
They pray to God. They exercise religious rituals regularly
and faithfully. They even go to religious retreats to seek the
higher spiritual altitudes of emotional experiences. Yet their
faith remains at the same level, and their lives fall far short of
productivity. The fruits of constructive Christian living seem
conspicuously absent. Missing from their faith is human
effort! Faith is climbing your way out and up, and *climbing* is
spelled w-o-r-k-i-n-g!

Faith is not merely believing—it's working!

God's plan is to get you so deeply involved that your total
commitment will be required before you can fulfill your divine destiny.

Many years ago, a wise minister said, "Pray as if it all depends on God, and work as if it all depends on you!"

Show me a person who is giving 110 percent effort to his
work and to prayer, and I'll show you someone who's really
climbing in his walk of faith. For the ultimate test of faith is
this: Are you motivated to get going and *do* the tough jobs you
have been praying about? Jobs that you know God wants you
to do today?

I watched an ant, brushed off a stone bench. Into a jungle of
bric-a-brac, he fell, confused, bewildered, lost. I watched him
madly race through the little passages, never giving up in spite
of the many blind alleys. Finally, he decided to climb up a
vertical cliff! And he found his escape. He surely and successfully climbed his way up and out.

Can you do less than an ant?

Checking in before anybody else

"For God is not unjust to forget your work and labor of love which you have shown toward His name."—HEBREWS 6:10

I've observed that there are strong connections among faith, ambition, and productivity. The person who really believes he is going to succeed goes the extra mile, applies himself, is extremely productive, stands out from everybody else, and understandably wins the promotions.

He's the first one to check in, and the last one to check out. He doesn't watch the clock.

I love the story of a little boy who wanted to be rich when he grew up. He noticed a man who drove a big expensive car, and always stopped at a construction shack next to a high-rise building that was going up downtown.

One day the little boy went up to the rich man and said, "Sir, excuse me, but can you tell me how I can be rich like you when I grow up?"

The man, impressed by the boy's ambitious attitude, said, "Simple, son, buy a red shirt and work like it all depends on you." The man continued, "You see, I am a developer. I buy property, build buildings, and sell them.

"When I started out I decided that if I wanted to get ahead, I'd have to work harder than everybody else. I did a little better job, got to work a little earlier, and stayed a little longer.

"But I also decided my efforts should be noticed. All the workers wore blue shirts with blue overalls. So I bought a red shirt! The boss noticed me. And I was rewarded! That's my advice to you, son."

God has promised that He will reward the good worker.

"For God is not unjust to forget your work and labor of love which you have shown toward His name."

133

Prioritizing your possibilities

"Let your eyes look straight ahead,/And your
eyelids look right before you./Ponder the path
of your feet,/And let all your ways be
established."—PROVERBS 4:25–26

134   **The biggest problem you face on your walk of faith is
finding yourself surrounded with more opportunities
than you can handle.**

How do you go about prioritizing all your possibilities?
After all, there are only a limited number of minutes and
hours in the day. Treat each minute of the day as if it were a
gem. Each minute is money that can be invested or wasted!

First, list your daily possibilities on paper. List all of the
things you *could* do today, *should* do today, and *would* like to
do today; review the basic objectives that you want to accomplish.

Now, begin to prioritize the possibilities by giving your best
time to the most important project. The morning hours will
be your most valuable time, while the day is still uncluttered
with uninvited irritations that can easily tarnish your happy
attitude.

Give your best time to your most important projects.

Now—if you still lack resources to take advantage of great
opportunities, consider this. Many possibility thinkers lack
the resources to execute all of their dreams. So they carefully
look for other possibility thinkers whom they can approach
with their projects. They'll share their opportunities along
with the potential profit before they abandon the dream for
lack of time or money. In business this is called "setting up
limited partnerships."

To make sure your priorities are in order begin to form and
forge an "unlimited partnership." . . . "Your Lord and you"—
thinking, planning, dreaming together!

Father, thank You for the many opportunities I have to serve
You and others. Help me schedule my time and energy in
order to accomplish all You desire of me. Amen.

Chipping away at the block

"He who deals with a slack hand becomes
poor,/but the hand of the diligent makes one
rich."—PROVERBS 10:4

I often define faith in these simple but important D's.   **135**

Faith is *deciding.*
Faith is *daring.*
Faith is *doing* the job.
Faith is *determination* and *dedication.*

The writer of Proverbs tells us that *diligence* produces
wealth.

It is amazing what enormous problems dissipate when a
person's mind is diligently focused on a goal.

The first time I saw Michelangelo's bronze statue of Saint
Peter, in Saint Peter's Cathedral in Rome, there was, as always,
a line of faithful peasants and plutocrats alike waiting to see
this revered statue. It has been a tradition for years for the
faithful to pause at the statue and kiss the bronze toe of Peter,
or rub it softly. Today, that solid bronze toe of Peter is worn
away so it is nothing more than a flat, sharp edge.

If soft and gentle kisses can wear away a bronze toe, what
will daily touches of positive thoughts toward your tough
problem do to that obstacle?

If you've got a project to build or a problem to solve, take
that first crack at it today. You will chip away and before you
know it, the sculptured piece will begin to emerge out of the
marble.

Dear Lord, I need to exercise the six D's of faith today to
keep chipping away. Give me the power to *decide*, the courage
to *dare*, the energy to *do*, the willpower to be *determined*, the
grace to be *dedicated*, and the patience to be *diligent*. Thank
You, Lord. Amen.

Chiseling away at the mountain

"But you, be strong and do not let your hands
be weak, for your work shall be rewarded!"—
2 CHRONICLES 15:7

136 How do you move a mountain? You move a mountain one truckload at a time. You chisel away one chip at a time.

I have stood at the Great Wall of China and marveled at the hundreds of years that were consumed to build this wall over the impossible mountain ranges!

I have walked beside the great pyramids of Egypt and been amazed at these magnificent mountains that were built—one block at a time!

Dallas Anderson was sculpturing a larger-than-life statue of Job out of marble. He invited me to his studio, where I looked up at a ten-foot-tall chunk of white granite marble that weighed many tons.

Dallas said to me, "Job is inside there—and we'll have to bring him out." Then he handed me a sledge hammer that appeared to weigh twenty pounds!

"Take a whack at it; you have to really hammer at it!" With that I swung the sledge hammer with all the power I could muster and saw only a small chunk of white marble chip away. That was many months and tens of thousands of chips ago.

Today, that statue of Job stands in all his inspiring glory.

I learned, once more, how you move a mountain—one truckload at a time. I learned how you take a big rock and turn it into a work of art—one chip at a time. I was reminded again of what faith is all about. We chip and we chisel at life's challenges with confidence and hope until beauty emerges.

Dear God, thank You for giving me this faith. I will chisel away at my challenges one chunk at a time. Amen.

Positioning yourself in the marketplace

"Where no oxen are, the trough is clean;/But much increase comes by the strength of an ox."—PROVERBS 14:4

A contemporary paraphrase of our text today could read, **137** "Where there is no market, the store is empty; but much increase comes by the strength of providing the goods that people need." As you anticipate future growth and struggle with decisions to expand your base, do not abandon your faith to folly.

For example, when the sixties gave way to the seventies, Americans suddenly lost interest in huge automobiles. However, Detroit ignored the pressures of the marketplace and continued to manufacture big cars. By doing so, they plunged the automobile industry into a recession of gigantic proportions. Japan captured Detroit's position.

Success often depends on selling something to someone. Selling is convincing people that you have the answer to their problem and the help they need.

Education sells knowledge.

Universities sell training or professional work.

Hospitals sell health care.

Even churches sell something—spiritual and emotional services—to people whose problems can only be solved through a personal relationship with God and Jesus Christ!

Does the need still exist or is it passé? Who else is filling this need? These are responsible questions you need to ask before you expand your base of service. If there is a need that no one else is meeting, then come up with a program to meet those needs. Position yourself in the marketplace of ideas to provide services that solve problems no one else is really tackling!

Faith in action is positioning yourself in the marketplace of human effort. I will solve someone's problem in the name of God.

Evolving upward

"Be faithful unto death, and I will give you the crown of life."—REVELATION 2:10

138   You have a dream, but the solid base you need for a launching pad is not yet established. What do you do?

You have to let the dream evolve.

The first level is the *nesting* level. Here you ask the basic question: "Who needs it?"

When you discover that someone can be helped by your forward act of faith, you enter the second level, the *testing* of the dream. Here you ask three basic questions: Will it help people who are hurting? Will it be a great thing for God and for the human family? Is anybody else doing the job? If so, can I do it better and cheaper?

The third level is the *investing* level. This is the level where you invest your resources. Put your money where your mouth is.

The fourth level is *divesting* yourself of negative thinking. Eliminate the fear of failure.

The fifth level is *arresting.* You encounter tough times. God always gives you a great new test before He gives you a great success! This is God's way of making sure He can trust you with success.

The sixth level is the *cresting* level. This is the uppermost level of the evolutionary process of the dream. Faith evolves upward until that moment when the dream is complete! The project is finished!

O Lord, today I shall take time to review each level of evolution my faith has experienced. I shall praise God that He was there all the time. He has not failed me yet. He will not fail me now. Tomorrow will be glorious, for God is there. Thank You, God. Amen.

Pacing your progress

"To everything there is a season,/A time for
every purpose under heaven . . ./A time to
plant,/And a time to pluck what is planted,
. . ./A time to break down,/And a time to build
up . . ."—ECCLESIASTES 3:1

Doesn't the walk of faith appear to be inflicted with contra- **139**
dictions or paradoxes? Doesn't it seem like a juggling act in a
possibility-thinking game? Then remember this:

Faith is an art—not a science. Faith advances for a season,
then retreats the next. You are ambitious for a season, then
relaxed; aggressive, then passive; giving, then taking.

As positive and negative wires generate the power of elec-
tricity, so in faith, negatives are used with positives to create
mountain-moving energy for the believer.

Faith is pacing your progress. The challenges come in knowing: when to push forward, when to hold back; when to dig in,
when to yield; when to hold on, when to let go; when to plan
alone, when to form a partnership.

Faith paces your progress through life with a rhythmic
steadiness regulated by an all-wise Timekeeper, God Almighty. When you walk the walk of faith, you are assured of
the divine guidance to

**Make the right move, in the right way, at the right
time.**

When you kneel before the throne of the almighty God in
respectful humility and cry out, "I need the wisdom of heaven
to walk this walk of faith," you reach the level of faith where
contradictions become constructive; paradoxes become truth.

So keep trusting God to give you His sense of timing. Pace
yourself. Now you wait. Now you move. Now you race! Now
you rest. Now you leap! Now you walk slowly. Possibility
thinkers don't quit—they change their pace to win the race.

Thank You, God for the exhilaration we experience in the
ebb and flow of faith's pilgrimage. Amen.

Triple-checking your position

"Examine me, O LORD, and prove me;/Try my mind and my heart."—PSALM 26:2

140

Late in the Vietnam conflict I found myself in Tachikawa, Japan, where the central command headquarters for the entire medical evacuation of the sick and the wounded was situated.

I was given a personal briefing by the general who was in charge. It was his job to establish systems and procedures to care for the patients from the time they fell wounded on the front line to their final hospitalization in America.

On our tour he said, "Dr. Schuller, we are very proud of the fact that of the multiplied tens of thousands of casualties we have seen in the Vietnam conflict to date, we have only witnessed *eleven fatalities in transit.*"

Astonished, I asked, "How do you do it?"

He said, "We *check, double-check,* and *recheck!* Before any wounded person is moved, we take the vital signs. If his vital signs indicate he can make it, he is loaded onto a helicopter. Before the chopper takes off, we double-check his vital signs. If he passes the check, we tell the pilot to prepare to take off. We wait a minute and triple-check! This triple check often becomes the key factor in survival!"

Faith is triple-checking the position. Many people succeed or fail here.

The possibility of suceeding increases drastically if you will
• check
• double-check
• recheck
You ordered it done? You expect a delivery? Somebody promised? Check, double-check, recheck!

Narrowing the path

> "Enter by the narrow gate; for wide is the gate
> and broad is the way that leads to destruction,
> and there are many who go in by it. Because
> narrow is the gate and difficult is the way
> which leads to life, and there are few who find
> it."—MATTHEW 7:13–14

141

The walk of faith is not the broad path. The truth is, most people choose the wide, safe road, which leads to despair, discouragement, and ultimate lack of self-fulfillment.

The narrow path is the walk of faith. It leads to excitement, adventure, and discovery, that adds up to *life!*

The exciting path is the narrow road that winds through the mountains. It's the narrow path through the garden that leads to the secluded little spots.

Most people take the wide boulevards. They completely miss the interesting places tucked away in the back streets. They are often like tourists who land at an airport and take the bus down through the main streets of town to see the old monuments and the biggest buildings. They return to the airport, never having felt the heartbeat of the people or the places that throb with charm and mystery.

It is easy to deal in broad strokes, for there is a certain safety in sweeping generalities. Instead, we must refuse to accept mediocrity, and we must keep narrowing the pursuit of excellence.

Philosophy and faith get tough and challenging when you try to apply them to the daily acts of human existence. Your prayers are safer if they deal with the broad platitudes. Dare to be specific today and take a very narrow definition in a dangerous request, and prayer will become exciting. What specific need do you have today? Dare to pray specifically!

God, help me today to narrow my path, to lead a more exciting life of faith. I pray specifically for _____. Thank You, Lord. Amen.

Maintaining equilibrium

"Everyone who competes for the prize is
temperate in all things."—1 CORINTHIANS 9:25

142   In the Christian walk of faith it is so easy to lose one's sense
of balance. It's easy to become religious extremists of either
the right or the left. We've all seen those who believe solely in
prayer and reject all forms of scientific and medical aid on the
assumption that seeking human help would be a lack of faith.

By contrast, there are believers who depend entirely upon
material and medical aid and reject the possibility of supernatural and miraculous intervention by God.

The walk of faith is a narrow walk.

It's a delicate task of remaining equilibristic.

By that, I mean one who maintains equilibrium, that remarkable ability to maintain balance when you walk on two
feet balancing a hundred or two hundred pounds.

Remaining spiritually equilibristic is a tricky task too. I believe in prayer for divine guidance, yet I do not recklessly
plunge ahead as soon as a positive idea comes to my mind.

I test the idea. How?

(1) I use the intelligence God has given me;

(2) I check with positive-thinking experts on the subject;

(3) I make sure it does not violate the moral and spiritual
principles taught in the Holy Bible—God's Word for my life!
And finally,

(4) I ask the question, "What would Jesus do?"

> **Dear God, is there some aspect of my faith that I have
> been neglecting? Today help me to realign the scales
> so that I shall have the poise of a well-balanced artist
> on the walk of faith. To Christ be the glory. Amen.**

Comparing the values

"How much better it is to get wisdom than gold!/And to get understanding is to be chosen rather than silver."—PROVERBS 16:16

On this walk of faith—how do you keep your balance? How **143** do you maintain equilibrium? You do so by carefully comparing competing values before you make unconditional commitments!

As a possibility thinker, you will spot so many opportunities you will be confronted with innumerable demands on your time, energy, thoughts, and money!

Here's a word of caution: you will be tempted more often by the good than by the bad.

The greater dangers on this walk of faith will not be the temptations to kill, steal, and commit adultery. The greater temptation will be

- to neglect the higher good for the lower good
- to choose the mediocre instead of the excellent
- to live on the "pretty good" level instead of the "super" level, and
- to take the easy goal instead of the impossible challenge.

Every time faith translates into action, what is really happening? Why, some person is making a comparison of values. Consciously or subconsciously, he or she is making a choice between alternative values. When people tell me they "lack faith" I often conclude that they're really confused. They can't decide between competing options.

Frequently there is a contradiction within their value system.

The spiritual and the carnal compete for control.

The ideal and the practical clash for allegiance.

The call to comfort, luxury, and ease competes with the call to sacrifice and commitment.

Decision making is easy if there are no contradictions in your value system.

Bottom lining

". . . seek the kingdom of God, and all these things shall be added to you."—LUKE 12:31

144 Quickly and with great regularity, successful people look to the bottom line. They review the profit and loss statement. In the same way, faith asks these basic questions:
- What do I really want to accomplish?
- If I keep going at it the way I am, will I make it?
- If I do, will I be satisfied?
- If I forfeit an opportunity to educate my mind, how will that benefit me socially, financially?
- At the end of my life, can I face my family, myself, and my God with pride?
- Or will I be ashamed and find that the victories are hollow in my hand?
- *What will the bottom line be?*

> **Faith specializes in looking ahead and projecting the outcome. Then faith makes the choices that ensure the odds that the bottom line will be great.**

Today I shall take the long look. As I calculate the price I'll have to pay, I'll also anticipate the rewards I shall reap.
- I am asking God for guidance.
- I am promising Him that I will follow His leadership.
- I'm aware that the most important thing in my life is the welfare of my soul.

O God, don't neglect to take the actions that guarantee the salvation of my soul. Now I accept You, Jesus Christ, as my Savior. I ask You to receive my soul, redeem it, guard it against temptations and sins so that I may be strong and successful! Amen.

Maneuvering your way skillfully

"You comprehend my path/and my lying
down,/And are acquainted with all my ways."—
PSALM 139:3

It's common in most ports for captains of ocean liners to **145** step aside and allow special pilots to come aboard. Every harbor has its own peculiar channels and hidden shoals under the surface.

I remember, on an ocean voyage I took, our ship passed through a narrow and precarious passageway in the Coral Sea, between Australia and New Guinea. The narrow S-shaped crevice that cuts through the coral reef below the water is only about sixty feet wide—just wide enough for an ocean vessel. It requires enormous skill from a captain who knows the passageway.

The voyage of faith is not unlike the passage through the Coral Sea. We need to bring a skillful pilot aboard, one who knows the water and hidden shoals. Our Lord is that special pilot who understands our past and knows us better than we know ourselves.

Faith keeps you moving forward by maneuvering between successes and failures, between accomplishments and setbacks, between victories and defeats.

> **Faith is no irresponsible shot in the dark. It is a responsible trust in God, who knows the desires of your hearts, the dreams you are given, and the goals you have set. He will guide your paths right.**

O Lord, give my faith the flexibility to maneuver between the highs and the lows, the ups and the downs, the ins and the outs. I am trusting that under Your skillful patrol my plans are moving in absolutely the best possible way. Thank You, Lord. Amen.

Buckling your safety belt

"The wise in heart will receive commands."—
PROVERBS 10:8

146 As a possibility thinker you buckle your safety belt not out of fear, but because you balance your faith with caution. After all, can there be faith without respect?

By faith you make commitments before you have solid guarantees of success. That is the essence of possibility thinking. You never wait to make the move until all risks are removed. But you do try to cover all bases. Then you use faith to minimize the risks—with a healthy respect for possible dangers.

You walk the walk of faith—but you still carry liability insurance.

You walk the walk of faith, but you still lock your doors.

You walk the walk of faith, but you still check credentials and credit references before making a big investment.

Faith is buckling your safety belts—*making a commitment to take the trip without guarantees of successfully arriving.*

You dignify your faith when you separate it from folly.

So keep walking the walk of faith—all the while, watching your step!

One negative thought, carelessly allowed to enter the mind, can undermine the unity of your faith.

Show me the person who buckles his safety belt, and I'll show you one who dares to take a chance,

is not afraid of flying,

and knows there can be accidents on the road.

Doesn't that sound like the kind of faith God will bless?

FAITH IS . . .
Scouting the territory

"If the LORD delights in us, then He will bring
us into this land . . . which flows with milk
and honey."—NUMBERS 14:8

Entertainers and athletes alike know what we mean when **147**
we speak of "scouting the territory." "Scouts" are always on
the lookout for new talent waiting to be discovered.

Faith calls out a new greeting to you today!

"Be a good scout! Hey, look around you! There's talent in
you waiting to be discovered. Check out the possibilities today."

**Thoughts are like roads; you never know where they
will lead you.**

Think through new ideas; discover new formulas. Scout the
territory beyond the horizon of your mind; consider the positive potentialities. Ask: where will this opportunity lead me?

As you scout the possibilities, be a good scout! Two persons
can scout out the same territory and each come back with a
conflicting report. There is a marvelous story in the Old Testament that illustrates the point. Moses sent out twelve
scouts to check the promised land of Canaan to see if the
territory could be conquered. Ten negative thinkers returned
with a despairing report, saying, "There we saw giants . . . and
we were like grasshoppers" (Num. 13:33). They saw only the
obstacles and recommended that the people of Israel remain
in the desert.

Two positive-thinking scouts, Joshua and Caleb, came back
bearing gifts of fruit—grapes, pomegranates, and figs. Their
report was an enthusiastic one. "Let's take the territory! We
are well able to overcome it!"

Faith is scouting the territory and reporting back enthusiastically. Faith is believing that with God's guidance and
blessing on your life, you can conquer the territory that flows
with milk and honey!

FAITH IS . . .
Creating new products and services

"Behold, the former things have come to pass,
and new things I declare; before they spring
forth I tell you of them."—ISAIAH 42:9

148   Faith finally adds up to this: We have to keep creating new
products and new services to meet the changing needs in a
shifting society. Creativity is always the ultimate act of believing.

It takes faith to launch a new idea, for there is always risk
involved. But there are ways to minimize the risk.

Market research may determine in advance whether a new
product will really succeed. Spot testing can predetermine
whether an idea is going to be effective. Field polls conduct
research of public opinion to project which candidate will be
the winner.

But in the final analysis, all creativity entails risk. Many
times the poll is proven wrong on election day; mass distribution didn't succeed as the tests predicted.

The element of the unexpected keeps us on our toes! God
never allows us to become so smart that we can be absolutely
confident our new creations will be successful.

**God does promise He will bless us if we are genuinely
creative and keep moving ahead in faith.**

For unless we keep creating new products or service lines
we will be out of business before we know it. For one thing,
the brightest and best people become bored and drift away
when nothing new, exciting, and challenging is happening.
Lose your best people and you're soon facing a disaster. Stop
all experimentation and life becomes stale!

When was the last time you tried to create something new?

Today, O God, give me the courage to be creative. Amen.

FAITH IS . . .
Competing constructively

"In You, O LORD, I put my trust;/Let me never be put to shame."—PSALM 71:1

Possibility thinkers thrive on competition; impossibility thinkers quickly and cautiously back away from competition. **149**

What do these impossibility thinkers fear? Are they afraid they will fail? Surely they don't think they can win if they never play the game. How will they ever know who they are if they never enter a competition?

You will never know what your abilities are until you put yourself to the test.

> **Surrendering to the fear of competition may leave you forever in the dark, unaware of hidden strengths you possess.**

Begin by competing against yourself. Set a pride-producing goal to achieve something measurable and worthwhile within a responsible time frame. Now when that's accomplished, compete against that achievement; set a larger goal. Faith calls you to competition!

Compete against the problems of this life by finding a ministry that will help people triumph over their tragedies.

Compete against mediocrity by committing yourself to excellence and inspiring others around you to artistic effort in their chosen profession and career.

Compete against lethargy by raising your awareness level so that you challenge social and spiritual sickness with a positive faith.

Compete against negative and sinful persons by living such a positive and beautiful life that you shall be a "shining light in a dark world."

As long as you've got the competitive spirit, you are walking the walk of faith and you are alive.

Compete in life today!

Tapping the untapped possibilities

"Launch out into the deep and let down your
nets for a catch."—LUKE 5:4

150 So you think you've taken your project as far as you can?
You think you've exhausted the market? You think you know
the answers on philosophy, psychology, and religion? Wait a
minute!

> **When you think you've exhausted all possibilities, re-
> member this—you haven't!**

There is a beautiful story in Luke 5:1–8 about the disciples'
fishing all night. As morning breaks the Lord greets them,
"How's fishing?"

"Master, we've fished all night and caught nothing!" is their
weary reply.

"Go out in the deep and throw out your nets," the Lord
directs.

They have every reason to doubt His advice. After all, they
have been fishing all night. But by faith they throw the net in
once more; and this time there are so many fish they can
hardly pull up the load.

It's a beautiful example of life today! Living is like fishing
on the surface of the sea. Even as schools of fish move from
one place to another, so opportunities are always on the move
around you.

There are untapped possibilities around you now. There are
religious experiences you haven't had yet. Encounters with
God through prayer are possible, even if you haven't experienced them.

There is a distinguishing quality about the possibility
thinker—he goes one step beyond everybody else. That extra
step is called the "mark of faith." It is the "winner's edge."

FAITH IS . . .
Spiraling your way upward

"I will go before you and make the crooked
places straight."—ISAIAH 45:2

Of all the misunderstandings about possibility-thinking **151**
faith, there is one point that must be reviewed again: Faith is
not a wild plunge into dangerous ventures. Faith faces risks
with the wide-awake awareness that success is uncertain.
Nevertheless, faith moves ahead, confident that you can arrive if you keep on keeping on. Faith believes that you can
maneuver your way around the obstacles and dangers.

You may not be able to remove the obstacle and you may
not be able to tunnel through the mountain that lies before
you, but no matter how steep the path may be—it can still be
conquered if you work your way around the obstacle.

Remember: A mountain road is seldom a straight path. The
road will twist, turn, curve, and wind. Not infrequently the
road detours for miles before a "switch-back" can be executed,
and you can start moving in on your destination once more.

The good news is that eventually—after compromising, adjusting, manipulating, and maneuvering—you do succeed!
The crooked place becomes straight. The mountaintop is
reached, and the village with its straight streets lies below.

> **Faith calls you to travel ahead in uncharted territory,
> exposing yourself to risk. But faith manages the risks
> responsibly through wise and cautious maneuvering.**

Affirmation: I shall keep spiraling my way upward. I shall
not fail. My strong spirit of determination is itself a victory
over discouragement! I am a success at this level—anyway!
My willingness to exercise patience is a victory over reckless
impulsiveness. Here, too, I am experiencing a success. Thank
You, Lord!

Redoubling the effort

"Be steadfast, immovable, always abounding in
the work of the Lord, knowing that your labor
is not in vain."—1 CORINTHIANS 15:58

152   When someone fails, is it because they've lacked enough
faith? Or was it because they didn't give it enough effort? Is
the problem laziness or is it a lack of faith?

Does effort inspire faith? Does faith inspire effort? Or do
they stimulate and sustain each other?

The answer is yes, they do stimulate and sustain each other,
for actually faith can be defined as "giving it all you've got."

There is no doubt that little effort is put forth without faith.
It is also certain that great faith motivates maximum output
of personal energy and investment.

All of the successful people whom I've met and studied
demonstrate this quality: they give their project everything
they've got. They invest more capital in the business. They
work overtime gladly and cheerfully. No wonder they are promoted!

**When we see someone redoubling their effort, we see
an inspiring person demonstrating a strong faith in action.**

When positive people are faced with temptations, they call
upon God and their inner selves for moral strength beyond
what they have previously tapped in life.

Again and again, spiritual, financial, social, educational, or
professional victory is the result of someone's redoubling the
effort.

Quadruple the output. Calculate the average cost for the
goal that you want to accomplish, then multiply it four times!
Now you join the inspiring team of men and women who
walk the walk of faith.

Today, O God, I'll double, triple, and finally redouble my
efforts! And I'll trust You to bless me. Amen.

Redoing the job

"Let patience have its perfect work, that you
may be perfect and complete, lacking
nothing."—JAMES 1:4

Faith is redoing a job after you've botched it the first time. **153**
It's removing the wallpaper because the wrinkles couldn't be
smoothed out. It's scraping the new paint job off because it
just didn't come out right. Faith is starting over!

I recall one summer when I was under contract to complete
a book for a publisher. Mrs. Schuller and I were scheduled to
attend a conference in Europe. We spent a beautifully productive week on the island of Madeira where I hand wrote a complete book. Finally, when the entire manuscript was finished, I
proudly put it in the mail in time to meet the publisher's
deadline.

A few weeks later I arrived in New York and telephoned my
editor. He gave me the terrible news: the manuscript had
never arrived! It was lost in the mail never to be found. Since I
had handwritten the manuscript, there was no carbon copy,
only scattered pieces of notes. I had no choice but to start over
again and completely rewrite the entire book.

That took a lot of faith! Faith (a) to find the energy to do it
over; (b) that I could write as well as I had done in a secluded
and creative setting; and (c) that I would still be able to finish
the project in time to meet my publisher's deadline—which
now they had extended a few weeks.

I rewrote the entire manuscript, and I have to admit that the
second writing was considerably better than the first.

> **"It's good enough" is an attitude that is not good
> enough for the person who is walking the walk of
> faith.**

Dear God, give me the faith to do the job over again. There
is a possibility that I can do a better job the second, or the
third, or the fourth time around!

Staying with it

"Let us hold fast the confession of our hope without wavering, for He who promised is faithful."—HEBREWS 10:23

154   *Stick-to-it-iveness!* That's what faith boils down to, doesn't it!

I don't know how many rejections I had from a variety of publishing firms before my first book was published. There were times in the nearly thirty years of my ministry when I was tempted to quit! Why didn't I pack up? Because I had made a commitment! That's another word for f-a-i-t-h!

> **Faith is staying with it through thick and thin, believing that eventually you will win.**

For years I kept a saying under the glass top of my desk: "When things get tough, don't move. People and pressures shift, but the soil remains the same no matter where you go." I read these words over and over. Wow! They have really helped me have stick-to-it-iveness.

Choose today to develop a reputation for being a person of emotional stability. When you make the decision that you're going to stay with it, you step up to a higher level of emotional maturity. In what area of your life do you need stick-to-it-iveness?

- The goals you know in your heart were given by God— like a life-long marriage to one person—cannot be abandoned.
- You're definitely going to continue the program of good body care.
- You are not about to give up on life.
- Your commitment to Jesus Christ is stronger than ever.

That's great! You're going to stay with it. That's faith. You'll never be sorry when you let faith make the move.

Forsaking ease and comfort

"When my father and my mother forsake me,/
Then the LORD will take care of me./Teach me
Your way, O LORD,/And lead me in a smooth
path."—PSALM 27:10–11

I first spotted my wife when she was nineteen years of age. **155**
She was a beautiful, vivacious, energetic, exciting young
farmer's daughter who played the organ on Sundays. I got a
date with Arvella DeHaan, and it was then that I found out
where she lived.

Arvella lived on a remote farm. The only way to get to her
house was by a one-lane driveway, a quarter of a mile long,
leading through a muddy corn field. As long as the driveway
was dry, there was no problem. But when it rained, it turned to
mud. In the wintertime it was often closed with drifts of
snow. No snow plows ever opened this private driveway. But I
wasn't about to let a muddy or snow-filled driveway keep me
from courting my girl! Often I had to forsake the ease and
comfort of my car in order to reach the girl of my dreams.

Such enthusiastic determination has really been the testi-
mony of my life. For every time I've spotted something that
caught my fancy, captured my imagination, and filled me with
passion, it was always something that was seemingly out of
my reach. Or at least the road to get there was tough!

Having a God-given, seemingly impossible dream is rarely a
comfortable spot. So, don't ever think that possibility-
thinking faith is a call to ease and comfort! It is exactly the
opposite. It is a call to a cross. Be willing to deny yourself, take
up the cross, and follow the Lord.

When He gives you a project, it will be tough. Be sure of
that.

**If your project seems impossible, the odds are, the
dream came from God!**

Paying the high price gladly

"The kingdom of heaven is like a merchant seeking beautiful pearls, who, when he had found the one pearl of great price, went and sold all that he had and bought it."—MATTHEW 13:45–46

156   A supersuccessful multimillionaire in California started his manufacturing and marketing business by selecting a small team of bright men. He shared with them the great opportunities he saw for the business and for them. He promised them a good salary and the opportunity to be very creative. He offered all the benefits on one condition: that they invest all of their money and capital in the company. Why? He wanted their 100 percent investment in the business. One of the men objected and was sure that the founder would compromise. He was mistaken. He was passed by.

All of the others who went along with the president's requirements went on to share in the success of the company that today is known throughout the country. All of them have become multimillionaires.

"I had to have the confidence that they had total faith in the company and what it was designed to accomplish," the founder-president said.

Faith is paying the price—gladly!

Do you believe in yourself, in your God, and in your God-inspired goals enough to give your all to Him and to His dreams for your life?

I'm a believer. I'll pay the price. Thank You for giving me this faith, Lord. Amen.

Striving for excellence

"Whatever your hand finds to do, do it with all your might."—ECCLESIASTES 9:10

Once you've achieved success, it takes a lot of faith to be- **157** lieve you can upstage your own accomplishment!

It takes faith for a C student to believe that he can earn B's or A's!

It takes faith for a straight-A student to believe that she can do an A + job in the career world.

Whether you are a low, medium, or high achiever, it takes a lot of faith to believe that you can do a lot better!

Striving for excellence is an act of faith.

God is not honored or glorified by mediocrity.

How can you motivate yourself or others to strive for excellence? If striving for excellence *is* faith, then today's prescription is aimed at building up your confidence so that you will not fail!

What excellent, superlative, outstanding goals would you go for if you knew you'd make it?

The strong assurance of a genuine possibility of success remains a major motivating force for excellence.

Motivate yourself today with the assurance that:

I can do it!

I can become a champion if I set my heart on it!

It is my sense of obligation to perform at my best before the Almighty! Yes, that's what drives me to excellence.

An attitude for opportunity stirs me to noble effort.

Be thankful you're alive! As an expression of your gratitude, give the Lord the best that you have. In so doing, your work will be your worship! Your outstanding effort will be your faith in action, praising God for His goodness.

Stretching the mileage

"If you walk in My ways . . . to keep My
commandments . . . then I will lengthen your
days."—1 KINGS 3:14

158 Do you suffer from a lack of energy, money, talent, or
power?

Before you assume you "don't have enough," learn how to
get more mileage out of what you do have.

You stretch mileage much in the same way you use a spoon-
ful of honey. It's hard to measure, much less stop it from going
on and on. It drips from the edge of the spoon, becoming a
liquid stalagmite, stretching unbroken until it becomes like
an exquisite gold thread glistening in the sun.

It's like the trained vocalist who is able to sustain a note,
delicate and fragile, yet strong, until finally it fades away. Faith
is stretching the mileage.

How do you stretch your assets to get the most mileage
from them?

Check out discipline and see the wonders it can do. Believable productivity is achieved by the highly trained and power-
fully disciplined person.

In the last years of my mother's life, she lived on an income
of only four thousand dollars a year. To many she was living
below the poverty level, yet she refused financial help from
any of the children. Happily, she managed to live comfortably
and still give four hundred dollars a year to her church.

She was an inspiration as she always had a birthday card for
each of the grandchildren with a crisp one-dollar bill in it.
Plus, she always managed to buy flour and sugar so she could
bake homemade cookies as gifts to the neighbors.

My mother stretched the mileage of her faith and her possessions. Her life was as beautiful as a drop of honey, a glistening strand of molten gold.

**Believe that you can do so much more with what you
have! You'll delight in the new discoveries that come
as you stretch the mileage on this trip of faith.**

Phasing in—phasing out—phasing up

"You have made known to me the ways of life;/
You will make me full of joy in Your
presence."—ACTS 2:28

Perhaps you have already passed through some of life's **159**
phases in your pilgrimage of faith. I've categorized six of them
with rhythmic verbs:

Phase 1 is *sitting:* Faith is to "Be still, and know that I am
God" (Ps. 46:10). Wait until you get God's direction before you
do anything.

Phase 2 is *splitting.* Leave your passive position, break with
inertia and get started.

Phase 3 is *flitting.* There is a certain amount of floundering
in the early days of your pilgrimage. Look at the child who
learns to walk. Consider the novice on the job. Don't give up.

Phase 4 is *gritting.* Decide you are going to settle down. It
may take longer than you hoped, but grit your teeth—and
make the commitment to success.

Phase 5 is *knitting.* Tie the loose ends together. Learn from
mistakes and take steps to improve yourself. Stitch by stitch,
you'll make it.

Phase 6 is *hitting:* You will be a hit! You will score successfully!

Faith is facing life's many phases positively!

You may find it takes more faith in the final phase than in
the first. Once you arrive, you discover new, unexpected problems. One thing is sure, the walk of faith is never boring.
There are always new challenges. For that be grateful.

**Variety is the spice of life when you make the commit-
ment to live with a positive belief.**

Moving ahead step by step

". . . you would have a walk worthy of God who
calls you into His own kingdom and glory."—
1 THESSALONIANS 2:12

160   How would you describe your movement today?
Are you in retreat? Retrenching? Moving backwards?
Are you at a standstill? In neutral? Coasting?
Or are you moving ahead? Are you actively making plans
and setting goals to move yourself upward and forward?
The kind of faith that God promises to bless is faith that is
expressed in dynamic action.
Meditation must be translated into creative activity.
Creative fantasizing must be transformed into muscle
movements.
The actions may be small, but they must be forward move-
ments. "Inch by inch anything's a cinch." Practice these small
significant movements. Say aloud:
"I must pick up the telephone."
"I must reach for the pencil or the pen."
"I must do something to move myself forward."
"I must hit the books."
"I must make the contacts and communicate."
"I must sell my ideas, and I must sell myself."

**You cannot simply wait quietly and piously for God to
drop miracles out of a cloud.**

What is the biggest problem that you face today?
What can you do about it today?
Answer these questions and get to work. Start by doing the
toughest job first.
By the time the day is finished, you'll be able to look back
and know that you have made progress.
That's walking the walk of faith.

Projecting future growth

"A mustard seed which, when it is sown on the ground, is smaller than all the seeds on earth . . . grows up and becomes greater than all herbs, . . . so that the birds of the air may nest under its shade."—MARK 4:31–32

I must never stop growing—or I will start dying! This is a **161** law of life. It is evident in nature. In my yard I have a pepper tree that is one hundred years old. I proudly shared this information with a tree trimmer who had come to prune it. "I'm sure that it's full grown by now!" I added.

"Oh, but it is still growing," he said. "Trees continue to grow—until they die."

I said, "Even the giant redwoods that are thousands of years old—are *they* still growing?"

"Of course they are," he said.

There is no life without growth.

This is a law of life. Should you decide to grow just for the sake of growth? Yes, because you must remain youthful and alive all the days of your life. There are psychological studies that show that senility may be in part the result of a decision made by tired old people to stop growing.

Faith is deciding to grow for growth's sake, projecting growth by carefully considering human needs.

When you believe that the secret of success is to find a need and fill it, then you must project growth plans to meet authentic market pressures and projections.

I know an old gentleman, keen and alert, over ninety years of age, who has a huge garden. "And it is bigger than ever this year," he told me with enthusiasm. "I belong to a little church through which I contribute fresh vegetables and fruit to people who need the food. It makes me feel so good to give the food away . . . no one could pay me for the good feeling it gives me."

Growing with tomorrow's possibilities!

"Mercy, peace, and love be multiplied to
you."—JUDE 1:2

162 The exercise of faith is the very process of growth! So long
as we are growing intellectually, emotionally, and spiritually,
we are still alive and youthful.

Life is growth.

To stifle growth is to initiate the termination of life. The
deceptive spirit of decay, decline, and death subtly and seduc-
tively enters our human spirit when we gradually or abruptly
stop growing. The seed of death is planted in an individual or
in an institution when growth is no longer possible.

But growth is always possible for the person who is walking
the walk of faith!

You can grow and discover new insights into yourself if you
welcome every problem as a possibility, every obstacle as an
opportunity, and every age as a new laboratory experience in
understanding the path of human existence!

Yes, every phase and condition brings with it a unique possibility for personal growth.

Faith spots positive opportunities. Faith welcomes each tomorrow with its pleasure or pain as an invitation to adventure.

Where are the opportunities and possibilities for my personal growth that I can work on tomorrow? I can become
more merciful! It's possible for me to be less judgmental and
critical! I'll try—tomorrow. Then I can expect peace and love
to really be multiplied in my life—tomorrow!

Thank You, God. Amen.

Exploring all possible alternatives

"There is nothing hidden which will not be revealed, nor has anything been kept secret but that it should come to light."—MARK 4:22

Wouldn't it be exciting to be the first person to discover a **163** new, previously unknown country filled with exotic birds, glorious mountains, rushing rivers, and strange but attractive human beings, previously untouched by civilization?

Life is never boring to the exploring mind.

The walk of faith offers this possibility to any person of any age. The walk of faith is truly an adventure in living. When you walk by faith you are in the process of becoming an explorer.

Faith is the mental process of exploring all possible alternatives in goal-setting and problem-solving activity.

The shocking thing is, faith honestly does move mountains. Don't deplore your situation; explore it—for hidden possibilities! When we move forward and assume that a way will open up to achieve the impossible, then suddenly it happens.

We discover an alternative route through what appeared to be an impenetrable mountain range.

What appears to be the *end* of the road suddenly turns out to be a *bend* in the road, leading through a narrow pass.

- A new route to happiness is discovered.
- A new path to prosperity is found.
- A new secret of success is learned.
- A new approach in communication is acquired.
- A new profession is developed.
- A new belief system moves into your thinking.
- A new experience with God is encountered.

Keep exploring and you'll keep discovering the secrets to exciting success.

God blesses the explorer, for this is faith in action!

Applying old principles to new situations

"That which has been is what will be,/That which is done/is what will be done,/And there is nothing new under the sun."—ECCLESIASTES 1:9

164 Is it possible to be really truly creative? If you said yes there would be those who would challenge your creativity. There are those who contend that to create is to come up with something *totally* and *completely* new.

We can, however, be innovative when we apply a proven principle in an area where it has never been contemplated or considered before.

W. Clement Stone said it:

"The secret of success is learning to observe principles and applying them in new and surprising areas."

When he said that I took notice, and I realized that he was right. I began to observe marketing principles that were operating in American business and then tried to apply them to our work in the church and to our ministry through television.

By the grace of God we have had a measure of success simply because we applied old principles to new situations.

Now we see how we can use our faith as we apply established principles in areas where they haven't been applied before! You see we need to break from our traditional Western tendency to deal with facts, and start dealing with principles as they do in the Orient.

Begin with this simple principle. The secret of success is to find a need and fill it. When we apply it in marriage, in family, in business, or whether in problem solving or decision making, we know we are on the way to success. Be innovative today. Apply what you know to something new!

FAITH IS . . .
Negotiating your way forward

"By humility and the fear of the LORD/Are
riches and honor and life."—PROVERBS 22:4

How do you sell your ideas successfully? **165**

How do you persuade people that they should accept the
help you want to give?

There's a lot of negotiating that must take place as you walk
the walk of faith. A wife and a husband will not have a happy
marriage for long until they learn how to handle the negotiable values.

There are negotiable and nonnegotiable human values. You
need to sort them out and determine what can be abandoned
without sacrificing your ultimate objective. For example, the
ultimate objective in any marriage should be to live happily
together until death, thereby providing a wonderful harbor of
happiness and hope and emotional health for children.

In our marriage, I have had to negotiate with my wife and
she with me on several occasions. Once, I wanted to vacation
at a certain place—she at another. So, we negotiated, for happiness and harmony is more important than having our own
way.

"I don't want my own way—I want to be a success."

This is a principle to live by. If I insist on having my own
way at every turn, I will be foolish; and I may ultimately win
only to find myself with a lonely victory.

Historians talk about a Pyrrhic victory. King Pyrrhus of
Epirus, a small state in Greece, defeated the Romans. They
won the battle, but they lost so many men and ships that they
were never strong again. Their victory defeated them!

Be prepared to negotiate anything—except your moral values and the God-given goal that He has entrusted to your
stewardship!

Accommodating yourself to others

"And whoever compels you to go one mile, go with him two."—MATTHEW 5:41

166 Make the decision today to be accommodating to people who ask you for a favor. Go the extra mile. Our Lord talked about this. "When someone asks you to go a mile, go two miles." It takes faith to go the second mile and to have an accommodating attitude when your plans are made and your systems, procedures, and policies are all established.

As difficult as it may be to be accommodating at times, this attitude of "going the extra mile" can be the key to your success—whether it's in business, marriage, or other personal relationships. We see how important this accommodating attitude is when we recall how irritating it has been when we've been faced with an unyielding person or situation.

Is anything more frustrating than a narrow-mined person who dares not adjust his firm policy to make room for an exception that was not considered or foreseen?

This "policy over people" mentality is the hallmark of totalitarian systems, such as communism. Anyone who makes a trip through these countries soon finds out that the lack of freedom is the nonaccommodating attitude that prevails in their "policy over people" ideology.

Of course, it is necessary to manage by maintaining control. Yes, it is important to establish policy, but

The person who lives by faith lives by the principle of Jesus Christ: "people over policy."

This marks a major distinction between Christianity and communism. Christianity says, "People before policy." Communism says, "Policy before people."

Faith commands us to develop an accommodating attitude in life, including in business. It is then that we become really creative, winning new friends and new customers in the process. No wonder faith and prosperity are linked together in the chain of life.

Sharing the power

"Two are better than one,/Because they have a good reward for their labor."—ECCLESIASTES 4:9

One of the marks of the truly high achievers is the ability to **167** accomplish much in a short span of time. How do they do it?

They learn the art of delegating authority, responsibility, and power.

Only the person with a strong self-image is inwardly secure enough to share the power.

People who suffer from a weak ego jealously hold to the power position without sharing it, because they lack faith in themselves and in others. They cannot bring themselves to share the power and the glory. The result? In trying to do it all themselves, they consequently get very little done. It takes a lot of faith to share power and glory.

"If I don't do it myself, it won't be done right," is a popular illusion that negatively holds a gripping power over the non-believer. Replace this negative illusion with the positive fact: "If I share the glory, the power, and the responsibility, I have a greater chance to reach my goals, and know that I have created opportunities for others to grow and to live!

"In the process I'll be rewarded with a mature self-respect! Today I will walk the walk of faith for it is the pathway to spiritual and material prosperity."

People who walk the walk of faith dare to believe that others are as responsible as they are. They have the faith to share responsibility. Yes, mistakes will be made. But you and I have a capacity for error, too.

Better to have something done imperfectly than to have nothing done perfectly.

Teaming up

"Let each of you look out not only for his own interests, but also for the interests of others."—
PHILIPPIANS 2:4

168   The beautiful fringe benefit that comes with this walk of faith is that it gives us a communal attitude. Possibility thinking that promotes rugged individualism does not reject the team spirit.

Our faith tells us that divine help will often come in the form of persons without whose skills and dedication we could not succeed.

God can do great things through the person who doesn't care who gets the credit.

We must sort through our motives and decide that we would rather succeed and share the glory than to fail and bear the blame alone. We must not be ego-involved as much as we must be success-oriented!

Even the genius has a limited perspective. Multiply your intelligence and magnify your clever abilities by teaming up with people who are smarter than you are. I am convinced that almost any human goal imaginable is possible.

When God trusts you with His dream, it becomes your job to call together persons with a variety of skills and talents until, through massive team effort, the mountain is scaled and the dream succeeds! Success becomes possible the moment you realize you can't do it alone.

Our Lord and I together are the beginning of a winning team!

I'm on my way to a successful life! For I have enough faith to trust others to work with me and share the great dream God has given me.

FAITH IS . . .
Delegating good jobs to others

"The body is one but has many members. . . .
God composed the body. . . . if one member
suffers, all the members suffer with it; or if one
member is honored, all the members rejoice."—
1 CORINTHIANS 12:14, 24, 26

It's easy to put together a winning team—if you're willing **169**
to delegate the good jobs to others! It takes a lot of faith to
make this move, for it's natural to believe that nobody else
can do the job as well as you can.

Will they drop the ball?

Can they follow through?

Do they understand how important the job is?

Yes, it takes a lot of faith to delegate!

The supersuccessful person trusts others to do the job as
well as he can, if not better.

Years ago I decided to refuse to do something that I could
hire someone else to do. This frees me to do the job that I, and
I alone, can do.

There are those tasks that cannot be delegated to others. I
have learned that I cannot delegate to anybody else the task of
writing my public messages. I cannot delegate the final decisions that reach my desk. But aside from these basic assignments, I have delegated almost all other jobs to other persons.

Until you delegate, you won't have time to plan ahead! If
you don't have enough faith to delegate, you will never be
creative. Great dreamers of great dreams are seldom good at
detail. If they were, they'd be too busy to think creatively. Affirm with me:

> **Today I'm going to give up some of the jobs I've always
> thought that only I could perform.**

And I shall relish the liberty and freedom to do beautiful
things I've never had time for before!

Thank You for giving me faith, Father. Amen.

Assimilating fresh opinions

"Now we have been delivered from the law, . . .
so that we should serve in the newness of the
Spirit, and not in the oldness of the letter."—
ROMANS 7:6

170 We all need to learn and to grow. We all need to add freshness to our lives. It is easy to assimilate new facts, but it requires a great deal of faith to assimilate fresh opinions.

Once you dare to relate to others you open yourself to fresh
thoughts that replace stale and worn-out opinions. Update
your life with current viewpoints, but don't abandon the
moral and spiritual guidelines that have brought you safely
and successfully to where you are. With that gentle warning,
be prepared to exercise faith. Assimilate new thoughts into
your old thinking.

Faith believes apparent contradictions can conceivably
form a symbiotic relationship.

According to an old Eastern parable, two beggars formed a
symbiotic relationship. The blind man was strong enough to
carry the legless man on his back. He became the legs for the
lame man. In return, the lame man became the eyes for the
blind one. Clinging to each other, they both benefited.

We are all weak in some area. But when we broaden our
thinking, we are able to assimilate ideas that can bring freshness to our own faith and life.

Without compromising, abandoning, or violating the integrity of your own position, have enough faith to see good in
others' opinions. Then draw lessons from them and positively
apply them to enrich your faith.

Faith assimiliates fresh opinions!

Dear Lord, give me a fresh experience in my walk with You
today. I admit that spiritual staleness has taken over, but now
in this movement there is a newness in my spirit. I know it's
Your spirit, assimilating mine. Thank You, God.

Hiring smarter people

"Thanks be to God, who gives us the victory
through our Lord Jesus Christ."—
1 CORINTHIANS 15:57

For every problem, there is a profession! Are you sick? There are doctors. Do you have problems selling your product? There are consultants in marketing. You name it, and there is some expert who can help you handle your problem in the smartest way possible.

The other day I discovered that I had locked the keys in my car. Being a possibility thinker, I decided to solve the problem simply and inexpensively with a wire coat hanger. I worked and worked, but I finally concluded that this was not my area of expertise. So I called a locksmith to the rescue. He pressed his nose against the windshield to read the numbers on the keys in the ignition. Then he scratched some numbers on a pad and stepped inside his truck. Two minutes later he opened the lock perfectly. My problem was solved. Expensive? That's not the right reaction. The height of folly is to fail because you didn't want to pay the price to hire expert help.

It takes faith to hire people. Mr. Danforth, the founder of Ralston Purina Company, hired a smart young man to head his company. At the annual corporate meeting the young man's report was so outstanding that a stockholder asked Mr. Danforth, "How does it make you feel to have this young man get all the compliments?" Mr. Danforth confidently replied, "Great! That's a compliment to me! After all, I hired him!"

The good news is that there is a professional who is skilled in solving your biggest problem—lack of faith! His name is Jesus Christ. He is *able* to save you from sin, negative thinking, and doubt! He wants to fill you with optimism and faith! His fee? His salvation is free!

Listening to wise counsel

"Without counsel, plans go awry,/But in the multitude of counselors they are established."— PROVERBS 15:22

172   When we walk the walk of faith, does it mean we have so much self-confidence that we never need to seek advice from anyone else?

Is opening yourself to constructive criticism a lack of faith?

Or, on the contrary, is it a demonstration of a remarkably mature faith?

The latter, of course, is the truth.

For it takes a great deal of faith in yourself, in others, and in God to expose yourself and invite others to share their opinion and wise counsel. Faith is the belief that God guides you to success, by giving you some smart suggestions through the wise counsel of others. In the process you win their respect as they share freely their most valued resource: their insightful wisdom.

You're walking a higher road of faith when you learn to listen.

Step 1: Listen to compliments and accept them!

Step 2: Listen to constructive criticism and be guided by it!

Step 3: Invite smart people to show you what's wrong with your plan. No one is perfect. Every proposal has its soft spot. No idea is without its problems. There's something wrong with the best idea.

Be smart and find out the points of vulnerability before you go too far.

You can plan to insulate, isolate, eliminate, or sublimate the negative possibilities in the positive proposal. *And you can go on to promote the positive possibilities in the whole scheme.*

That's real maturity in faith! We call it "wise faith!"

Clarifying expectations

"I will make you an eternal excellence,/A joy of many generations."—ISAIAH 60:15

It is most important you remain steadfast in your expectation that success will be realized. **173**

Faith is clarifying your expectations to insure success.

It is at the expectation level that tremendous things happen—both positively and negatively. It is well established that conflict in interpersonal relationships is usually a result of a confusion of expectations. In counseling, I frequently address two conflicting personalities by asking both of them questions such as:

"What did you expect from him/her?"

"Do you have a right to expect this from him/her?"

"If you revise your expectations, do you believe you'd be able to make your relationship work?"

"How many revisions can you make in your expectations and still survive in your partnership and friendship?"

> **Faith is clarifying nonverbalized, confused expectations, thereby setting the stage for success.**

Faith is expecting to succeed. How?
• Clarify your expectations.
• Visualize them clearly in your mind.
• Write them upon your subconscious.
• Hold to them with discipline and determination.
• Nurture them with enthusiasm.
Then expect success!

Dear God, forgive me when I am confused in my expectations of You. You give me all I need to know in order that I can succeed, and You are more than generous with all the blessings You send my way. I will remain faithful in my walk with You today. Thank You for being my Friend. Amen.

Removing growth-restricting obstacles

"If the ax is dull,/And one does not sharpen the edge,/Then he must use more strength;/But wisdom brings success."—ECCLESIASTES 10:10

174   It is time to remind yourself every day that you have a choice—to walk by doubt, or by faith; to be a believer or a cynic; to be filled with a positive mental attitude or be controlled by a negative mental attitude.

By this time, you have scored some victories; you have realized some successes. You have made progress in your personal life. You have grown!

And you have learned another lesson: When you succeed, you produce a new set of problems.

Growth always generates a new set of tensions.

Be careful! Now is the time you are tempted to become negative, and ask the question: "Was it really worth it?" You can easily become cynical about your own success and vote against continued progress.

The most common growth-restricting obstacle is to become stagnant. "I've got enough." "We're big enough." "I know enough." These are all negative reactions to success.

As you keep walking the walk of faith, you must *continue* to press for personal growth. *For when growth stops, death and decay are just around the corner.* Keep on believing in progress.

Today's affirmation: Today I will proceed in an all-out effort to remove any obstacles that would keep me from growing. Failure to do so will be to surrender leadership of my future to a stifling force. I will not allow that to happen.

The obstacles that keep me from growing today are _____

_____.

I will walk the walk of faith and tackle them with determination!

FAITH IS . . .
Following the positive voices

> "Whoever hears these sayings of Mine, and does
> them, I will liken him to a wise man who built
> his house on the rock; and the rain descended,
> the floods came, . . . and it did not fall, for it
> was founded on the rock."—MATTHEW 7:24–25

Faith is a two-sided power. On one side is the activity of **175**
rejecting negative inputs. On the opposite side is the activity
of following positive voices.

Even an electric cord has both a negative and a positive
wire. So even as you reject the destructive negative stimuli
that enter your brain, also accept and listen to the positive
emotions and incentives that whisper in the back of your
mind.

Seek out friends, acquaintances, literature, books, television programs, and movies that will entertain, amuse, inspire,
uplift, educate, motivate, and challenge you to become a better and more productive person.

**I know of no positive voice of any living person that is
more helpful to me on a moment-to-moment basis
than that of my closest Friend, Jesus Christ!**

How can you follow the positive voice of God?

Constantly ask God questions and wait for His answer in
the hidden corner of your brain. Read what He said, what He
did, and how He lived in the Bible. Seek His advice and expect
Him to answer. The still, small voice will come into the silence of the holy chamber of your subconscious. It is the voice
of your Friend, Jesus Christ.

He nudges you forward. He affirms you can be forgiven of
all sins. He instills new passion to do His good work. He is
speaking to you through this moment of meditation. Simply
listen, then follow. That means you will take action.

Sorting things out optimistically

"He who follows righteousness and mercy/
Finds life, righteousness and honor."—PROVERBS
21:21

176   By now you've discovered that the road of faith isn't always smooth. In fact, it can be downright jarring. The jolts can get to you if you don't watch out.

I've had to ride over some rough roads in my life. One of the most famous—or infamous—is the Hana Road, on the island of Maui in Hawaii. I remember almost bouncing through the roof when I hit a hole in the road. I'm sure that not a few of my readers have driven the same route themselves and likewise found their teeth almost loosened in their jaws. I was terribly tempted to quit and turn around. But I hung in there. And was I ever rewarded!

When I finally reached Hana, I saw the most beautiful waterfall in the world! The serenity at this spot made the torturous trip worthwhile. I'm sure that's the reason Charles Lindbergh chose to be buried there.

You must keep on believing that even the jolts on the rough road of life can have a positive influence on you.

Faith is sorting things out optimistically. That's exactly what happens when you optimistically see the jolts that come your way as the impetus to re-examine your life.

Years ago I told the story of the potato farmer who sorted out the big potatoes from the little ones by riding to town on the rough roads. "Big potatoes ride to the top on rough roads," he said.

My daughter loves to sort out the raisins in her raisin bran cereal and she has discovered that if she shakes her bowl of cereal, the raisins bounce to the top.

Welcome those rebuffs that can bring out the deeper qualities of life.

Reading the good between the lines

"You know in all your hearts and in all your souls that not one thing has failed of all the good things which the LORD your God spoke."—JOSHUA 23:14

"Reading between the lines" is something we all do. It's like **177** "putting two and two together," a mental activity in which everyone engages. The difference between the person who's living by faith and the negative-thinking person is that the pessimist reads only bad news between the lines where the optimist reads good news.

Two birds—a vulture and a hummingbird—fly over the California desert. One sees a rotting carcass; the other, a fragrant flower. Each sees what it looks for!

If you are a believer and have received guidance from God Himself, you don't blind yourself to upcoming problems; but you do keep your eye on the possibilities! You never allow problems to overpower the possibilities.

The truth is you can always read either good or bad between the lines. There is something negative and something positive in every person, proposal, and project.

The most fantastic idea contains the seeds of problems as well as the seeds of possibilities!

Both success and failure exist in every project. Your vote can go either way, but you cast the deciding vote and determine the destiny positively when you choose to read the good instead of the bad.

Here is a powerful truth: What you see is what you will be. Our firmly focused imaginations tend to become self-fulfilling prophecies.

The vulture finds a carcass, while the hummingbird finds honey in a flower half-hidden in a cactus behind barren roots.

God's Word tells us to believe the best in the worst of times. Question: Are you practicing positive thinking or negative thinking today? Here's the test:

Believe the best! And live with zest!

Resolving conflicts creatively

"Avoid foolish and ignorant disputes, knowing
that they generate strife. A servant of the Lord
must not quarrel but be gentle to all, able to
reach, patient."—2 TIMOTHY 2:23–24

178 Walking the walk of faith will ultimately lead you to a clear-
ing where the sun can shine gloriously upon your well-lived
life! How can you be sure that the walk of faith will lead to
such a happy ending? By its very nature, faith cultivates a
positive mental attitude toward conflicts.

If you anticipate problems and tensions after making a commitment, you are not necessarily guilty of negative thinking.

For the truth is, any time you press forward toward your
goal, you will create conflict.

You can be sure most everyone will agree with you!

Conflicts are inherent in creative accomplishments.

Notice here the difference between the person who has a
positive mental attitude and a negative mental attitude. The
positive person has a creative attitude toward problems,
whereas a negative person has a destructive and complicating
attitude toward conflict.

Negative thinkers become defensive when they face conflicts.

Positive thinkers become peacemakers when they face conflicts.

**When you walk the walk of faith, you discipline your-
self to resolve conflicts.**

Resolving conflicts always starts with a resolution: I will
manage the conflict and not allow the conflict to manage me!

I will not allow the conflict to collide, clash, or collapse the
commitments I have made.

I will be more patient and determined to turn the conflict
around and in the process become healthier and happier than I
was before!

I am resolved to win out over the conflict!

Fixing problems

"My grace is sufficient for you, for My strength is made perfect in weakness."—2 CORINTHIANS 12:9

One of the greatest basketball coaches of all times was John **179** Wooden of UCLA, a fantastic, positive-thinking Christian. One of his great motivating statements to his players was: "Nobody is a real loser—until he starts blaming somebody else!"

Faith believes there is a solution to every problem. Even when the problem defies solutions, faith believes that we can be positive anyway!

Affirm with me:

- Today I shall exercise my faith to seek solutions immediately, instinctively, impulsively, and intelligently.

- I'll look upon this not as a problem, but as an opportunity to grow up and be more effective as a manager of my own life.

- I will categorically reject all arbitrary, negative judgments, and I believe that with the help of God there will be a solution to the problem.

I'll go to work right now and fix my problem, just as soon as I fix my attitude!

Dear Lord, I'm aware that the biggest part of any problem is my attitude toward it. I thank You, that You and I together can fix that today. Your strength is my strength, so I'm trusting You. Help me, O God, my Father, to bloom with such faith that I will be surprised, and so will everybody else who watches me go through this trying time. Thank You, Lord. Amen.

Inventing solutions

". . . always pursue what is good both for
yourselves and for all."—1 THESSALONIANS 5:15

180 Years ago when my children were yet small, our family
spent summer vacations in Iowa, visiting our relatives. One
summer, as we drove the long road back to California, we
heard an enormous explosion! My left rear tire had blown out!

I stood dejectedly on the shoulder, looking at the tire, now
in shreds. Fortunately, I had a spare tire, jack, and crowbar
readily available. I promptly put the jack under the car and
began to pump it up. Just as the flattened tire rose a few
inches, the jack suddenly started bending as if it were made of
rubber! I couldn't believe my eyes. Never had I seen or heard
of that. The tire slowly settled down again on the hard adobe-
like surface.

What could I do? I had no jack! There was no gas station for
miles and miles! Suddenly I had an idea: "If I can't raise the
tire, why don't I lower the ground?"

I took my only tool, the crowbar, and proceeded to chip
away at the hard ground around the flattened tire. It was hard
work, but after almost an hour, I could remove the bolts, lift
the tire off, and slip the spare tire on!

**The walk of faith can be fun! When something seems
impossible just invent new products or new procedures.**

God gave you the only tool you need—your brain. We can
all be inventors on this walk of faith. We won't necessarily
dream up new gadgets, but we can invent new ideas that will
prove to be the solution to our problem. Faith is inventing
solutions, pursuing "what is good both for yourselves and for
all."

Negotiating your way around obstacles

"May our Lord Jesus Christ . . . comfort your hearts and establish you in every good word and work."—2 THESSALONIANS 2:16–17

Dedicated possibility thinkers stubbornly refuse to accept defeat. Rather, in the face of apparent catastrophe, they seek creative solutions. Possibility thinking is a process of creatively negotiating around obstacles.

Begin the process by believing you will not accept defeat. Hang in there and decide you're going to make it within to the rules and laws of God and country. Creatively calculate new and innovative schemes to achieve what appears to be unachievable. Consider all constructive compromises. It may even require retreat in order to advance later on. Rework, revise, rewrite, reorganize, reschedule, or refinance; and thereby creatively negotiate your way to ultimate victory. Begin with these affirmations:

- I am open to new strategies.
- I will review the price.
- I will call for a review of the proposal.
- I will break the stalemate.

After all, I don't want to have my own way; I just want to do the right thing. For I am a possibility thinker. I exercise faith. I am a courageous and wise negotiator.

I believe that I will ultimately salvage and save the most valued part of my life's work.

I believe in myself and in my God-given dream. I, and only I, have the power to kill my dream. I do that if I'm unwilling to negotiate. God has entrusted a dream to my care and keeping. I will nurture it carefully. I will protect its life at all costs. I will prove faithful, O Lord.

Catching the blame

"So then each of us shall give account . . . to God."—ROMANS 14:12

182   When the finger points at you and criticism falls at your doorstep, when you catch the blame and are held responsible for a mistake, look upon this as a left-handed compliment. You have tried your best; you are willing to be held accountable!

It's hard to find people who are brave enough to accept responsibility. The fear of being held liable for mistakes is enough to frighten many a person from a leadership position.

Faith is "catching the blame." When you walk the walk of faith, you accept responsibility with a tremendously serious attitude. You are able to face the reality that you may make a mistake. But your positive-thinking faith gives you enough confidence in your own abilities to be willing to be held accountable!

> **Until you're able to conquer the fear of "catching the blame," you probably will not have enough courage to become the entrepreneurial person you ought to be.**

Do you dare to become an effective manager, a successful supervisor, or an inspiring leader in your church or community? All you need to do is overcome the fear of failure by looking for the positive, exercising optimism, stimulating positive emotions in people, and inspiring and encouraging people.

Today have the faith to believe that these responsibilities of life are steps upward. You are maturing in the walk of faith. You will not be afraid of the blame and criticism that comes with accountability. Criticism won't mean you will get fired—it will mean you'll get inspired—to do and to be better!

Affirm today: "I have the courage to be accountable!"

FAITH IS . . .
Allowing for error

"He is able to save to the uttermost those who
come to God through Him, since He ever lives
to make intercession for them."—HEBREWS 7:25

A famous British statesman had his formal portrait done. **183**
When it was finished he took a look at what was a most remarkable likeness. The artist, expecting compliments, instead received this rebuff: "You didn't paint the wart!"

The artist meekly replied, "But, sir, I think you are more
attractive without it. Don't you find this so?"

The politician answered, "Paint me as I am—wart and all!"

Accepting yourself with your imperfections gives evidence
that your faith has achieved a remarkable level of maturity.
Until you and I are able to allow for error in ourselves we will
lack the grace to allow error in others.

Your faith is able to spare you from what psychologists call
"projection"—projecting your feelings toward others. If you
feel good today, you treat people well. If you feel bad, you treat
others badly.

The positive approach does not demand perfection. We have
faith in people, anyway!

When you make a mistake after doing your best, be thankful to God that you're able to perform at all: Have faith that
you are doing a worthwhile job, *anyway!*

Now project this positive attitude toward your family, your
friends, and your business associates.

Allow for error in yourself and others. Until you do, you
will never be able to have a strong relationship with anyone—
including God Almighty.

> **If you can't believe that God accepts you with your
> obvious sins, shortcomings, and errors, you may find
> yourself subconsciously leaning toward agnosticism.**

Faith allows for error. The Lord accepts you anyway!

Hearing what your critics say about you

"Listen to counsel and receive instruction,/That
you may be wise."—PROVERBS 19:20

184 I'd rather succeed than have my own way! You agree with
me, don't you?

You are moving strongly forward on this walk of faith. You
have made commitments. The public announcement is out.
It's not secret what you intend to do. Now, for the sake of our
God, you had better make it happen.

In order to do that you need to make sure you have not
forgotten something. You don't know all of the answers. You
can't do everything perfectly. You still are a human being subject to error and fault.

So, if there's something wrong with your project, your
plans, your timetable, or your team, you'd better find out
about it—now!

I learned long ago that if I live by faith, I will listen to what
my critics say. My friends may be blinded to my shortcomings
by their own devotion, loyalty, and affection. In truth, my best
friend may well be my most severe critic. I listen and carefully
evaluate his or her critique.

You are also a person of great faith! If there is something
wrong with a project or performance, it's not too late to correct the problem or compensate creatively for the drawbacks
you may have neglected to notice.

Insecure people are defensive people who refuse to respect
their critics. But you are inwardly secure. You have your calling from God. You are confident.

**You are strong in your faith. You are strong enough to
listen to your critics. For you discover that even they
are sent as friends from God!**

Thank You, Father, that You are protecting me from the
blindness that comes through ego involvement. Thank You
for everything You're doing to guide me to success. Amen.

FAITH IS . . .
Changing your mind

"Put on the new man who is renewed in knowledge according to the image of Him who created him."—COLOSSIANS 3:10

Today's theme sounds like a contradiction, doesn't it? If I change my mind, isn't that instability? And isn't instability a lack of faith?

Think of it this way.

People who never change their minds are either perfect—or stubborn.

One day when I was checking a building under construction on our church campus, I was surprised at how dark and gloomy the room was. "Why isn't there a window over there?" I asked the superintendent.

"That's the way you planned it, Reverend," he replied. I admitted that I had. I looked at the freshly plastered wall; and suddenly I walked over and with a ball-point pen wrote in letters three inches high, "People who never change their minds are either perfect or stubborn." Then I turned around and said to him, "Put a window right there!"

Never surrender to a mistake. Faith, committed to excellence, gladly allows you to change your mind if there's a better way!

How do you avoid the embarrassment that comes with admitting you made a mistake? Simple. Announce you are a human being, and not too proud to do the best possible job. If that means changing course, you'll do it.

It takes a great deal of faith to change your mind.

Dear Lord, I know it's not a mistake when I believe in You. There is no better way to live than to trust You completely with my life. I will dare to "put on the new 'me,'" renewed in Your knowledge. Thank You for creating me in Your image. Amen.

Learning from past mistakes

"Strengthen the weak hands,/And make firm
the feeble knees. Say to those who are fearful-
hearted,/'Be strong . . .'"—ISAIAH 35:3–4

186 By now you have made more than one mistake on your
walk of faith.

Every artist messes up a canvas at one spot or another.

Every accountant uses a pencil with an eraser.

No baseball player ever had a batting average of a thousand,
getting a hit every time he was at bat.

Consequently, you cannot allow your mistakes to master
your mood and cause you to lose enthusiasm.

Begin to program yourself positively. You cannot surrender
leadership to your past failures. You must take a positive attitude toward them for they can prove to be wise teachers.

> **The person who never makes a mistake is the person
> who is a total failure, for that person never tries to do
> something worthwhile.**

Affirmations for today:
- My mistakes only prove to me that I'm not a total failure.
- I did not fail to try!
- I did not fail to dream!
- I did not fail to decide!
- I did not fail to make a commitment.
- I did not fail in courage.
- I will not fail to learn from my mistakes.
- I will not fail to make corrective changes in my life.
- I will not allow my mistakes to cause me to take my eyes
off my goal.

Help me, O God, heavenly Father, to learn from my sins,
my shortcomings, and my mistakes. Help me to turn the mistake from a stumbling block into a stepping stone, through
the help of Christ. Amen.

Congratulating your competitors

"LORD, You will establish peace for us, for You have also done all our works in us."—ISAIAH 26:12

Congratulating your competitor when he does a better job, **187** when he outpaces you, or when he runs off with the prize is a concrete statement of faith.

> **It shows mountains of faith when you have enough internal pride and self-esteem to give your competition a pat on the back after he has defeated you soundly and squarely.**

In the summer of 1983, at the sixty-fifth PGA Championship in Pacific Palisades, California, Hal Sutton and Jack Nicklaus exercised fantastic faith.

Sutton wanted the world to know that it was possible for him to be a winner. Only two weeks earlier he had had an embarrassing failure at the Anheuser-Busch classic.

Nicklaus, at forty-three years of age, had played poorly all season. Sports writers were declaring he was "over the hill." They were suggesting he pack up his clubs.

As the tournament neared the end the battle was between Nicklaus and Sutton. In the end Sutton won—by one hole! Nicklaus lost by one stroke.

Both proved something terribly important to the world. One proved that he could be a winner. The other proved he still had it! In the process Nicklaus broke his own record.

But Nicklaus had his greatest success when he went up to twenty-five-year-old Hal Sutton, shook hands, and said to him bravely and beautifully, "That will be the first of many for you!"

That's the faith that moves mountains! Mountains of failure, jealousy, resentment, and all other negative emotions disappear when you are confident enough in your own talents to congratulate your competitors.

Swallowing your hurts

"If I say, 'I will forget my complaint,/I will put off my sad face and wear a smile.'"—JOB 9:27

188 Here's some good advice on how to handle the rejections, defeats, or failures you probably have experienced. You may have collected enough hurts to keep you from wanting to press forward. Setbacks can take the joy out of faith if you don't watch out! Even success—steady, solid, and exceptional—can make you the target of criticism from colleagues who are jealous of your achievement.

Careful! Hidden hurts in the heart can nurture and nourish negative thinking. Often the most painful wounds are not the scars that are outwardly seen but the hidden wounds deep in the heart. Because they are hidden they are often the most dangerous.

Swallow your hurts and stimulate a new spirit and spurt of growth!

If, in fact, your drive to grow has lost its passionate power, if the flush of enthusiasm has mysteriously diminished, then check the accumulation of negative emotions that have attached themselves to you, much like barnacles that attach to whales.

Along the shoreline in California it is a common sight to see whales stopping alongside rocks to scrape off barnacles as they migrate from Alaska to Mexico.

In the walk of faith we too will pick up a collection of personal hurts that will attach themselves to our souls like parasites sapping the life and vitality out of us!

Ouch! You can't let these negative emotions get to you!

By faith, learn to swallow hard. Imagine all polluted thoughts being drained from your mind, body, and spirit.

Lord, with Your help, I swallow the hurts. They will pass on and out. Thank You. Amen.

Sensing success in dark times

"We know that all things work together for
good to those who love God."—ROMANS 8:28

How can you describe the experience of faith you have been **189** experiencing? It's an inner sense that things are going to work out all right, isn't it? You can almost call it intuition.

Deep down within yourself you know with a solid know-ingness that the worst times will pass.

- Better days are around the corner.
- The storm is not eternal.
- The clouds have a limited lifespan.
- The mountain has a peak.
- Dark times will give way to bright days. Somehow you intuitively sense that the tragedy can turn into a spiritual triumph.

No matter how difficult the time may be, remember:

God has no wastebaskets.

He makes no mistakes. He never bungles a job. So He will somehow be able to take the torturing experiences and turn them into diamonds that will sparkle in the crown of your life. God will not allow the suffering, the sorrow, the pain, to be fruitless.

John Greenleaf Whittier put it well, "I know not where the islands lift their fronded palms in air./I only know I cannot drift beyond my Master's love and care."

Prayer: O God, thank You for the faith I have today. In spite of all the suffering, sin, sickness, and unspeakable tragedies that exist in the human family, I sense deeply and irrevocably that love will triumph. The sun is stronger than the clouds. God is more powerful than evil. I shall succeed in spite of dire predictions, gloomy forecasts, and depressing projections! I sense success in the dark times. This is my faith operating. Thank You for giving me this gift. Amen.

Marching on—nevertheless

> "On the seventh day [Joshua] . . . marched
> around [Jericho] seven times. . . . when the
> priests blew the trumpets, Joshua said to the
> people: 'Shout, for the LORD has given you this
> city!' "—JOSHUA 6:16

190

• From thinking—to action!
• From meditation—to marching.
• From the classroom—to the main street.
• From the church—to your daily life and business!
• From reading a book—to living out the principles!

These are the challenging times of life—when you apply the faith. Life starts when you stop talking and start making it happen!

David Hartman, the anchor man of "Good Morning, America," always closes his morning program with the challenge: "Make it happen. Make it a great day!"

Almost always when the sun sets and you look back on a well-worn day with the happy review, "It's been a great day," you have to admit—you made it a great day! God blessed you. Unexpected good things happened to you, and you responded positively to the opportunities that hit you unexpectedly!

Some other persons had a similar day, but they came to their sunset discouraged. The only difference is that you made it a great day. You had some tough assignments. You ran into some binding predicaments. But you kept marching on—nevertheless!

When at first you don't succeed, like Joshua you keep marching on! A second time, a third, a fourth, a fifth, a sixth, and then on the seventh try, the walls came tumbling down!

"Shout, for the LORD has given you this city!" Praise God right now! For He is giving you victory today!

Insulating against the negatives

"The lamp of the body is the eye. If therefore your eye is good, your whole body will be full of light."—MATTHEW 6:22

Once you have declared your intention and entered the contest, be prepared for an attack from negative-thinking people! As much as possible, insulate yourself from their influence on you.

191

Insulation is a wonderful thing! We put it in the walls of a house to insulate from the summer heat and the winter cold. How can you insulate yourself from the inevitable negative criticism you can expect, as you move forward, upward, and onward?

"The lamp of the body is the eye." Begin by focusing on the Bible. Go back through this book and find Bible verses that give you courage, confidence, and conviction. Then when negative forces attack, they will bounce off you like sparks off cement, desert sand, or asphalt pavement.

"The lamp of the body is the eye."

The mind that is filled with a visual eye on God's promises of prosperity and power and peace will see sparks of negativity bounce off! We are insulated!

(1) Feed your mind with all the positive literature you can read.

(2) Choose as your closest friends and collaborators, dynamic possibility thinkers who will encourage you and keep boosting your spirits!

(3) Attend a positive-thinking house of worship every Sunday.

(4) Program your mind with a possibility-thinking treatment every morning.

Finally, insulate yourself through positive prayer. Affirm today: Thank You, God, that my eyes are focused on my dream which has come from You! As I focus on You, I am insulated from all negativity. Thank You, God. Amen.

Reversing a negative situation

"Do not be overcome by evil, but overcome evil with good."—ROMANS 12:21

192   Faith doesn't immunize you from difficulty. But it does radically alter your attitude. The negative person takes a bad experience and *curses* it. He takes it out on his best friends and innocent people! He *nurses* the affliction and tells people how bad the situation is. He talks up his tough times. He *rehearses* the miserable history that got him into the predicament.

Then there is the believer—the person who looks for positive possibilities. He *disperses* the gloom-and-doom mentality.

He disperses negative thoughts with positive ones: "The sun is stronger than the clouds. And my God within me is more powerful than any depressive mood that surrounds me. Light is stronger than darkness; therefore, the sun will shine again in the new morning!"

The believer waits for the sunrise, with a positive faith he *reverses* the negative situation and turns it into something positive! How do you overcome evil with good? By believing there is good in every situation!

My friend, Denis Waitley, displays on his wall an airline ticket to a flight he missed. By the time he reached the gate, the DC-10 was pulling away. He was terribly dejected! Then it happened! The plane had hardly taken off before it exploded. All passengers on board were killed.

> **Troubles today? Don't curse them, don't nurse them, but disperse them, and even reverse the negative situations into a positive possibility. Trouble is only a blessing in disguise!**

Putting up with the disagreeable

". . . In quietness and confidence shall be your strength."—ISAIAH 30:15

Today you may encounter disagreeable confrontations with **193** negative situations. How will you react when you experience rejection or insult? How will you handle frustrations when everything seems to go wrong?

Will you be put out, put off, or will you put up with the problem? Touchy people will be *put out.* Arrogant people will be *put off.* Positive people will *put up* with the problem, patiently enduring the unpleasant scene, quietly riding out the storm.

By faith you can duck a lot of problems, avoiding some of them and facing sudden cloudbursts the way ducks do. They simply sit still, waiting patiently, knowing the storm will pass. The sun will break through again, soon.

Something amusing will happen shortly, and you'll be laughing again.

Anticipate humorous moods that will replace the time of tension. This is faith—putting up with the disagreeable. Remind yourself that your reaction can exaggerate, aggravate, or tolerate the sorry scene. You can make matters better—or worse.

So faith tolerates the scene patiently. This does not mean you remain apathetic in the face of injustice or approve of mediocrity. Instead, you must not allow yourself to be drawn into troublesome quarrels over petty causes.

Develop the skill of separating the important from the insignificant before you make a mistake and waste your emotional energy and creative power.

Don't fret over the frivolous and get tense over the trivial.

Faith is putting up with the disagreeable.

Riding wild horses

"Indeed, we put bits in horses' mouths that
they may obey us, and we turn their whole
body."—JAMES 3:3

194 If I were to list ten books that changed my life, I would have
to include, high on the list, a book by the late J. Wallace
Hamilton entitled *Ride the Wild Horses.* Wild horses are
emotional impulses that, at face value, appear to be negative
and destructive.

Is fear negative? Yes, but we have learned how to turn it into
a positive.

Is anger negative? Yes, but take the temper out of steel, and
its strength is gone.

So it is with the ego. We have all seen demonic and destructive forces of egotism. Does that mean we should squeeze
every bit of the ego out of the human being? Not at all! To do
so would kill the drive that can accomplish glorious things for
the human family and for God. The ego is to be redeemed, not
destroyed! When channeled into the drive to do God's good
work, the ego becomes our self-esteem!

What about jealousy? William Shakespeare called this destructive force "the green-eyed monster." But even jealousy
can be a healthy force. Become jealous over the beauty of the
environment and work to protect it. Become jealous over the
beauty of a piece of architecture or a fine garden and work to
preserve it.

> **Destructive forces in life—almost all of them—can be
> turned into positive values.**

That's what happens when we really want to walk the walk
of faith. Faith is turning negatives into positives. It's deciding
not to shoot the wild horses, nor to break them of their noble,
prancing, virile spirit, but to harness them and ride them
gloriously!

That's possibility thinking! That's practicing the walk of
faith!

FAITH IS . . .
Gambling God's way

"I am the LORD your God, who teaches you to profit, who leads you by the way you should go."—ISAIAH 48:17

Among the wild horses that need to be bridled is the gam- **195** bling instinct. The Christian church has long opposed gambling. It has been looked upon purely as a negative impulse. Its potentially destructive influence has been well studied and documented.

Gambling is a destructive force when it takes someone's property without paying for it. Gambling, then, is borderline theft.

But it is possible to turn this instinct into a controlled and positive force!

The farmer turns the gambling instinct into a positive force as he throws the seed on the ground and hopes and prays that it will return in multiplied numbers.

The researcher working in medical research may invest millions of dollars gambling on the hope that he or she can find a cure for cancer. That's turning the gambling instinct into a constructive force.

The developer who buys property and designs a beautiful habitat of comfort for humans takes a big gamble as he or she pledges a great deal of front money.

The walk of faith recognizes that the gambling instinct is a divine quality placed within God's children.

Challenge the winds!
Scale the heights!
Welcome the gambling instinct. Do not destroy it.
Give God a glorious life.
What an exciting way to live—walking the walk of faith!
Give God the glory of a positive life that dares to live by faith.

Encountering opposition positively

"Uphold my steps in your paths that my
footsteps may not slip."—PSALM 17:5

196   Success often requires clever strategy to maneuver your
way around negative obstructions or negative impossibility
thinkers. And this must be done, for not even the greatest
ideas are unanimously accepted upon the first announcement. Every project I've ever been a part of—building a
church, the Crystal Cathedral, or the television ministry—
has encountered opposition from intelligent people.

Should you abandon your dreams to those who lack the vision?

Should you crudely and callously attack your critics face
on?

Or should you maneuver your way around them?

It's frightfully easy to be intimidated by negative people.
Fearful that you might incur the displeasure of a friend or that
your ideas might not be accepted you quickly become the victim of intimidation. In the process, you slip off the path of
faith. That is not an acceptable option. Obstructions, whether
pressures, person, or property, must never abort your divine
calling.

So the best defense is an offense!

Today go on the offensive in a kind but forceful way. Believe
that your positive dream has the built-in power to attract support and enthusiastic backing.

Do not allow the fear of criticism to stop you. Rather
strengthen your dreams until your project will intimidate the
opposition.

Negative voices will be silenced by your enthusiasm.

Obstructionists will not dare to resist the growing support
that God is sending your way.

Opposing forces will shrink and shrivel in the face of your
God-given success!

The Lord and you are winning today!

Rejecting negative advice

"Blessed is the man Who walks not in the
counsel of the ungodly."—PSALM 1:1

There are all kinds of negative thinkers who discourage us, **197**
impugn our motives, insinuate that we are insincere, and intimidate us to retreat.

What kind of friends do you have? Are your teachers positive thinkers or negative thinkers? How about the coworkers
and associates with whom you associate?

And what kind of material are you allowing to enter your
brain? Check again the movies you watch, the books you read,
and the voices that penetrate your conscious mind.

Negative counsel is poison to faith.

The back side of faith is the process of rejecting negative
advice. You walk the walk of faith and exercise dynamic possibility thinking when you sort out and throw away negative
thoughts and emotions from the control positions in your
mind.

No human being can prevent negative stimulations from
attacking his faith-filled mind. You live in a universe that is
saturated with evil and sin. At no point is this more conspicuously clear than when you stop and consider how often your
mind and moods are assaulted with negative forces.

You will be blessed with a blossoming and fruit-bearing
faith as you reject negative advice and separate yourself from
destructive acquaintances. Immunize yourself from the germs
of negativity. It's up to you to keep your faith sanitized and
sterilized. Today, double-check what you allow your mind and
moods to be exposed to.

Begin with this affirmation: I will clean up my mental act,
starting *now!* And I will be blessed appropriately and forthrightly. The very moment I reject a negative thought, I will
immediately sense an inner cleansing invigorating the health
of my soul!

Separating yourself from negative pressures

"What part has a believer with an unbeliever? Come out from among them and be separate."—2 CORINTHIANS 6:15, 17

198   There is such a thing as a divine divorce. By that I mean, sometimes it is necessary to sever relationships that are mutually self-destructive.

In the culture of Christ's time and locality a husband and wife promised to hold to each other until death separated them.

In the Christian church through the centuries it has been maintained that divorce in marriage is a sinful act. I have never met anyone who went through a divorce who did not admit that it was the most self-esteem-shattering experience they had ever gone through. And I've never met anyone who bragged about the fact that his or her marriage fell apart. Divorce is always viewed as a failure.

Yet, Jesus indicated that there would be times when even the divorce of a married couple would be an acceptable course of action. An adulterous affair by one of the two mates gives ground for divorce.

The divorce of a married couple is always a shattering experience, but if you are to have a tough-minded faith there are some persons that you should divorce from your circle of important relationships.

- Never invite a negative-thinking person to the power center of your life.
- Never appoint a dyed-in-the-wool impossibility thinker to be a member of an important committee.
- Never create a platform for enemies to launch their proposals or projects.

It takes a lot of faith to say good-by.

Utilizing suspicion positively

"Therefore let us pursue the things which make
for peace and the things by which one may
edify another."–ROMANS 14:19

What will you do with that negative emotion—suspicion? **199**
Suspicion is one of the more unreliable forms of mental
activity and one of the more difficult mental habits to uproot
once it has established its malignant tentacles in the mind!

Suspicion is a pregnant demon, giving birth to fear, jealousy,
depression, and anger!

You _must_ check negative suspicion! It can ruin you!

Suspect that others think negatively about you, and they
will!

If you think people don't love you, you will freeze up, withdraw, and actively sow the seeds of alienation!

Suspicion can easily become a self-generating, self-
propagating, self-fulfilling prophecy.

A possibility-thinking faith believes that we can turn negatives into positives! Can we apply this to suspicion?

Yes, faith can turn this negative mental activity, called sus-
picion, into positive mental activity. Turn paranoia inside out!
Reverse your suspicions! Try practicing positive suspicion.
Here's how:

- I suspect that somebody is going to give me a boost!
- I suspect that people I don't even know are defending me
  behind my back.
- I suspect that people will not condemn me for my faults.
  In fact, they will love me more once they see I'm imper-
  fect just as they are.
- I suspect somebody is going to support me. And faith tells
  me that "somebody" is Jesus Christ.

Yes, turn suspicion, an expression of human imagination,
into a positive mental force. Believe that the best will happen,
not the worst. Before you know it, you will cxpcct a miracle—
and you'll get one!

FAITH IS . . .

Reacting positively to a negative situation

". . . If God is for us, who can be against us?"—
ROMANS 8:31

200 What do you do when the bottom falls out?
When the bubble breaks?
When the market is saturated?
When it looks as if your dreams are turning to ashes in your hands?
Remember this. Keep on believing!

> **You've not lost everything until you've lost your faith!
> And that's a choice . . . never an accident!**

You reserve the right to choose your reaction to whatever happens. You always have the choice to react positively or negatively.
Decide today to react positively . . .

- I'm going to be thankful to God—anyway!
- I will be rejoicing—nevertheless!
- My dreams may be frustrated; nevertheless I will keep standing on my strong feet of faith!
- This could turn out to be my shining hour!
- I can turn a tragedy into a triumph!
- This is my opportunity to build the greatest treasure a person can possess—a fantastic reputation!
- I shall choose to inspire people in my time of suffering.
- I shall achieve respect because of my courage in this enormous difficulty.

Faith is reacting positively to a negative situation.
Thank You, Father, for this gift of faith. Amen.

Burying old grudges

" 'Love your enemies, bless those who curse
you, do good to those who hate you, and pray
for those who spitefully use you and persecute
you.' "—MATTHEW 5:44

Faith is trusting that God will settle the accounts with **201**
those who have been unjust and unfair with you. No one
travels the road of life without being affected by injustice at
one time or another.

But the worst thing that can happen to you is to develop
victimitis.

Victimitis is carrying your grudge and nursing the hurts.
This only produces a whole new batch of emotional demons
to torment your soul! Resentment, anger, self-pity, and even
vengeance become a mixed-up recipe for messed-up feelings.

But if you walk the walk of faith, you'll recognize that upon
occasion you'll be treated unfairly. You've got the faith that:

God can handle the injustice a lot better than you can.

You've got the faith that He'll settle the score in a way that
will be helpful and not hurtful to everyone concerned. So
don't *carry* the grudge, *bury* it.

You can be positive about one thing. God knows the ins and
outs of the entire upsetting situation a lot better than you do.
God knows how to pull weeds without killing the flowers!

He understands your opponents, adversaries, and enemies a
lot better than you do. God knows how to turn an enemy into
a friend, too!

Affirmation: Today I shall drop all resentments, all in-
justices, into the deepest sea of God's power and mercy and
love as I pray that He will settle the matter in the best way!

Thank You, God, for taking over this problem before it does
untold damage to my spirit! Amen.

Coping creatively!

"In all these things we are more than conquerors through Him who loved us."— ROMANS 8:37

202 Let's take a look at two different lives: one walks the road of doubt and one walks the road of faith.

Negative people cry, complain, moan, and groan. They look at their losses instead of their victories. They look at what's wrong instead of what's right.

This naturally leads to a state of low self-esteem, which in turn produces an entire new set of problems. As they try to cope with life's hurts, they resort to chemicals, compulsive gambling, or immoral sex.

By contrast, people of faith cope creatively through possibility thinking! This is what Saint Paul did when he confidently wrote the words of our text today.

Positive-thinking people cope creatively by seeing the possibilities, even in the dark times. Instead of becoming pessimistic they start counting their blessings. They see stumbling blocks as stepping stones; obstacles as opportunities. They turn their negative temptations into positive passions.

Possibility thinkers focus all their efforts toward turning wild impulses into sanctified service.

What hurt do you need to conquer today? "We are more than conquerors!" Is there a wild passion you need to control? "We are more than conquerors!" What problem do you need to solve? "We are more than conquerors!" What obstacle do you need to move? "We are more than conquerors!"

How do we know we can conquer? The promise is through Christ who loved us!

Faith is coping creatively!

FAITH IS . . .
Smiling—anyway

"How beautiful upon the mountains are the feet of him who brings good news, . . . who proclaims salvation."—ISAIAH 52:7

"Dr. Schuller, you smile all the time on television. Are you always that happy?" The answer is no. But when I'm not smiling, I cease to be as helpful as I ought to be.

When I was a student in theological seminary, the professor of practical theology, Dr. Simon Blocker, taught us: "Students, when you get in front of an audience, give them a lift; don't give them a load. Help them with their problems; don't dump yours on top of them! Give them a breath of fresh air! Give them good news, or you're not preaching the gospel!"

Think of all the positive values revealed in the life and faith of our Lord Jesus Christ, and you'll be able to smile—anyway!

To the best of my ability I have tried to live up to that directive. The result is that many people tell me that when they were undergoing stress and crushed with sorrow, my smile was enough to give them hope!

The talent to smile is given to every living human being.

Exercise it. Get all the mileage you can out of it! The amazing thing is that if you keep on smiling, you really will feel happy in a little while anyway! Even as the mind affects the body, the reverse is also true. If you *physically* act out the exercise of positive emotion, you can, in fact, awaken those feelings that are within you now. Positive feelings are waiting to be awakened within you. You simply need to exercise them through positive talk and constant smiling.

One dear old soul was credited for bringing many people into the church. Her secret? She simply stood at the entrance of her church each week, "smiling them in and smiling them out!"

Absorbing jolts naturally

"What woman, having ten silver coins, if she loses one coin, does not light a lamp, sweep the house, and seek diligently until she finds it?"— LUKE 15:8

204 "Absorbing" is an important quality of life. People who walk by faith develop the art of absorbing. There are times when we need to be like a sponge—absorbing disappointments, rejections, setbacks. The woman Jesus talks about in today's Bible verse succeeded because she stayed with it. The ability to absorb the initial disappointment gave her come-back-ability. Nine times out of ten:

Success comes to the person who refuses to give up.

I remember the time my wife lost her diamond from her engagement ring. One afternoon she looked at her ring and saw an empty setting. The stone was gone! Since she hadn't been outdoors all day, she searched the house high and low, to no avail.

I suggested we might have better luck looking for the diamond in the black of night. With all the lights off, we aimed the flashlight at every corner of the house. Suddenly we saw a flash of color! I reached down and there it was. The light in the darkness had done the trick.

I took it to the jeweler the next day, but he took one look at it and said, "This isn't a diamond; it's only a rhinestone!"

Glass! I was horrified. I said, "But I bought it from a respectable jeweler."

He smiled, "This stone did not come out of this ring. It's almost the right size, but not quite."

We never did find the diamond. My wife learned to take the jolt, absorb it, and go on. Faith is absorbing the jolts.

O God, enable me to keep walking by faith despite life's disappointments. Give me the ability to absorb and then give me the courage to keep going—anyway.

FAITH IS . . .
Manipulating the rough course

"I will make each of My mountains a road,/And
My highway shall be elevated."—ISAIAH 49:11

Faith is manipulating your way upward and forward. Manipulation is a negative concept in the minds of people today, but it does not always mean treating people as puppets for personal pleasure. It does not necessarily suggest using them as tools to satisfy your needs.

205

Manipulation can be a positive form of human behavior. Such is the case when a human being follows the Holy Spirit down the walk of faith which sometimes twists and turns, rises and falls, circles and backtracks in its relentless drive to keep moving upward.

Remember, the walk of faith can be compared to a curved mountain road which circumnavigates in mysterious twists and manipulative turns upward to reach the mountain top.

We are managers of responsibilities given to our care by God. And management is the *positive* manipulation of resources to achieve the impossible!

Faith is *positive* managing and manipulating of ideas and projects through God's all-wise, all-knowing guidance. God will guide you until each mountain becomes a road and each highway is elevated. That's the promise to the people of faith in the Bible verse today.

God promises that He will make *His* mountain a road; He will elevate *His* highway. Be sure He is your guide today.

Then possibility thinking really works miracles, for God will give you the wisdom to know how to use it. Manipulate the rough course with God's help until you reach the top of the mountain.

Bearing your cross—constructively

Listen to these words of Jesus Christ: "If anyone desires to come after Me, let him deny himself, and take up his cross daily, and follow Me."—LUKE 9:23

206   What did Jesus mean when He made this statement? He was teaching a fundamental principle for successful living. To succeed you have to grab hold of God's dreams.

God's dreams will always appear humanly impossible. The fear of a shameful failure and criticism from colleagues may be enough to cause you to reject the call of God. If you follow God's call, you expose yourself to ridicule, criticism, and harassment in the pursuit of His plan for your life. Yet, in the process you will experience a constructive crucifixion as you build cathedrals, establish universities, develop research centers, and launch programs to help people in need.

To fulfill God's dream requires willingness to sacrifice the comfort of the sheltered life, rather than remaining faithfully aloof from any possible criticism and rejection by your peers.

Anyone who attempts to do anything positive is going to be criticized.

That is a price we're called to pay as followers of Jesus Christ.

The cross is implicit in possibility thinking!

There is no possibility of walking the walk of faith without being willing to bear a cross.

> **The cross is a positive symbol of success, not a negative reminder of failure.**

The cross is a minus turned into a plus!

It is the biggest plus sign in the world!

Affirmation: If I have enough faith to bear my cross, I shall leave something wonderful behind me when I'm finally called to leave this life. That's success!

Keeping on—anyway

"... he who endures to the end will be
saved."—MATTHEW 10:22

We are not on the walk of faith long before we encounter **207**
frustrations, obstacles, and obstructions. Then what? Then
it's time to hang on to one powerful, positive word—*endure!*

To endure means: "Inch by inch, anything is a cinch."

To endure means: "There is no gain without pain."

To endure means: "When faced with a mountain, I will not
quit. I will keep on striving until I climb over, find a pass
through, tunnel underneath . . . or simply stay and turn the
mountain into a gold mine, with God's help!"

To endure means: "I have to look at what I have, not at what
I've lost."

So you are unemployed? To endure means you're going to
keep on living a meaningful life anyway.

So you have people problems and are frustrated with regula-
tions and road blocks and negative forces? You are so tired of
fighting you'd like to throw in the towel and quit?

What does it mean to endure? It means to remember that
when you face problems, you keep this point in the forefront
of your mind: people, problems, and pressures are constantly
changing, so don't split. You'll run into the same basic frustrations no matter where you go.

So you are grieving over the loss of your wife? Your husband? To endure means you keep on being positive about
life—anyway!

Never forget this wise warning:

Never make a negative decision in a down time.

This is only a phase that you are going through. It will pass.
When it is over, you'll be glad you hung in there!

Thanking God always

"Giving thanks always for all things to God the
Father in the name of our Lord Jesus Christ."—
EPHESIANS 5:20

208   Deep in the heart of gratitude is a nugget of tremendous
faith. For the truly grateful person is the one who is walking
the walk of faith. He believes that his prosperity, peace, and
goodness come from forces and sources outside of himself.
Thanksgiving and trust are Siamese twins.

It's amazing how an unbeliever somehow assumes that it
was luck or his own cleverness that caused him to get to
where he is.

In contrast, the believer who thanks God for blessings will
also be able to thank God when the blessings don't come.

I remember visiting a young Chinese Christian in his office
in Hong Kong. Above his desk he had a huge sign made up of
only two words:

Hallelujah anyway!

"What does that mean?" I asked.

"Well," he said, "I believe God is blessing me always, and I
must be thankful at all times."

It's amazing how this attitude works miracles. Instead of
complaining when things go wrong, thank God anyway.

Believe that God will turn a tragedy into a triumph.

Once you begin to believe that God can turn an evil event
into a blessing, you will begin to relax. When your attitude
changes, your mood changes. When your mood changes, you
arise above the difficulty. That is the point where the miracle
takes place! Your mountain suddenly turns into a miracle.

Your optimism attracts great and good people! With this
kind of support you can't lose. Be thankful anyway—and expect a miracle!

Playing it down

"We are hard pressed on every side, yet not crushed; we are perplexed, but not in despair."—2 CORINTHIANS 4:8

Five years ago, my wife, Arvella, and I were thirty-five thousand feet over the South Pacific flying home from Seoul, Korea. Our hearts were bleeding, and our spirits, crushed, knowing that our thirteen-year-old daughter had just had her left leg amputated in a Sioux City, Iowa, hospital.

209

I called out to God for emotional strength. Into my mind came one of the most beautiful sentences He has ever given me.

Play it down—and pray it up.

Play it down—I was exaggerating the seriousness of her motorcycle accident. She lost only one leg, not both of them. Her spinal cord was not severed. She had no head injuries, no brain damage. She didn't lose her sight or her hearing. She still has a beautiful face. She has a beautiful figure. She will have an exciting life. She wasn't killed!

Play it down—that's faith's counsel in the face of tragedies that can overwhelm you.

- If you surrender to negative thinking, you will *exaggerate* the problem.
- When you exaggerate the problem, you will *aggravate* it.
- You will never *alleviate* the problem until you put it in proper perspective.

Faith is playing it down—and praying it up.

Praying it up

"Blessed be the . . . Father of our Lord Jesus
Christ, the . . . God of all comfort, who
comforts us in all our tribulation, that we may
be able to comfort those who are in any
trouble."—2 CORINTHIANS 1:3–4

210 Faith is playing it down—and praying it up. Praying it up
means giving your problems to God. Let Him turn your tears
into pearls.

As soon as my wife and I started praying about Carol's accident, we demonstrated faith again in the providence of God.
We exercised the belief that all things work together for good
when we love God and are faithful to Him.

**Pray it up, and give God a chance to strengthen you in
your sadness, sorrow, and sickness.**

As soon as I surrendered the broken body of my daughter
who was lying in pain thousands of miles away, I left my airline seat and made my way to the lavatory. There, I broke into
loud sobbing.

Compassionately, God met me in the shadows. I felt His
warm arms, like the comforting, gentle hug of a strong father.
I knew we would not only survive but also know His blessing
in the situation. Faith is playing it down and praying it up.

• Is there *sadness*? God can gladden your day.
• Is there *sickness*? He is the Great Physician.
• Is there *sorrow*? Heaven can heal.
• Is there *sin*? Christ alone claims the power to forgive sin.
• Is there *stress*? Christ can touch the nerve center and be-
stow peace.
• Is there *struggle*? Christ can strengthen you to succeed.
• Is there *scarring*? Christ can turn the scars into stars.
• Is there *scorching*? Christ can heal the searing hurts.

Then *surrender* your brokenness. God is able to pick up the
pieces and mend you again. His strength is all-sufficient!

Praising God anyway

"Continue earnestly in prayer, being vigilant in it with thanksgiving."—COLOSSIANS 4:2

Our daughter Carol had been in a motorcycle accident. My wife and I were flying to her side from a speaking engagement in Korea, when suddenly I felt grief well up uncontrollably within me. **211**

In the solitary confinement of an airplane lavatory six miles above the Pacific, in the middle of my sobbing, I was moved by a most miraculous positive thought.

The thought came like a clear message from Jesus Christ: *Schuller, if you are going to make a lot of noise, turn it into something positive. Let your lips shape the sounds that are coming.* I found my lips and tongue reshaping the wailing, sobbing sounds and turning them into the word *Alleluia.*

Tears rolled down my face, but the *Alleluia* was repeated. I kept repeating it—"Alleluia, alleluia"—until all of the audible crying sounds were out of my tortured soul.

It was amazing! The last "Alleluias" were offered in a hushed whisper. I found myself looking upward with my hands raised in a gesture that said, "I give this painful event, along with the broken body of my daughter, to You, God, and I praise You.

• I praise You for your comfort,
• I praise You for Your healing,
• I praise You for turning our tears into pearls,
• I praise You for turning her scars into stars."

The next time your life is torn apart from stem to stern, try praying "Alleluia." If you can repeat no other word, keep repeating it again and again.

Then wait for God to come like a sweet dove of peace to bless you. A soft spirit will kiss your tortured soul with tender mercies!

Thank You, Father, for Your faithfulness. Amen.

FAITH IS . . .
Biting the bullet

"Though He slay me, yet will I trust Him."—
JOB 13:15

212 The phrase "biting the bullet" comes, of course, from the Old West when there were no pain-killers.

I once asked the late actor, John Wayne, a university graduate and a keen student of history and contemporary affairs, about this. He offered this insight: "It's really true, Schuller. People literally put a bullet between their teeth and bit it to help distract them from the pain. It's hard for us to comprehend the pain they had to endure without the benefit of our modern pain-killers."

Faith is bearing the unbearable by biting the bullet!

I was invited to a home of a shooting victim who had been left a paraplegic. I have never seen a more pathetic person. His mind and eyes were glazed with the drugs to which he had become addicted. All around his wheelchair were evidences of enormous wealth. He lacked nothing that money could buy. But there was an overwhelming spirit of darkness and doubt. He has made a decision to be a cynic, not a believer. He has chosen to publicly reject all belief in God. The Great Soul, the Eternal God, who charismatically sends out vibrations of an indwelling Holy Spirit, simply is not in his life.

Faith bears the unbearable by biting the bullet. That's what Job did when he lost his family and when his friends forsook him. Sitting alone in the ashes of his dreams, He still believed, saying; "Though He slay me, yet will I trust him!" That's inspiring faith!

You can have that kind of faith and so can I. We can bite the bullet, we can accept the disappointment, endure the pain, and in the process we will be an inspiration to all those we meet.

Turning pain into gain

"When I am weak, then I am strong."—
2 CORINTHIANS 12:10

There is no gain without pain. Everything nice has its price. **213**
Max Cleland, as a soldier in Vietnam, lost both legs and an
arm when a grenade exploded. He could have come back to
the States a broken man, physically and spiritually. But there
was an inextinguishable spark of faith within him that turned
into a flame of burning desire.

Max tells the entire, painful, struggling story in his book
Strong in the Broken Places. A strong voice deep within his
spirit called him to greatness! "You can turn your scar into a
star! You can become *Strong in the Broken Places.* This unspeakable tragedy can be profitable to your soul."

Because Max Cleland was moved by faith to take a positive
attitude toward his crushing experience, he was able to look
positively toward his future. His hopes, rather than his hurts,
set his goals.

Today, let your hopes, not your hurts, set your goals!

Begin by setting a *reasonable* goal that you can be sure to
realize within the immediate future. With the enthusiasm
that will come with this fresh victory, you will be ready to set
a newer and higher goal.

Remember, anybody can have faith when the sun is shining—but you've got enough faith to be positive even when
you have good reasons to be negative!

You're destined to be above average!

Your courageous response alone will be a tremendous inspiration to yourself and to others. And who can measure the
value of that?

FAITH IS . . .
Surviving against all odds

> "For I am persuaded that neither death nor life,
> nor angels nor principalities . . ., nor things
> present nor things to come, . . . nor any other
> created thing, shall be able to separate us from
> the love of God."—ROMANS 8:38–39

214   Today I saw something you have probably seen many times—a vibrant, solitary blade of grass standing proud and alert in the crack of a concrete sidewalk. All of the odds were against this blade of grass growing in such an unlikely habitat.

In the same manner, have you not seen a tree growing strong and rugged in a granite cliff? How can this tree survive against all odds and thrive on the side of a stone mountain? Where does it get its water?

> **If a blade of grass can grow in a concrete walk and a fir tree in the side of a mountain cliff, a human being empowered with an invincible faith can survive all odds the world can throw against his tortured soul.**

There is an explanation for this marvelous miracle. *God plus one believer is a majority!* With faith in your Lord you can outnumber the enemies that may attack you.

You manage your problems, you don't let them manage you. You choose what kind of an attitude you are going to have.

> **One possibility-thinking believer, plus God, equals survival power!**

Dear God, today I imagine my hand with fingers spread wide open. I imagine Your hand approaching mine until our fingers interlock and we grip each other firmly in faith. I will never let You go, and You will never let me go. You are my Lord. We will see this through together. Thank You, God.

So I need never be discouraged.

I'll never let anything get me down.

I am a survivor! Thank You, God!

FAITH IS . . .
Sublimating your sorrow

"O Death, where is your sting? . . . Thanks be
to God, who gives us the victory through our
Lord Jesus Christ."—1 CORINTHIANS 15:55,57

I'm often asked: "Dr. Schuller, do you really believe in this **215**
possibility thinking?

"How can you really subscribe to such a positive attitude
when the world is in such a tragic mess?"

As a pastor for over thirty years, I bear witness to the truth
that sorrow either turns people into sweeter souls or into sour
and cynical spirits. The choice is up to the individual. When
loss has occurred, you must accept the finality of it. You can
either turn sorrow into a living enemy to torment, bedevil,
and finally consume you in its poison; or you can make
friends with your sorrow.

Sorrow colors a person's life permanently. The hues never
fade. Rather, they grow deeper in tone every passing year.
However, you can choose the colors. The colors are either rich
or they portray emotional impoverishment.

The word *sublimate* comes from the word *sublime.* I have
seen great people walk the walk of faith and go through the
deepest sorrows you can possibly comprehend. They arose
from their grief more compassionate, tenderhearted, and em-
pathetic than ever. They have sublimated their sorrow.

If you walk the walk of faith, there is no doubt you will
become divinely different after drinking the cup of tears.
When you remember this, it will help you choose how you
will react to sorrow. The loss you experience is horrible.
Don't compound it by allowing your life to be destroyed, too.
How inspiring was the faith of Saint Paul when he said,
"Thanks be to God, who gives us the victory . . ."!

Yes, walk the walk of faith; and when sorrow strikes, you'll
know that weights can turn into wings!

Polishing the silver lining

> "Can anyone understand the spreading of clouds,/The thunder from His canopy? . . ./God thunders marvelously with His voice;/He does great things which we cannot comprehend."—
> JOB 36:29; 37:5

216   People who walk the walk of faith give the world this positive thought: "Every cloud has a silver lining."

Men and women of great faith learn to polish their silver with positive thoughts. They affirm God is bringing good out of evil. They affirm nothing will befall them unless it is a beautiful blessing in disguise. They affirm there is a silver lining to every cloud.

When it rains—they look for the rainbow!

Today I will polish the silver lining of my darkest clouds when the thunder is the loudest, and the waves crash most violently! Today I shall discipline myself to pray a prayer with at least ten sentences, each one beginning with "thank You."

- Thank You, God, that I am alive!
- Thank You that I have friends!
- Thank You that I have the faith to see it through.
- Thank You that there is help available for the problem, even though I see no solution to it today.
- Thank You that there are people who love me and are praying for me!

That's right—keep at it. Make a list of ten thank-you sentences. In the process you will be polishing the silver lining of the dark clouds.

God can work miracles through His people whose hearts are broken in love.

Waiting for a breakthrough

"If anyone competes in athletics, he is not crowned unless he competes according to the rules."—2 TIMOTHY 2:5

What distinguishes the person who walks by faith from the person who basically walks the walk of doubt?

217

People who walk the walk of faith always expect a breakthrough.

People of faith anticipate that someone will offer them a "lucky break." When problems produce log jams, those who walk by faith listen for the crack of wood that clears the river for free-floating logs. When experiments fail to produce the magic cure, people who walk by faith keep working on new formulas, intuitively expecting that the big break will come.

Anticipating a breakthrough is enough to keep you going. Persistence ultimately finds the loopholes in an entanglement which threatens to strangle success.

A runner who competes in a race knows that to win he will need to push himself beyond his own limits. He'll need that "second wind," the breakthrough in order to be crowned a winner. He competes expecting a breakthrough!

Beware of crude, complaining voices of cynicism that whisper to you: "Throw in the towel. It's no use. It's never going to happen. Go ahead and quit."

Rather, plant your feet firmly on the high, hard, and holy road of faith. No matter how impossible the project may appear, keep on believing in your "second wind." Tell yourself that a breakthrough is going to happen!

- Wait for it,
  - work for it,
    - and be ready to receive the reward when it comes!

Adding up your assets

"Bless the LORD, . . ./And forget not all His
benefits:/Who forgives . . . heals . . . redeems
. . . crowns . . . satisfies . . . So that your youth
is renewed like the eagle's."—PSALM 103:1–5

218   Are frustrations, failures, and fears coming back to depress
and fatigue you today?

Faith looks at what you have left, never at what you have
lost. Faith adds up the assets. It doesn't surrender leadership
to liabilities.

- Consider what you really have going for you.
- Add up your assets.
- Measure your strength.
- Take account of your power.

The psalmist gives us the clue to begin by blessing the Lord.
What has the Lord done for you? What can you expect Him to
do for you in the future? He forgives. He heals. He redeems.
He crowns you with loving kindness. He renews your
strength! With a God like that, who can fail?

Now begin to add up the other assets that you may have
taken for granted. List your friends, your education, your cit-
izenship.

There is no more helpful therapy for depression or fatigue
than the exercise of adding up your assets. Retreat from the
hectic style of life. Find a quiet time and place and list on
paper everything you have going for you. You will be surprised
how rich you are. Your capacity not only to survive your present condition but to succeed is formidable indeed! Now, before you add up the bottom line, reread the Bible verse.

**God promises that when you remember daily what
benefits He has sent your way, you will have renewed
strength like an eagle!**

FAITH IS . . .
Counting your blessings

"Godliness with contentment is great gain."—
1 TIMOTHY 6:6

It's amazing how many opportunities must have opened up **219** to you yesterday when you stopped to reevaluate your net worth:

1. You discovered you had friends whom you did not know a year ago.
2. You discovered that the value of your property has inflated and you are richer than you thought you were.
3. You have discovered that you have maneuvered your way around a treacherous conflict this past year. Only God could have made it possible.

As you practice counting your blessings, you will find that your faith is being suddenly revitalized.

Of course! Faith is the practice of counting your blessings!

The cynic exposes bleak and barren stupidity when he feeds his doubt! No joy ever sprouts from the soil of cynicism!

By contrast, the process of counting your blessings strengthens faith and produces a contentment in the most adverse circumstances.

When our daughter Carol went through the pain of an amputation of a leg, she spent seven months in bed. Yet, she counted her blessings every day. She thanked God for the nurse. She thanked God for the bed, for the clean sheets, for medication, for pain-killing drugs, for shelter from the storm.

What blessings can you thank God for today? List no fewer than ten: _____

_____

_____

_____

Coming back after defeat

"Let us not grow weary while doing good, for in due season we shall reap if we do not lose heart."—GALATIANS 6:9

220   Even saints have their low times! A great Scottish pastor, Peter Marshall, once said, "There are times when my prayers never go above the top of my head."

There are seasons of the soul, you know.

There is the wintertime when all the trees appear to be dead. I remember one winter when my father cut down a dead tree only to see new sprouts grow from the stump in the springtime. "Never cut a tree down in the winter," he said to me. Then he added, "I shouldn't have cut it down. It had more life in it than I thought."

The principle?

> **Never make an irreversible *negative* decision in the dark times. Never set your goals when you are at a low ebb. Believe that the springtime will come.**

- This depressing season will pass.
- Positive new feelings will return to you.
- You will come back again.

Yes, your faith will pluck you from the ashes, and you will be resurrected once more. Youthful enthusiasm will return.

Burned out?

Then refuel.

Take a break.

Seek a retreat.

Find renewal and replenish—you can go on again!

Never make a move from weakness. Always move from strength.

And the spring will turn to summer and the summer to harvesttime! You will reap successfully simply because you didn't give up!

Reconstructing after ruin

"Then the nations . . . around you shall know
that I, the LORD, have rebuilt the ruined
places. . . . I, the LORD, have spoken it, and I
will do it."—EZEKIEL 36:36

What happens when life strikes you a blow? What happens **221**
when you "blow it"? When you are too weak to resist temptation?

> **When you stumble, don't crumble. Admit you're
> human. God doesn't expect you to be perfect. He does
> expect you to be dependent on Him.**

Faith is reconstructing after ruin. It probably takes more
faith to rebuild for a second time than to build the first time.

When a tornado completely demolished our farm home, I
saw faith in action as my dad rebuilt the buildings one at a
time, slowly but steadily. And he was in his mid-sixties at the
time.

There's something infectious and inspiring about the in-
domitable human spirit that wades through the flood waters,
rakes through the ashes, and then makes the decision to rebuild.

Faith looks at ruin and says, "This only means that you
have a chance to build something better in its place."

The terrible hurricane that hit the island of Kauai in Hawaii
in 1982 was devastating. The full force of the hurricane lifted
the larger-than-life-size sculptures of Allerton Gardens and,
like torpedos, hurled them through the walls of the owner's
private home. Then flood waters followed, washing out to the
sea a priceless collection of first-edition books from Mr. Allerton's private library. Books—many the only extant copies—
were lost forever. How has he handled the ruin? He has re-
paired his home and planted new trees. He is reconstructing
after ruin.

> **That's how God is with you and me! He is the Master
> Artist, reconstructing beautiful lives from ruin.**

FAITH IS . . .
Awaiting your turn—especially after crushing disappointments

"The end of a thing is better/than its beginning,/And the patient in spirit is better/than the proud in spirit./Do not hasten in your spirit to be angry,/For anger rests in the bosom of fools."—ECCLESIASTES 7:8–9

222

He was passed by for a promotion that he was sure he would receive. His first impulse was anger. He ranted and raved and stomped in the privacy of his home, and decided he'd quit the next day. He said, "Let's see how they get along without me!"

Then he read the Bible verse that we are using today. Faith took over. He thought, *I won't quit. Instead I'll wait my turn. Perhaps I'll get another chance later.*

The person who had been brought in from outside the company to receive the coveted promotion resigned within six months, and the patient person's turn came up. This time he was offered the position. He's doing great today!

It takes faith to hang in there after you have been hurt, especially if you cannot justify the loss.

Another friend of mine was an ambitious political candidate with integrity. In the closing days of the campaign, his opponent resorted to smear tactics. And my friend was defeated. The dishonesty made him say, "I'm finished with politics."

I urged him to hang in there. "Voters have a way of being very wise," I advised him. "If I didn't believe that, I wouldn't believe in the democratic system." The story has a happy ending. Three years later he ran for office again. This time he made it.

Faith is waiting your turn.

O God, give me patience in spirit. If I'm tempted to pick up my marbles and run because I did not win the game, I am really too proud. Replace my anger with Your understanding spirit, and save me from the self-destruction that I could bring upon myself by my negative reactions. Thank You, Lord. Amen.

FAITH IS . . .
Regrouping after a setback

"Do not remember the former things, nor
consider the things of old. Behold, I will do a
new thing. . . . I will even make a road in the
wilderness."—ISAIAH 43:18,19

223

Regrouping may mean little to you, but it is a very meaningful term in military strategy. When the enemy lines collide
and the battle (not the war) is over, the side which suffered the
apparent defeat does not contemplate surrender, it speaks
about "regrouping." They analyze why they lost, calculate the
weak spot in the enemy's lines, and develop a new strategy for
effective counterattack.

The regrouping strategy is of course mostly known in
sports, especially football. The opposing teams are allowed to
huddle and regroup to discuss a game plan they hope will surprise and beat their opponent.

Businesses do this when they go through periods of recession. They may permanently discontinue some unprofitable
lines they carried at a loss. They may cut overhead, trim their
personnel, and regroup their resources.

> **Regrouping is an act of dynamic faith!**
> **It is possibility thinking in action.**
> **Do not dwell on old mistakes; concentrate on new**
> **ideas.**

What do you do when you've had
• a nonproductive day?
• a streak of ill luck?
• a poor semester in the classroom?
• a stagnant relationship?
When you face setbacks, don't send up the white flag. Don't
throw in the towel. Rather get your best thoughts together.
Reorganize, retool, or regroup! Then go back at it again with
vengeance!

That's faith, and it moves mountains.

Redeeming a lost cause

> "Fear not, for I have redeemed you; I have
> called you by your name; you are Mine. . . .
> you were precious in My sight."—ISAIAH 43:1,4

224   **A "lost cause" simply doesn't exist in God's mind!**

And it must not exist in our mentality as possibility thinkers either! Jesus came not to condemn, but to save.

When you see what appears to be a lost cause, instead see a challenge to be miraculously redemptive!

Any act of redemption is a beautiful display of faith. I really admire people who take old automobiles and restore them to the original condition. Or those remarkable artists who have the incredible ability to restore a damaged work of art.

Here is a list of all the lost causes that were redeemed by possibility thinking.
- Eliminating child slavery laws.
- Eliminating segregationist laws in this country.
- Taking a company that was hopelessly bankrupt and turning it around until it turned a profit again.
- The person who was dying from cancer, but is alive today because of medical research.
- That marriage which was threatened, but now is renewed.
- The drug abuser who now is a rising young executive.
- You and I were lost, until Christ redeemed us!

What "lost cause" do you need to turn over to God today? Is there a possibility that you consider yourself to be a "lost cause"? When faith comes into your mind and heart, something wonderful happens. Under the power of your Lord, you are not condemned—you are redeemed! Write your name in the blanks below.

God calls me by name, _____.

I, _____, belong to Him.

I _____, am precious in His sight.

Now—say these affirmations—aloud.

Thank You, Lord, for redeeming us!

Bouncing back after failure

"Every valley shall be exalted,/And every mountain and hill shall be made low;/The crooked places shall be made straight,/and the rough places smooth."—ISAIAH 40:4

Flexibility. That's the word that describes this walk of faith. **225** The pathway of possibility thinking is not flat. The trail of positive thinking twists and turns, rises and falls.

In a way the walk of faith is like those exciting moving sidewalks at major airports in the world. I love to walk as fast as I can on those moving sidewalks! And if I'm the only one on the horizontal escalator, I will often jog. How fast I can move! I bounce up and down with every footfall. I almost feel like I'm flying! What a marvelous feeling!

The walk of faith is a moving sidewalk! It gives bounce-back-ability!

After a defeat, there are the down days and moments of discouragement; yet you must resist the temptation to give up on life. Faith finds you bouncing back with new enthusiasm.

Doubt whispers with a devilish voice: "Well, you've learned your lesson; be smart. Give in. Quit."

But the still, sterling whisper of God nudges and lifts us, saying, "O.K., learning to walk is learning to bounce back after you stumble and fall. Step up again. I'll walk with you. Try again, we'll make it!"

With this definition of faith in mind you can see why the people who walk the walk of faith are never ultimately defeated. They simply refuse to take up a permanent residence at a point of failure.

Failure is a juncture in the road. It must never become a campground. So pack up your tent and move on to greener pastures. Affirmation: I have an invitation from God to start over again! Today I have been born again! My new life started this morning. I have the freedom now to bounce back.

Saving the broken pieces

"The Spirit of the LORD is upon me. . . . He has sent Me to heal the brokenhearted."—LUKE 4:18

226 At the Royal Palace of Teheran in Iran, you can see one of the most beautiful mosaic works in the world. The ceilings and walls flash like diamonds in multifaceted reflections.

Originally, when the palace was designed, the architect specified huge sheets of mirrors on the walls. When the first shipment arrived from Paris, they found to their horror that the mirrors were shattered. The contractor threw them in the trash and brought the sad news to the architect.

Amazingly, the architect ordered all of the broken pieces collected, then smashed them into tiny pieces and glued them to the walls to become a mosaic of silvery, shimmering, mirrored bits of glass.

Broken to become beautiful! It's possible to turn your scars into stars. It's possible to be better because of the brokenness. It is extremely rare to find in the great museums of the world objects from antiquity that are unbroken. Indeed, some of the most precious pieces in the world are only fragments that remain a hallowed reminder of a glorious past.

Never underestimate God's power to repair and restore.

And when restoration is not in His plan, expect Him to replace what has been destroyed with something even more beautiful. God has ways of filling the empty spots with His love. With God the fragments of our happy memories are like precious gems.

Dear God, mercifully bless me in the broken times, and I shall rise up to praise Your name. And thank You, Father, that through Your love something precious is being salvaged from sorrow, and I shall soar again on eagles' wings. Amen.

FAITH IS . . .
Elevating your hopes

"I [God] dwell in the high and holy place,/With him who has a contrite and humble spirit,/To revive the spirit of the humble."—ISAIAH 57:15

Do you need a lift today in your walk of faith? Are you in need of a rebirth of hope? Let's consider an elevator of faith and hope to elevate your spirits!

First, you have to believe there is an elevator. There are those who can't imagine that there's an easier way to the top than climbing each step painfully, slowly. They feel that a great deal of effort is necessary to raise your spirits. Too many people strive at being happy when they could be riding the faith elevator to the top.

Once you believe in an elevator, you've got to have enough faith to step into it. For if you don't step into the elevator, you'll never make it to the top of the skyscraper.

After you are in the elevator, remember to push the button. More than once, I've suddenly realized that I'm in an elevator that is going nowhere, because we all forgot to push the button. Everybody assumed somebody else was pushing it.

Finally, make sure you are in the *right* elevator. High-rise buildings often have elevators that only go to certain floors and bypass the others. Get on the wrong elevator and you'll never get to where you are planning to go.

Faith is elevating your hopes. Don't sell yourself short. Set higher goals, or you'll surrender leadership to your past accomplishments. Who wants to be stuck in an elevator that isn't going anywhere?

Press the button and step on an up elevator called F-A-I-T-H.

Look for the arrow pointing upward, and you will experience a rebirth of hope.

FAITH IS . . .
Opening yourself to new opportunities

"I know your works. See, I have before you an
open door, and no one can shut it."—
REVELATION 3:8

228 You know what is so exciting about the walk of faith?
It's knowing that some mistakes can actually be profitable!
Failures and even setbacks may prove to be positive pos-
sibilities in disguise.

My faith sharpens more to spot opportunities in both
failure—and success.

Surely success creates new opportunities.

Success starts a whole cycle of margin successes. The *peak*
to *peek* principle is set in motion. For once you have climbed
a mountain you gain greater self-confidence.

So each new success experience gives your self-image a new
boost.

You are more than you thought you were.

When you conquer a challenging problem you feel like you
are standing on a mountain top! This "peak" experience produces a "peek" experience—you see farther and spot new hori-
zons, and new opportunities.

Now you experience a *"peek"* experience: Your vision ex-
pands; your faith grows! You imagine accomplishing more
than you ever thought you could: "If I could scale this peak—
maybe I could. . .?!"

The higher you climb, the farther you see. From the top of
the hill you can see a valley waiting to be explored. You find
that you are a lot stronger than you were when you started
this walk of faith!

You gain a new sense of self worth! You now have more
money, more friends, more knowledge, more self-confidence,
and more faith than when you started your climb.

O God, open my eyes to see the incredible opportunities
that are before me today and give me enough common sense
never to slam a door shut that you have just opened for me!
Amen.

Laminating the life for strength

"O God, You are my God. . . ./Because you have been my help. . . ./My soul follows close behind You,/Your right hand upholds me."—PSALM 63:1,6–8

When you walk the walk of faith, you experience the "laminating principle." Let me illustrate what I mean.

When we built our first chapel, I discovered how laminated wood beams are built. A layer of wood about an inch thick is glued under pressure to another piece of wood of equal thickness. Several other layers are glued under pressure on top of that. This creates a laminated beam that may be as thick as three feet and conceivably able to span a width of over one hundred feet without supporting columns.

Amazingly enough, these beams are stronger than steel and are virtually fire resistant. Flames lick around the outside but cannot penetrate, for there are no hollow cores where the flame can continue to draw oxygen and create a roaring fire.

Steel beams, on the other hand, melt under the heat of a burning wall, unless they are wrapped in fire-resistant plaster!

> **The kind of faith that moves mountains**
> **doesn't come from one simple religious event**
> **in your life, but through layer upon layer**
> **of experiences, one upon another—**
> **until your walk with God through months and years**
> **becomes an emotional and spiritual**
> **beam that can span the deepest chasm**
> **and the most ghastly gorge**
> **that your path will encounter.**

Thank You, God, for the way You are building my faith stronger and stronger.

Laminate my life for strength so that I need never fear the future. Amen.

Filling the tank

> "The wise took oil in their vessels with their lamps. . . . the bridegroom came, and those who were ready went in with him to the wedding; and the door was shut."—MATTHEW 25:4,10

230   Faith is filling the tank—especially when it's a rental car! "Fill 'er up." Now that's faith, isn't it? How do you know you'll take the whole journey and won't change your mind soon after you start out? And if you can't, what a waste it is to have all that gas sitting in the tank. When you return the car, you don't get more for it because there's gas in the tank!

Notice how possibility thinkers fill the tank—before they're sure how long the trip will be. Isn't that what you did when you took that special training course?

"Filling the tank" becomes a key element in success, for it activates an inner commitment. It sets in concrete ways the hopes and dreams you have.

Read carefully the passage from Matthew, chapter 25, verses 1 through 13. The wise women were those who filled their vessels with oil and took extra oil along! There is a warning in this parable: Opportunities will come in unexpected times and places, so be prepared.

Make sure your tank of faith is full of gas so you can be prepared for the unexpected opportunity that wasn't in your plan. Faith is filling the tank so you can be prepared for an unanticipated emergency along the road, helping a lonely wounded person along the road of life.

There's also a promise in this principle. The promise is that God gives great opportunities to those who are prepared.

Inspiration + preparation + saturation = success.

Yes, fill the tank. It won't be wasted. Someone will benefit from it!

O God, in a changing world I want to be prepared for the unexpected. Fill my tank of faith today with Your promises and Your wisdom so that I will not miss the opportunities before me. Amen.

FAITH IS . . .

Bracing yourself against the storms

"O LORD, You are my God./. . . a strength to
the needy in . . . distress,/A refuge from the
storm."—ISAIAH 25:1,4

Are there stormy forces of sin and doubt that are confront- **231**
ing you today?

Are the waves of cynicism threatening to capsize your ship
of faith?

How will you confront these negative storms?

Is it possible to avoid them?

Not always.

There are the storms of wrong and evil that the believer
must face. There are moral positions you can never compromise without sacrificing your soul.

Sin is still sin! Wrong is still wrong!

Faith is bracing yourself against the storms of doubt, where
lightning may flash, tornados may drop out of the sky, hur-
ricanes may hit the shore, the storms may lash against the
garden of your life. But the faith that God gives stands firm,
bracing you. His voice stills the waves of sin. His hand calms
the wind of wrong.

Practice these positive affirmations today to give you "bracing" power!

• I can brace myself against any storm of doubt, temptation,
sin, and despair, for God is at my side.

• God will not allow me to be defeated.

• God has entrusted me with a holy treasure, a divine idea. I
will guard it with my eternal soul!

• I will not take my eye off the walk of faith.

• This storm shall pass away. The winter season of my soul
will turn to spring with God's help.

• I will not abandon faith in my God, for He will allow the
sun to rise again tomorrow in my faith.

Focusing on God's power

"O LORD, our Lord,/How excellent is Your name. . . ./When I consider Your heavens, the work of Your fingers."—PSALM 8:1,3

232 Did you ever take a magnifying glass and allow the sun to shine through it, adjusting it all the while in your hand until it focused a burning white dot on a piece of cloth or paper or dry leaf? Do you remember how the magnified rays of the sun on the dry paper suddenly created a wisp of smoke?

There is tremendous energy generated in the powers that are created through the "focusing principle."

Is there a malfunctioning in your soul? Is there a source of disharmony that is upsetting you? Is there an illness in your body? Is there a negative factor or faith that is disrupting the normal, happy rhythm that should be characteristic in the life a person who is walking by faith?

Then exercise the power of "focusing." Focus on the power of the God who created the sun. Visualize the incredible immense globe of molten fire that the sun actually is.

Can you begin to comprehend the power of the God of *all* the ages? Focus all your thinking on His power.

Allow God's power to magnify your faith until it burns its healing force into the problem area of your life.

Continue to focus God's power on the obstructions in your life, and visualize the sizzling, smoking problem being consumed by the enormous power of God. Nothing can resist His redeeming forces!

Thank You, Father, for faith in this focusing power of healing that I exercise now in the name of Jesus Christ, my Lord and my Savior. Amen.

Connecting with power sources

"The God of Israel is He who gives strength and power to His people."—PSALM 68:35

"He's very well connected" is a sophisticated statement **233**
that analyzes personal power. Powerful people in the world are
those who are well connected with power sources, such as
faith, freedom, knowledge, opportunity, wealth, and other
people around them.

With what power sources are you connected?

**Today, connect with the power source of the most
beautiful and wonderful people alive—the positive-
thinking people!**

When you choose to become a believer, you suddenly find
yourself moving out of the circle of cynics and into a new
company of optimistic people.

When you step out of the society of skeptics and into a circle of trusting souls, an incredible transformation takes over.

Enthusiasm replaces boredom.

Excitement replaces lethargy.

Faith-producing energy replaces doubt-producing fatigue.

Youthfulness replaces weariness.

That's being connected with the *real power people.*
Through their minds flows an energy that has its source in
positive ideas flowing from the eternal God. That's exciting!
That's ultimate living.

Thank You, Father, that You're giving to me today the greatest gift possible—freedom to choose my friends! I am choosing today to connect myself to the most beautiful, positive-
thinking people I can meet. I pray that You will lead me. I
thank You that I'm connected to You, for You are the ultimate
Power Source. You give me the motivation to laugh, love, and
lift myself to higher and happier living. Thank You, Lord.
Amen.

Relaxing under pressure

"Be still, and know that I am God."—PSALM
46:10

234 Imagine a balloon filled with air. You maintain the balloon's
full pressure by tightly pinching the opening closed.

Now separate your fingers to allow the air to rush out. The
balloon completely deflates until it is limp and empty of its
pent-up pressure. It lies lightly in the palm of your hand.

Release the pressure inside you that has blown up like a
balloon ready to explode.

> **Exhale deeply.**
> **Blow out the tension.**
> **Deeply breathe in the presence of God's peace.**
> **Blow out the poison of stressful pressures.**

"Be still, and know that I am God." Can you know God
without being still? Probably not. Tensions can block the freedom of God's flow into your soul. Often in my ministry I have
spiritual experiences high in the mountains. As I relax among
the tall pines I feel God's presence. The secret of dynamic
spiritual power is right here. *First relax!* Defuse those tension
bombs within yourself by blowing out the pressures that have
been pumping up your blood pressure!

Now throw open the sun roof of your mind and let the sun
tranquilize your spirit. Be still—and then you may be able to
hear the voice of God.

I once asked Viktor Frankl the question, "How can you have
a religious experience?" He answered with a question, "How
do you catch a dove?"

The way to catch a dove is to open the palm of the hand and
reach upward with a grain of wheat or a bread crumb in your
hand. If you sit very quietly, the dove will come and rest in the
center of your palm. Be still—and you will catch the faith!
Quiet your spirit, and you will feel God's presence. Relax under pressure, and you'll tap into God's power!

FAITH IS . . .
Dissolving anxieties

"Do not worry about tomorrow, for tomorrow will worry about its own things. Sufficient for the day is its own trouble."—MATTHEW 6:34

As you walk the walk of faith and discipline yourself to seek positive possibilities in every situation, you will still face such realities as sickness, separation from loved ones, and even death. **235**

You can't escape the raw realities of life, but you can shape them!

You either shape life's realities, or they ravage your mind until you're devastated with worry.

How can faith help you dissolve life's anxieties?

Faith faces the worries and anxieties one at a time. If you imagined all of the possible painful experiences you might encounter from birth until the end of your life all at once, you could not handle it. A bridge cannot handle all the traffic that passes over it at one time. Bridges are designed to handle moving traffic. So faith is designed to handle anxieties, one at a time. Deal with only your immediate pressures. Let tomorrow's worries wait until then.

Faith erases anxieties and worries. By the time you've spaced your anxieties, you will have erased many of them! Many anxieties that remain can be erased by transferring them to a Higher Department. Turn them over to God. He specializes in problems you are incapable of handling.

Faith replaces anxieties. If anxieties and worries still remain after prayer, then faith replaces them. It says: I'll replace worry with work. I'll replace anxiety with ambition. I'll replace depression with new drive. I'll replace stress with success!

Faith and I together will win. Thank You, Lord.

FAITH IS . . .
Replacing worry with hope

"Do not worry about your life. . . . Which of
you by worrying can add one cubit to his
stature? . . . Your heavenly Father knows that
you need all these things!"—MATTHEW 6:25–32

236   Our Bible text today is one of the most beautiful prescriptions for the traveler on the road to faith. It comes from our Lord Jesus Christ. According to His definition, faith is replacing worry with hope.

Somebody said, "worry is like a rocking chair: It gives you something to do, but it doesn't get you anywhere."

Worry doesn't put a twinkle in your eye, a whistle on your tongue, or a happy gait to your walk.

You are the manager of your moods, with the responsibility and the freedom to manipulate your emotions. You can elect to go out today with worry or step forth with hope.

Many Christians have tried this therapeutic experiment: They write down what they're worried about on their daily diary. They pray about it and turn it over to God. A year later they see how beautifully the Lord took care of the situation, or with the passing of time, discover that it was actually incredibly inconsequential!

Hope is a phenomenon. Faith replaces worry with hope, and no psychiatrist knows what it is. We only know what it does to people. It makes gray skin pink, dull eyes sparkle, and releases healing forces in the body itself!

Affirmation: Today I'm going to walk the walk of faith. My faith will take action as I replace worry with hope.

And what's hope? *Holding* on, *praying* expectantly!

Good-by, worry! Hello, hope!

Leaning back with casual confidence

"Rest in the LORD,/and wait patiently for Him;/
Do not fret."—PSALM 37:7

237

Faith takes a tough look at rough spots and asks the responsible question: "Is it my fault? Is this the responsibility of my department?"

Not long ago I missed a flight to Japan because my visa was not in order. This was serious, for I would be a day late, missing the first series of lectures in Tokyo. Not all the positive thinking and talking in the world could get me on that flight. I had no choice but to wire my host in Japan and express my regrets that I would be arriving a day late.

Then I proceeded to lean back, take a casual attitude, and have a great time enjoying this unplanned day of leisure. When I made that decision, my problem was transformed into a joyous experience.

Faith is a wise instructor, counseling you to stop torturing yourself with irritating attitudes. Faith is leaning back with casual confidence, letting positive thoughts stroke the stress away until a mellow spirit comes over you softly, gently, and peacefully.

God is far more concerned about your welfare than you are, for you are His child. He knows how to turn this rough spot into a serendipity, a blessing in disguise. Praise Him for His faithful love and concern for you in this trying condition. He understands it so much better than you do!

Now that you've talked it over with Him, close the door.

It's time to lean back and let God take over.

He will handle it in the most responsible way possible. Give yourself a break by believing positively!

Comparing conditions and choices

"I will sing to the LORD,/Because He has dealt
bountifully with me."—PSALM 13:6

238   "How do you like your wife?" a Vermont farmer was asked.
"Compared to what?" he answered.

Life is made up of values that are relative.

"How do you feel today?" Answer: "Compared to *when?*
Compared to *whom?*" Before you answer negatively remember this: You feel great compared to some of the really painful
days and times in your life.

Faith is comparing your conditions. Compare your present
condition to the conditions of those pitiful human beings in a
Siberian labor camp, without any hope of ever getting out.
Compared to them you should really feel great!

After all, you have the freedom to make a telephone call.

You have the opportunity to have visitors (even if you are in
one of America's prisons)!

You can boost your faith by using this process of comparing
conditions. You make your condition better or worse. You aggravate it or sublimate it.

The first condition you face today is a realization that

You alter your condition by altering your attitude.

Faith is also the process of comparing choices. What are
your options? By exercising possibility faith, list all the positive possibilities that can conceivably come your way if you
became positively aggressive!

Affirmation: As I compare choices today, I will make a list
of all possible uses of my time and efforts and achievements!

O God, I compare my walk of faith with the walk of doubt
that I once experienced—with all of its negative fears, frustrations, and failures. Thank You for releasing me from these
negative conditions. I am singing with the psalmist: For You
have "dealt bountifully with me." Thank You, Father. Amen.

FAITH IS . . .
Framing your awards

"Where your treasure is, there your heart will
be also."—MATTHEW 6:21

Let's review again the steps in the process of mountain- **239**
moving faith.
- God sends an idea into your mind.
- He calls you to courageous action.
- He challenges you to attempt the impossible.
- The idea suddenly grips your attention. How does faith
  handle this inspiring possibility?

(1) Faith *forms* the idea carefully in the mind—shaping,
sculpturing, rolling it around like clay in a potter's hand—and
then takes a good look at it to see what it is!

(2) Faith *firms it up.* The idea becomes solid; the potential
appears realistic. The idea has been formed; now it will be
firmed up! You'll make the commitment. You're going to go
for it.

(3) Faith *farms it.* Faith has formed it, firmed it, now it
farms it! This means you give your attention to developing
the new growth to full fruit-bearing maturity!

(4) Finally faith *frames it!* The harvest comes. You are successful. You put the award on the wall and accept the compliments. Do not deprive yourself of the joy of feeling proud over
an achievement made possible by the grace of God! Now you
look forward to greater achievements, greater successes and
greater accomplishments, because you're walking the walk of
faith!

**So long as you keep moving forward in the realm of
this faith you can expect to accumulate more victories, more awards to frame and hang on the wall!**

Thank You, Father, for calling me to such an exciting way of
living! Amen.

Relying on your source

"And my God shall supply all your need
according to His riches in glory by Christ
Jesus."—PHILIPPIANS 4:19

240 She sat at the breakfast table this morning. I don't know her
name. She was obviously blind, but she relied in trust on her
companion, who read the menu to her. Gracefully, politely,
with an elegant charm, her fingers found the utensils and the
napkin. She ate her intricate breakfast without an accident. I
was proud of her!

Faith is trusting the sources that we will never see.

We take the doctor's prescription to be filled by the pharma-
cist. Then we take it home and follow the directions, consume the drugs, trusting and relying on the doctor and the
druggist—including those who produced the ingredients before they were mixed and bottled for our consumption.

We listen to a believer in the Christian faith give a testi-
mony. If there is no reason to doubt a sincere confession of
faith, we will believe the witness.

Over five hundred Christians saw the resurrected Christ at
one time! Several others testified to seeing our Lord following
His crucifixion and burial. We believe in the resurrection of
Jesus Christ because we are relying on the sources.

Can we believe the Bible to be the Word of God even
though it has been copied and recopied through the centuries? Yet its marvelous miracle power of generating and
sustaining life transforming faith is obvious. There is power
in the Holy Book. Can we believe that God is morally obli-
gated to reveal Himself to us? Yes, God owes it to us. He has
"put it in writing"! If not the Bible—then what?

And where does our faith itself come from? Beyond the
Holy Scriptures does it not come from our positive observa-
tion of life around us? Can we not sense that there is a
Source beyond ourselves? Rely on God.

FAITH IS . . .
Exposing your colors

"And whoever believes on Him will not be put
to shame."—ROMANS 9:33

Faith isn't faith unless it makes a commitment in the face **241**
of possible ridicule and rejection.

Do you dare to expose your belief?

Is it possible that you have not publicly declared yourself to
be an enthusiastic believer because it might prove embarrassing in your business or social circle? Do you want to be all
things to all people? Are you a fence-straddler? Or is it because you sincerely are afraid of making a mistake? You really
want to make the right move but you can't be sure. What if
faith is all wrong? Is this why some of your friends claim to be
agnostic? Perhaps you are one. Then listen carefully.

When it comes to faith, there are only two choices:

(1) To choose to believe that *there is a God,* that in this
unlimited universe, there is an Intelligence! It is *Good!* It is
God!

(2) The other choice is to be an atheist, a believer in
nothing!

The third possibility is really not a choice, for an agnostic is
one who *refuses* to choose.

No one can be positive that he is right. But one thing is
sure, either the believer *or* the atheist is right. Certainly the
agnostic is wrong, for he has avoided choice altogether!

> **How do we make right choices? By following the in-
> stinct of faith, not the compulsion to fear.**

The play-it-safe agnostics are not the ones who are leading
the world upward and onward. It is the dreamers who are the
uplifting source of society!

FAITH IS . . .
Choosing the best option

"A good name is to be chosen rather than great riches,/loving favor rather than silver and gold."—PROVERBS 22:1

242   If I can create a verb to be a synonym for "possibility thinking," it is the word *optionalizing.* For when you examine all of the possibilities, you actually are listing all of the options. You are "optionalizing"! It starts when you consider your first option: to be a believer or an unbeliever.

Once you and I choose to walk the walk of faith, we will continually encounter those intersections where the road ahead separates, and we need to ask the question: "Which road do I take now?" Then you need to "optionalize." Ask: "Where do I want to go?" and "Which road will take me there?" Be careful what you choose.

The Bible text today gives guidance for choosing the best option: "A good name is to be chosen rather than great riches."

George Beverly Shea was a young man with his heart set on a great career that could bring him fame and fortune. His mother was concerned for him. One day as he went to practice, he found a poem placed by his mother on his piano. The poem was entitled, "I'd rather have Jesus," now a well-known religious song.

After reading the words George Beverly Shea dedicated his talent totally and completely to Jesus Christ. The result? His singing has led untold tens of thousands of people to Jesus Christ.

Today you have many choices to make. Some of them will be small and some may affect your entire future. Choose carefully. Choose prayerfully.

Opting for the optimum

"Now may the God of hope fill you with all joy
and peace in believing, that you may abound in
hope by the power of the Holy Spirit."—
ROMANS 15:13

Yesterday we created the word *optionalizing*. Today let's **243**
learn more about *opting*—the beautiful verb that comes from
the same root as the noun *options*. Faith is choosing the best
option. It opts for the optimum. It selects the wisest alternative from a noble value system.

"You mean they are getting married—again—to each
other?" The news sent shock waves through the social circle.
They had divorced nearly three years before and neither had
remarried. Someone commented, "Remarriage after divorce.
That's real faith."

I counseled with them before I reunited them in marriage.
They explained: "We simply didn't have the right foundation
for our relationship. We didn't have a religious faith or value
system. Now both of us are Christians. We have a more mature attitude toward each other and toward life.

"Meanwhile we've considered our options. We've thought
about them very carefully. Neither of us chooses to grow old
without anybody; that's a road that leads to loneliness. We
have chosen the option of genuinely forgiving each other and
loving each other with our mistakes."

Why settle for anything less than the best possible alternative? Faith opts for the optimum. It opts for the very *best* possible alternative, and it believes that the best alternative is
possible!

**Settle for nothing less than best! Philosophically, re-
ligiously, psychologically, that means you go with
Jesus Christ. No person that I've ever met claims to
surpass Him in faith, love, and courage!**

Harmonizing your inner self

"The LORD your God in your midst, the Mighty
One, will save; He will rejoice over you with
gladness, He will quiet you in His love, He will
rejoice over you with singing."—ZEPHANIAH
3:17

244   Let's stop to think today about the many different people
who live inside you.
• There is the brave one.
• There is the cautious one.
• There is the dashing, daring adventurer. (Yes, there really
  is—even if you haven't met him or her!)
• There is the saint who would be hcly.
• There is the sinner who would indulge in the lusts of the
  flesh.
• There is a person who would move forward ambitiously.
• And there is another person who would seek the easy way
  out.
We experience wholeness when we achieve harmony within
ourselves. Imagine that several persons that live within each of
us are like spokes in a wheel. A rim and a hub hold the spokes
together. Without them, the spokes would collide and clash.

**Christ is the hub of the wheel. He is the power that
integrates our life until we achieve an inner harmony.
Our Christian faith is the rim.**

Is there a power struggle in your soul today? Between good
and evil? Between the positive and the negative? Between the
Lord and the forces of Satan? Faith is letting Jesus Christ har-
monize your inner self.

Thank You, Jesus Christ, that You are able to take command and settle the internal power struggles within me.
Through Your Spirit now, I feel an inner harmony. And it is
beautiful. Amen.

Sacrificing your arrogance

"Whoever humbles himself as this little child is
the greatest in the kingdom of heaven."—
MATTHEW 18:4

Humility. What is it? It's the opposite of arrogance. What is **245**
arrogance?
- Arrogance assumes that because you can't imagine how
  something can be done, you can declare without reservation that it's impossible!
- Arrogance does all the talking and none of the listening.
- Arrogance rejects advice, simply because someone else
  said it or because your mind is already made up or you
  don't want anybody else to get the credit.
- Arrogance is refusal to accept help unless you've earned
  it, and inability to accept a compliment when you have
  earned it.
- Arrogance stubbornly refuses to change a mind when it
  knows it is wrong.
- Arrogance is the opposite of faith.
- Arrogance spouts off without reservation: "There is no
  heaven. There is no hell."
- Arrogance is an unwillingness to consider the possibility
  of making the 360-degree turn in your life that will allow
  Jesus Christ to come into your life, converting you into an
  authentic Christian.

> **Faith sacrifices your arrogance on the altar of authen-
> tic humility.**

What a change it will make in your life! You'll be left with a
confidence that's been purged of cockiness. It's easy to see
why this kind of faith moves mountains and leads to genuine
prosperity.
"Whoever humbles himself as this little child is the greatest
in the kingdom of heaven." That's God's promise to us today!

Admitting your inadequacies

"Whom have I . . . but You?/. . . My flesh and
my heart fail;/But God is the strength of my
heart and my portion forever."—PSALM 73:25

246   Only the people who have a strong faith in themselves, in
their God, and in their best friends dare to admit their shortcomings.

As you continue in the process of positively programming
your mind, and ridding it of conscious and subconscious negative thoughts, it is important to admit your inadequacies.
That is an act of faith, too!

Once you have enough faith to admit your inadequacies you
experience incredible liberation! From that time on, you develop an immunity to hypocrisy.

The word *hypocrisy* is bantered around irresponsibly today.
Hypocrisy is not the human frailty that keeps you from practicing what you preach. Hypocrisy is not the failure to live up
to your own ideals.

Hypocrisy is pretending to be perfect, and in the process,
imposing a sense of judgment and guilt on those around you.
Hypocrisy is giving everybody the verbal assurance that *you*
are living up to your own standards, when you really are not!

**Christians aren't perfect. We know where we must go
for forgiveness!**

Therefore, go to God, on an hourly basis! Your flesh and
heart may fail, but God never gives up on you! That's why you
can dare to be open and honest.

Dear God, I thank You that Your adequacy atones for my
inadequacies. I thank You that Your strength takes over where
my weakness begins. I thank You that Your forgiveness is sufficient for my sins. Thank You, Lord. Amen.

Waving at a mystery

"How precious also are Your thoughts to me, O God!/How great is the sum of them!/If I should count them, they would be more in number than the sand;/When I awake, I am still with You."—PSALM 139:17–18

The walk of faith is a command to march straight into a mystery!

247

The Christian faith is based on facts and mysteries. There are several facts upon which our faith is built. It is a fact that Jesus lived. It is a fact that He died. We *accept* His Resurrection as fact. But the Resurrection *remains* a *mystery.* How did it happen? How can it possibly have happened? It's a mystery. Is He alive today? We believe He is.

That's why we call our religion faith, not science. For faith is waving at a mystery!

Faith assumes that the unknown, the mystery, is not a hostile element but a kind providence!

"How can you believe in God?" I once asked Viktor Frankl in a long wide-ranging conversation in my office. I'll never forget his answer.

"I see living as being an actor on stage. The house lights are off; since I am blinded by a bright spotlight, I cannot see the audience. Nevertheless, I will give them my best performance. The mysterious darkness keeps me from seeing and fearing what I am facing. Then, when the curtains drops, I hear the applause. The house lights come on and the curtain rises. There they are—my friends!"

So it is with God. He is there, in the darkness, watching me perform. I cannot see Him, yet I know that He is urging me onward and motivating me to do my best.

FAITH IS . . .
Surmising with the soul

"I am the LORD . . . there is no God beside Me.
I will gird you, though you have not known
Me. . . . I am the LORD, and there is no
other."—ISAIAH 45:5–7

248   What synonyms can you give for the word *faith?* George
Santayana, the poet and philosopher, used a word I like very
much. It is the word *surmise.*

> O, World, thou choosest not the better part!
> It is not wisdom to be only wise,
> And on the inward vision close the eyes,
> But it is wisdom to believe the heart.
> Columbus found a world, and had no chart,
> Save one that faith deciphered in the skies;
> To trust the soul's invincible surmise
> Was all his science and his only art.*

Faith is applying positive thinking to solve problems, spot
opportunities, and make decisions. Somehow you "surmise"
that there is a universal principle that could unlock the problem you're wrestling with.

It's strange, mysterious, marvelous, yes, miraculous how
faith operates in your daily life. Once you turn your thinking
in the direction of an "invincible surmise," you begin to imag-
ine breakthroughs. You begin to think
- "It might be possible *if* . . ."
- "It could be possible *when* . . ."
- "It might be possible *after* . . ."
- "It might be possible *in conjunction with* . . ."
- "It might be possible *for God* . . ."
- "It might be possible *but* . . ."
- "It might be possible *so* I'll keep on surmising—and I'll
  soon be surprising."

---

*John Bartlett, *Familiar Quotations*, Boston: Little, Brown and Co., "O, World,
Thou Choosest Not" (1894), George Santayana.

FAITH IS . . .
Preempting the negatives

"[God] who is in you is greater than he who is in the world."—1 JOHN 4:4

What does it mean to "preempt"?

Imagine a party happening in a ballroom. Suddenly the President enters! Every eye turns on him. That's what you call "preempting the scene"!

Imagine a starry night in the desert. The Milky Way is spectacular. The Big Dipper can be seen clearly. Then, suddenly, above the horizon comes a full harvest moon! That's called preempting.

When irritations and frustrations possess you, use your faith to rise above them! Come up with a bigger idea! That's called "preempting the negatives."

For example, consider jealousy. Jealous people are people who never learned how to use their faith to preempt negative thinking. I cannot recall ever being jealous of anyone in my life. I was so afraid I would be jealous of pastors with larger churches that I decided I'd go out and start my own church and pray that God would make it as large as He wanted it to be and as effective as He would like it to become.

I didn't realize I was actually using the preempting principle. It has served me well for many years1 I have no problem delegating important jobs and glamorous assignments to others—simply because I use the preempting principle.

When we spot bigger opportunities and carve out greater assignments for ourselves, thus meeting our needs for challenges, that's preempting a negative with a positive idea!

When you are tempted toward discouragement, defeat, or depression, simply think bigger! Upstage the negative thought with a new and exciting positive thought.

Call for a change of command within yourself. Power is shifting constantly in this political world. Let there be a power shift in your life. You call the shots! Replace the negative thoughts with the positive thoughts.

Here's to you! Your tough-minded faith is making a way!

Considering all possible resources

"In [Christ] are hidden all the treasures of
wisdom and knowlege."—COLOSSIANS 2:3

250   Mountain-moving faith is like a magic formula! There are
vital ingredients that make the recipe outstanding. Leave out
a single spiritual chemical, and you diminish the positive results proportionately.

One major ingredient in the walk of faith is *humility.* Big-
thinking people have an amazing capacity for humility. They
are humble enough to listen to advice from anybody who
makes sense!

A chief executive of one of America's top corporations was
approached by a janitor who said, "Sir, I've noticed you seem a
little on edge lately."

"Well, John," the executive replied, "if I am, it's because I'm
carrying an enormous load. Under the circumstances, I think I
have a right to be anxious."

As he turned his back to unlock his door, he heard the janitor say, "But, sir, if you believed in the God I believe in—you'd
be on *top* of the circumstances, not *under* them."

Stopped short by this sentence, but too proud to turn
around and acknowledge it, he walked into his office. He put
his head in his hands and prayed: "God, are You out there? Or
are You here? Have I been missing You all this time?" Then he
called the janitor in and asked him what church he went to.
The next Sunday the janitor took the executive as his guest to
church. And he became a believer!

Faith is willing to accept help from all sources. What pride
and prejudice might be holding you back from developing pro-
fessionally, personally, or spiritually?

**Be humble enough to take help from anybody. You'll
be surprised what God will open up for you!**

FAITH IS . . .
Repenting the positive way

"Repent therefore and be converted, that your
sins may be blotted out, so that times of
refreshing may come from the presence of the
LORD."—ACTS 3:19

Of the incredible assortment of religions in the world, why **251**
have I chosen Christianity? Because it is true. Because it deals
with the problems of sin, negativity, antisocial behavior, and
psychological aberrations in the most redemptive, positive
way possible! It forthrightly recognizes the reality of sin. It
does not try to explain it away, permitting us to keep indulging in lusts that deprive us or another person of our dignity.

> **Positive Christianity has at its heart a God who dem-
> onstrates perfect love. He loves us after He has seen us
> at our worst. That's forgiveness.**

And forgiveness requires repentance. Repentance obviously
includes regret, remorse, and a genuine sorrow for negative
behavior. But it is not self-condemnation. The word *repentance* is used to translate a Greek word, *metanoia*, meaning to
"turn around." Repentance means to change directions—set
new goals and establish new standards. Pick up on God's
dream for your life! (1.) Positive repentance recognizes doubt
as the real sin. So repentance is a decision to share faith. (2.) To
make daring decisions; to seek to fulfill God's plan for my life
regardless of the price!

Lord, forgive me for not having the faith to live the life I
should have lived. I am now ready to dream Your dreams, to
carry the cross, and to pay the price. I am going to live right,
think right, pray right, and do right! I am trusting You to give
me the power. Together, we shall succeed. Thank You, Lord.
Amen.

Converting to belief in God

"Most assuredly, I say to you, unless one is born
again, he cannot see the kingdom of God!"—
JOHN 3:3

252   It's good to review the realities we've discussed this far on
the walk of faith.

Reality #1: Real faith always leads to commitment.

Reality #2: Commitment always demands and results in
            conversion.

Reality #3: Conversion is the process of radical change.

Reality #4: The ultimate experience of faith is the process
            of making a commitment to believe in God
            and devoting your life to serving Him as He
            leads, encourages, and empowers.

**Faith's noblest move prompts a person to convert from
doubt to faith, from immorality to morality, from self-
aggrandizing behavior to unselfish and charitable conduct.**

Is it really possible for human beings to be born again? Does
human nature really change after the age of twenty-one? Is it
possible for a person's character to be turned around 360 degrees? The answer is yes!

Of course it's a miracle. Conversion happens by the grace of
God.

Conversion is the process of making an irreversible, no-
holds-barred commitment to believe in God and to walk according to the light of His Word. Have you been converted?
Let faith call you to make a complete surrender of your life to
the Lord Jesus Christ. Confess your sins to Him. Ask His forgiveness. Accept His cleansing.

Feel the rush of holy life coming into your soul. Do not be
afraid to announce to the world, "I am a Christian. I have been
born again!"

Thank You for the gift of saving faith, O God, my loving
Father. Amen.

Trusting a stranger

"Because you have seen Me, you have believed.
Blessed are those who have not seen and yet
have believed."—JOHN 20:29

Is it really possible to trust a stranger?

253

Well, that's what happens when two people marry, for you really don't know your mate until you live together through years of happiness and tears.

Even then, do you ever really know each other? For you are constantly changing and growing, aren't you?

I've been happily married to my wife for thirty-three years, yet I'm constantly amazed at how I have guessed her wrong many times. It is these surprises that keep our relationship from growing stale.

When you walk the walk of faith, you need to trust others. When you trust someone, you bring out the best in him or her. Even the worst person will manifest good qualities when another person trusts him or her.

But what happens when you try to trust people only to have them let you down? Guard yourself against the cynical reaction of the negative thinker: "I'll never trust anybody again." Such a decision is an invitation to a haunting hollowness and devastating loneliness.

Instead, place your trust in Jesus Christ. Trust Him—even though you may not understand who He is, where He is, or what He can do for you. Trust Him—even though He may yet be a holy Stranger to you.

Trust Him. He will draw greatness out of you that you never knew was there.

Dear Lord, there is so much I don't know about You. But I do believe You are the reflection of the eternal God and so I trust You to be my Friend. I ask You to be my closest Companion as I walk the walk of faith.

FAITH IS . . .
Going home after sinning

"My son was dead and is alive again; he was
lost and is found."—LUKE 15:24

254 There isn't a single one of us who will not fall short of our
own standards, stumble, and sin.

**A shameful act of sin is made worse by the negative
reaction it can set off within our lives.**

The danger is that we'll be too embarrassed to go back
again. Consider:

—the student who flunks out and never returns to the
classroom!

—the entrepreneur who suffers a business failure and never
starts another business!

—the church member who sins, drops out, and never goes
back to the fellowship again.

—the preacher who fails to practice what he preaches and
leaves the ministry.

—the hometown boy who hasn't made good and doesn't
dare return to his roots.

Think of the damage that happens in the life of a person
who lacks the faith to come home. But once he's returned in
honest confession, he no longer needs to run, hide, and avoid
certain people.

When you demonstrate an immense act of faith through
genuine repentence, you discover again the goodness of God.
Like the father who killed the fatted calf for the feast of his
returning son, so God embraces you with understanding affection!

O God, spare us from the temptation to choose the path of
fear. Give us the faith to face up to You, always believing and
trusting that You will understand, forgive, save, and welcome
us home again! Thank You, Father. Amen.

Returning to my spiritual homeland

"'Father, I have sinned against heaven and in
your sight, and am no longer worthy to be
called your son.' But the father said . . . 'Bring
out the best robe.'"—LUKE 15:21–22

We have seen that faith is a mark of mental and emotional **255**
health. We have seen that faith releases creative powers. Ag-
nosticism, atheism, cynicism, and negative thinking are the
abnormal mental activities of the soul that has wandered
away from God.

Faith, then, is the process of coming home again. It is a
returning to the God who created you in the very beginning,
when the cells creatively collided to cause life to spring forth
in the silent chambers of a woman's womb.

If you have a problem believing, if your faith stumbles and
falters, then you must ask the question: "What is separating
me from a loving friendship with God?"

Begin by checking your private life. Do you have some secret sins? Is there some conscious or subconscious guilt
within your life?

**It only takes a little bit of guilt to produce a large
amount of doubt.**

Doubt is the defense mechanism of a guilty person fabricated by an insecure, subconscious mind to protect itself
from belief in someone or something that could impose a
judgment on him.

Every time I've encountered an atheist or a boastful agnostic I challenged him, "Are you sure there is no sin in your life?
Are you positively sure there is absolutely no guilt within
your soul for deeds done or left undone?"

Faith comes when you return home again like the prodigal
son, begging God's forgiveness. You not only receive forgiveness but also the robe of real faith!

Confessing your sins

"Search me, O God, and know my heart/. . .
And see if there is any wicked way in me,/And
lead me in the way everlasting."—PSALM 139:23

256   The choice is so simple: choose to follow the voice of faith
or listen to the voice of fear. The path of faith always leads to
freedom and peace, whereas the path of fear always leads to
oppression and tension.

For example, consider the problem of your own sins and
shortcomings. The natural inclination is to hide from failure
and try to give the impression that you're perfect. You fear
that if your sins are exposed, you will be publicly rejected. The
enormous complexities of human behavior that are motivated
by a fear of exposure that might reveal imperfections makes
an interesting study!

- What mask do you wear?
- What misleading impressions do you try to leave behind
  you?
- What games do you play?
- How long do you think you can keep up the act?
- What will happen when the curtain is finally lifted?

Until you develop the faith that God forgives you when you
confess your sins, you will never be a truly honest, well-
integrated personality.

Confession is good for the soul. There's enormous healing
that happens in confession.

Alcoholics Anonymous has wisely recommended that healing will never come until a person finds at least one essential
friend. Find one person to whom you can confess your sins, to
whom you can open up all of your faults. Get the garbage out.

Jesus Christ is that kind of friend to me.

**Confession is an act of faith that begins enormous div-
idends of incredible peace of soul.**

Asking for forgiveness

"And forgive us our sins, for we also forgive
everyone who is indebted to us."—LUKE 11:4

To ask for forgiveness after you've confessed your sins is an **257** unsurpassed profession of faith.

You're at the mercy of the judge now.

You are without defense.

Can any act really reflect more faith than open and honest confession of sin and guilt?

Everything you are or could hope to be is on the line; for without forgiveness, integrity is impugned.

When you ask for forgiveness, you really ask for people to trust you again. You encourage them to once more see you as a wonderful human being.

I'm sure this is why Jesus Christ is so extremely effective with people around the world. He encourages everyone to come to Him and ask for forgiveness.

Jesus Christ has never failed once to forgive anyone who honestly and sincerely asked for forgiveness.

Jesus Christ has a 1000 percent record of keeping His word.

One of the classic translations of the petition of the Lord's Prayer uses the words "forgive us our debts" (Matt. 6:12).

That is what happens when Christ forgives you.

He pays the mortgage off.

He eliminates the moral and spiritual debt you added up against Him.

Your full line of credit is restored with Him.

Ask Jesus for forgiveness.

He promises to give it to you!

What an unsurpassed blessing!

How wise you were to decide to take this walk of faith!

Wiping the slate clean

"Create in me a clean heart, O God,/And renew a steadfast spirit within me."—PSALM 51:10

258   Once you start thinking, living, and moving by faith, you open an almost bottomless well of refreshing water.

Of all the blessings that come from living by faith, none is more valuable than salvation from guilt and sin.

The peace of soul that comes when you realize you are pardoned by God is the single most priceless gift you will ever receive!

We are promised in the Bible that "by grace, you have been saved through faith, and that not of yourselves; it is a gift of God." (Eph. 2:8) What could be better news than that?

Human beings sin, make errors, and fall short of *our* standards, to say nothing of the standards of a Holy God, who does not wish for us to perish in our sin.

God wants us to be His happy, helpful servants, spreading love and encouragement in the world. We are of little value as long as we carry a negative self-image. Now faith wipes the slate clean!

Wipe the slate of your own soul clean every night. How? Approach your Lord Jesus Christ with this simple prayer:

Jesus Christ, You have promised forgiveness of sins. I accept this offer. I can feel you wiping clean the blackboard of my soul. I go to sleep, knowing there is no guilt attached to my record.

I am exercising my faith by affirming and believing, by the grace of God, that I am declared to be a person made clean in heart and soul. Thank You, Jesus. Help me to be so grateful for my pardon that tomorrow I shall dare to dream great dreams and do a good work for You! Amen.

FAITH IS . . .
Forgetting your forgiven sins

"As far as the east is from the west,/So far has He [God] removed our transgressions from us."—PSALM 103:12

Faith is a spiritual force—the eternal God, moving in and through your life. Nothing blocks the fresh flow of God's spirit more than a sense of guilt. No human being is perfect. Everyone is infested with sin and exposed to it continuously. The glorious good news of the Christian faith is that God waits, moment by moment, to cleanse us of all guilt and to forgive us of every sin. **259**

When God forgives, He forgets.

When God buries the hatchet, He doesn't leave the handle above the ground.

Sin is any act that robs you of your God-given dignity. Shame is the first symptom that sin is operating in a life.

When God saves you from your sins, He totally and completely removes all shame and replaces it with a youthful sense of holiness and righteousness. You feel washed, cleansed inside and outside! It is now your job to forget the sins that God has forgiven. How?

No longer repeat self-denigrating confessions of sin. No longer practice destructive repentance by putting yourself down as a horrible sinner.

Jesus Christ died on the cross to save me from the penalty, the power, and the pollution of sin.

I walk the walk of faith by practicing mountain-moving faith as I affirm: Christ has forgiven me of every sin.

I am spiritually whole. God is flowing through my life with power again, for I am forgiven. My faith has fresh new power! Thank You, God.

Yielding yourself to God

"Do not let sin reign in your mortal body. . . .
but present yourselves to God."—ROMANS
6:12–13

260 Faith is crowning Christ as King of your life. It is accepting His imperial command over your thinking. It is acknowledging the lordship of Christ over your life. It is yielding the leadership of your life to the winds of the Holy Spirit—the way tender trees yield to the breeze.

It takes a lot of faith to surrender leadership to someone you have never touched, never talked to—except in prayer. On the twenty-two-acre campus of the Crystal Cathedral we have planted Italian cypress trees and Australian eucalyptus trees. Both were selected because they create a tranquilizing emotion in the landscaping plan.

Landscape architects recognize that there are two basic types of planting—dramatic and tranquilizing. Cactus plants are categorized as dramatic plantings. They stab the air; they rigidly resist the wind. They confront, from an "attack" position, nature around them.

By contrast, the tranquilizing landscape relaxes, yields to space, breeze, and gravity. The weeping willow, the coconut palm, the Italian cypress, and the eucalyptus tree all send out vibrations of tranquility. The tips of the tall eucalyptus and cypress trees reach upward as they sway every so delicately, sensitive to the slightest breeze. Then they bow gracefully and respectfully, bending to the wind. No wonder they survive storms that destroy rigid, brittle trees.

Yielding is surrendering. Surrendering is the ultimate act of faith. As the tips of the trees bend to the wind, so will you and I respond to the winds of the Spirit of God.

Faith is yielding yourself to God—to the higher Power, to the loving Presence of our precious Friend, to our loving Lord, to our gracious God.

Overcoming all fears

"God has not given us a spirit of fear, but of power and of love and of a sound mind."—2 TIMOTHY 1:7

When you and I have yielded ourselves to God, and He has wiped the slate clean, does this mean we will never face fear again? Of course not, but God's promise to the believer is that we *can* overcome all fear through the power of His love and faith.

Where does fear come from? Not from God! But from the source of all universal negativity—the devil. Philosophically we refer to this source as evil.

Neurotic fear that destroys your creative and constructive planning and productivity does not come from God! "God has not given us a spirit of fear" (2 Tim. 1:7); rather God empowers you with a healthy mind.

How do you overcome fear that encircles you? Read today's Bible verse over again and again. Draw close to God in prayer. Ask Him to possess you with His Spirit of

confidence,

courage,

conviction!

Under the leadership and lordship of Jesus Christ, command that negative thought, that destructive emotion, to get out of your life!

Call upon almighty God to fill your mind and mood with healthy thoughts, loving emotions, and powerful motivations. God will answer your prayer! You will overcome your fears! For God is more powerful than any negative thought.

Thank You, Father, for being so good to me. Thank You for coming into my life to remove all my fear. Thank You for filling me with this kind of faith.

Quieting the storm

"Then He arose and rebuked the wind, and said to the sea, 'Peace, be still.' And the wind ceased and there was a great calm."—MARK 4:39

262   One of the most beautiful stories ever written is the account of Christ's crossing the Sea of Galilee with His disciples.

Our Lord had gone to sleep in the boat.

Suddenly a storm arose.

The disciples were panic-stricken.

They awoke the Lord.

Christ stood, calmly faced the winds, extended His arms to the troubled sea, and with authority commanded the winds and the waves to subside. "Peace, be still."

Faith assures you that unexpected storms will subside if you take control over them!

Picture yourself standing under the cross of Jesus Christ, where the Savior died for your sins! Here He has paid the price to earn the right to pardon you completely and eternally from all guilt. Beneath the cross of Christ face all guilt within you and affirm, "My sins are forgiven! Peace be still!"

Now, from this position, face the storms of your sin and guilt, and command all negativity and evil to release you from their bondage in the name and by the authority of your Lord. "Peace, be still." Now picture yourself standing before the open tomb on Easter morning. The resurrected Christ, who walked out of the tomb leaving prints of wounded feet in the soft sand, now stands beside you. He promises to be with you always—even unto the end of the world. With Him beside you, you can face the storms of anxiety and worry about today and tomorrow with a quiet confidence. Now, command your fears to leave you with this divine benediction, "Peace, be still."

Peace of mind—deep, abiding, powerful, and pervasive—is yours when you accept Jesus Christ as your personal Lord and Savior.

Bonding a friendship

"I have loved you with an everlasting love;/
Therefore with lovingkindness I have drawn
you."—JEREMIAH 31:3

When my grandson, Christopher, was only ten months old I
traveled so much I had little time to become acquainted with
him. One day, to my surprise, I reached out my arms to him
and he stretched his arms to me. He invited me to pick him
up. He sat on my lap, turned, and looked to me with a most
trusting look.

263

Then came a beautiful moment when he peacefully rested
his left cheek against my right shoulder as if he was sleeping
in his own bed.

Suddenly he lifted his head, and looked up to see who was
holding him. His big wide eyes searched my face, with an "I
know-who-you-are" look.

He realized who I was! His mother interpreted and explained his look: "Dad, you know I edit and review the 'Hour
of Power' television program before it is aired across the country. Christopher often sits beside me as I work. He knows
yours is the face he has seen on television every day for most
of his life."

The child recognized me as someone familiar. In that moment a bonding was formed between a grandfather and grandson. It was wonderful.

**Faith brings you to a moment when suddenly you real-
ize you are on solid and safe ground with a Friend!**

Faith is bonding a friendship with Jesus Christ! Let this be
the day when you rest your eternal soul on His heart. He will
encircle you with His love and embrace you to give you eternal spiritual security. That's faith! That will make a difference—always and forever!

Ruling out disqualification

"My sheep hear My voice, and I know them, and they follow Me. And I give them eternal life, and they shall never perish; neither shall anyone snatch them out of My hand."—JOHN 10:27–28

264 When we walk the walk of faith we rule out the possibility of ever being declared disqualified in the spiritual race of successful living.

My daughter Carol is determined to become an award-winning skier in national competition even though she has had her left leg amputated. It is nothing short of divine inspiration to see how she disciplines her body to qualify for the competitions sponsored each year by the National Handicapped Sports and Recreation Association.

It took Carol two years to meet the rigid standards to qualify. I will never forget watching her participate at the Twelfth Annual National Ski Championships in Squaw Valley, California. We watched her win a gold medal in the downhill race and a silver in the giant slalom. Then the slalom race was announced. We were waiting for her to come down the hill when the announcement was made: "We have a DNF ('Did not finish') at the top of the hill: Carol Schuller." She did not qualify! There is enormous disappointment when you are disqualified.

When we are saved by faith, Christ redeems us. He doesn't put a short-term lease on our spiritual welfare! Christ saves us—forever!

He doesn't select us for His team only to disqualify us if, and when, we fail to live up to His holy standards. He has written our names in heaven's Book—in indelible ink! He has adopted us as His children—not just accepted us as "foster children" for a season!

He holds us and never lets us go! We may be tempted to let go of Him, but He will not let us ever be disqualified from the family of God!

Dear God, today I commit my life and soul to Jesus Christ. Forever and forever! Amen.

Trading off anxiety for peace

"Peace I leave with you, My peace I give to you;
not as the world gives do I give to you. Let not
your heart be troubled, neither let it be
afraid."—JOHN 14:27

Life is made of trade-offs.

265

When you started this pilgrimage called "the walk of faith,"
you traded off safety and security for stimulation and success.

When you accepted God's gift of salvation by grace through
faith, you traded off arrogance for faith.

When you made a commitment in marriage to love, honor,
and respect your husband or wife, you traded off freedom for
friendship.

When you decided to believe in the promises of God, you
traded off anxiety for peace.

> **Worry doesn't bring happiness. Stress only brings ill
> health, and anxiety robs us of peace of mind.**

So today let's trade off anxiety for peace. Give yourself a
therapeutic meditation.

Picture yourself on a lonely and isolated island.

A long stretch of beach rolls out before you like silver carpet.

Now you see the only other living person on this island.

He is walking toward you.

Suddenly you recognize who He is! He is Jesus Christ.

He walks with strong, swift strides toward you.

He is opening His arms, throwing His head back, His hair
blowing in the wind.

His suntanned face breaks into a wide welcoming smile.

His greeting is strong.

"Peace I leave with you, My peace I give to you; not as the
world gives do I give to you. Let not your heart be troubled,
neither let it be afraid."

You respond to His appealing and attractive greeting.

You embrace as friends forever!

You have just made one of life's wisest trades:

His peace—for your anxiety.

Displaying the flag

"For I am not ashamed of the gospel of Christ, for it is the power of God to salvation for everyone who believes." —ROMANS 1:16

266 I saw a little fellow in the grocery store, who proudly wore a Los Angeles Dodgers baseball cap. At the time, the Dodgers were on a miserable losing streak. I went up to the little fellow and said, "So you're a Dodger fan, right?"

He smiled back and said, "You bet! And they're going to win the pennant!"

It doesn't take much faith to wear the cap and publicly declare yourself a strong supporter of the winning team. But when they have one setback after another, then it is a beautiful demonstration of confidence to stand in the limelight and reaffirm your trust in them.

I've always admired a certain courage in the political activist who is the first to fly the flag and flash the bumper sticker of the candidate whose campaign is just being launched.

Can we begin to imagine what it meant for those first twelve apostles to publicly declare their love and loyalty for that young, unknown religious leader called Jesus of Nazareth? When Christ was betrayed, and marched off carrying His own cross to a public execution, the apostles were nowhere to be found.

It was not until after our Lord was raised from the dead that this itinerant band of apostles became inflamed with an all-consuming faith in the divine Person and mission of our Lord.

Can you find any person who offers more than Jesus does?

To the lonely, He is a Friend; to the sinful, a Savior; to the dying, the promised Guide across the troubled waters; to the enslaved, the Power to be free again.

Offer your life to Jesus Christ today. Volunteer your services to the campaign headquarters. Dare to be known as one of His friends. Display the flag of belief.

FAITH IS . . .
Going out without looking in a mirror

". . . glorify God in your body and in your spirit, which are God's."—CORINTHIANS 6:20

What well-dressed person dares to step out into the public limelight without checking himself in the mirror? Have you ever been in a position where you had to do that? I have. I blindly fingered my tie: "Is it adjusted correctly?" With that, I marched onto the center of the stage into the spotlight to deliver the lecture.

What do I really mean when I say, "Faith is going out without looking in a mirror"? To begin with I'm not condoning the crude, unclean lifestyle of socially rebellious persons. There are those anti-social reactionaries who dress to attract attention, "make a statement," or provoke an argument. The person who takes the attitude, "I don't care what people think," is surely not making a constructive Christian statement! Certainly he's headed for failure and trouble.

What does matter profoundly, however, is an awareness that my success and self-esteem are rooted in my positive attitude more than in my style of dress. My hope for social acceptance and personal success depends more on the moral and spiritual values my life style reflects than upon the "label" clothing I wear.

In the final analysis you must believe that you will be judged by character, more than clothing or connections. And that self-confidence will make you a very persuasive personality on the road to success.

For when you walk by faith you develop profound moral integrity which is reflected in your face.

I can go out today without checking the mirror if my heart is right, for I am following the lordship and leadership of Christ Jesus.

Sustaining your self-esteem

"Cast your burden on the LORD,/And He shall sustain you;/He shall never permit the righteous to be moved."—PSALM 55:22

268 Wouldn't it be wonderful if you were perfect! How do you judge between the better and the best? How do you keep the lesser human value from taking priority over the higher human value?

Faith moves in to act as referee, blowing the whistle and calling you to attention with the command: "You can do better than that! Start over again and be great!"

When you drop the ball, lose the game, and head for the locker room with humiliation, then faith becomes your coach, who slaps you on the back, turns you around, and barks out tough encouragement, "Come on, now. You can't win them all! You're great—anyway! Don't be so hard on yourself!"

Faith is the referee; faith is the coach, and faith has become your best friend who goads you on when you want to take the easy way.

Now you know why the walk of faith is so beautiful and effective. It's a lifestyle that sustains your own self-respect. You are learning to say yes to challenges that lift your dignity, and no to negative involvements that degrade yourself and others.

Today's affirmations:

I have become a more beautiful person because I have chosen to live by faith. Through the positive attitude that my faith gives me, I find it easier to make friends. I am not as lonely as I used to be. Through my belief in a beautiful God, I am opening up like a flower. Because of my positive self-esteem, I am attracted to good people and good people are attracted to me. As faith sustains my self-esteem, I become a wonderful person.

Jesus Christ, I have to thank You for being at the heart of my faith. Faith has become a friend with a face; it is the face of my Lord, and I love You. Amen.

FAITH IS . . .
Broadcasting good news

"Behold, I bring you good tidings of great joy which will be to all people."—LUKE 2:10

The secret of happy living is to give yourself all the good news you can, as often as you can! Start the day by reporting all of the positive events that have happened since you awoke.

269

Faith is broadcasting good news to yourself: *I am alive!* I survived the night. I did not die in my sleep. I have been given—free of charge—the gift of another day, fresh and clean. It affords me wonderful and marvelous opportunities to think, plan, execute, advance, build, love, and enjoy.

Tune your mental dial into radio station TGNT.

There's **G**ood **N**ews **T**oday!

Scan the papers for good news. Believe it or not, you might have to begin on the sports page, the women's page, or the entertainment section.

If you can't report good news, then make your own good news. That's called "living" the gospel. For the word *gospel* literally means "good news."

The good news you, as a Christian, can report is that God lives!

- He came to this world in the person of Jesus to tell us that He loves us.
- He died on a cross to save us from our sins.
- He promises to live in our hearts through the Holy Spirit.
- He will do this by giving us ideas, dreams, and opportunities.

> **Give yourself this good news—right now—"God has a plan for my life today!" I'm going to be open to wonderful things that are about to happen. I will be optimistic, pleasant, cheerful, and hopeful today!**

FAITH IS . . .
Forming a partnership

"Abide in Me, and I in you. As the branch
cannot bear fruit of itself . . . neither can you,
unless you abide in Me."—JOHN 15:4

270 What happens when we become Christians? We have formed a holy partnership. You will now live a more productive life. In the final analysis God wants us to choose the path of faith that will maximize our productivity.

Who has more faith— the person who is confident he can make it all by himself or the person who shares the power, the credit, the risks, and the rewards with a partner?

Both avenues require great faith.

Life requires different styles for different miles.

On part of the road you may be challenged and tempted to travel alone—challenged, because you can't find the help you need; or tempted, because you enjoy and relish the freedom of operating as an independent entrepreneur.

Forming a partnership will restrict your freedom—to some degree. To trade off greater productivity for more privacy may be tempting, but it's a bad deal!

There is an interesting story in the New Testament where Jesus Christ noticed the solitary fig tree, resplendent in luxuriant leaves. There was no fruit—only leaves. And our Lord cursed the tree.

What's the point of it all? Style without substance is shallow, show without service is sinful; freedom without fruitfulness is folly.

In a world where so many people are hungry there's no excuse for luxuriating in selfish solitude.

It gets down to this: "Can I accomplish a great deal more in my lifetime if I am willing to limit my freedom, restrict my privacy, swallow some pride, and take on a partner?" Yes, certainly, if the partner is my Lord Jesus Christ.

FAITH IS . . .
Linking up with winners

"'If you abide in Me, and My words abide in
you, you will ask what you desire, and it shall
be done for you.'"—JOHN 15:7

Faith links up with winners. Doubt links up with losers. **271**
What trumpet do you respond to? What drum do you follow?

Faith links up with a Winner—Jesus Christ.

What is *your* relationship with Him? Do you link up with
Him in prayer? Through the Bible? Through His Holy Spirit,
who can give you high and holy thoughts?

Faith links up with other *winners*—positive people who
walk the walk of faith with you.

A family I know moved, in desperation, to California from
New Jersey because their sixteen-year-old daughter was being
influenced by the wrong kind of friends in school. No sooner
did they reach California than she found the same kind of
friends there. Why? Because she had such a negative self-image that she was attracted to losers. She felt successful according to their standards.

The family began attending our church, and we joyously
watched this young teen-ager accept Jesus Christ as her Savior. When that happened, her new Christian friends became
her closest friends. Most of them were diligent in school and
had high moral and spiritual standards. Now that she was in a
new circle and had a new faith, she found that the new linkage
changed everything!

I can't recommend anything stronger to you today than
this:

Link up with a good church.

Visit the churches in your community until you find a fellowship of believers that feeds your faith.

Join the only club that is committed to sharing the love of
Jesus Christ for the building up of human character.

Aligning yourself with positive people

". . . that I may be encouraged together with
you by the mutual faith."—ROMANS 1:12

272   Faith is fantastic! The positive fruits and by-products that
will spring up in our lives as we walk this walk of faith are too
numerous to count. Yet, let's examine just one of the assets of
this risky business called faith. When you make the decision
to become a believer, you put yourself in the company of brave
people, the possibility thinkers. That carries an immediate reward. Every time you make a new commitment, you meet
new friends. You have the joy of the company of people who
laugh, sing, pray, and are generally enthusiastic.

Faith is aligning yourself with the up-and-comers.

The believer is drawn into the circle of eagles when the
doubter is siding with the lame-duck crowd. The insecure person who hesitates to make the plunge finds himself in the
company of shrinking violets and withering flowers. The price
he pays for his security is a creeping awareness that life is
passing him by.

Today reaffirm your commitment to be a believer! Don't
miss the chance at excitement in life.

There is a train pulling out of the station. On it I see people
who are laughing, excited, and enthusiastic. I'm going to jump
on board with them—now! I'm joining the crowd of positive
people who are going places and doing great things.

I choose to be a believer. I am parting company with the
losers. Thank You for leading the way, Jesus Christ. I am aligning myself with the up-and-comers. I feel an aliveness with
me now. Is this Your presence, Lord? This keen and energizing
vibrancy within me? Thank You, Lord!

Combining contradictions creatively

"According to your faith, let it be to you."—
MATTHEW 9:29

Possibility thinkers who walk this walk of faith are success- **273**
ful because they have learned yet another principle:

Contradictions that creatively clash often open a treasure box of undiscovered values.

Designers, architects, musicians, and chefs sometimes combine contradictions creatively. They creatively use colors and materials that at first seem to clash to bring about amazing beauty. Chefs do this with sweet and sour sauce.

On our church grounds we have a statue of Jesus. The right hand is open, inviting, offering food to hungry sheep, making a statement of tenderness! The left hand and the strong, muscular forearm hold a staff: a statement of toughness. Tough and tender—contradictions? Yes, but combined creatively they are beautifully harmonious.

How often have we heard the questions asked about a couple: "What can those two have in common? What holds their relationship together?"

In many ways the personalities and lifestyles of a couple can seem to contradict each other. Yet their relationship combines the contradictions creatively and the combination works!

Take a look at a church and you will find a judge and an ex-convict, a sinner and a saint, rich and poor, working and worshiping together creatively.

Can God bring good out of evil? Can He combine tragedy and triumph and produce something inspiring? Of course, He can!

Finally, take a look at your own life. Everybody has some internalized contradictions. When we walk the walk of faith and give Christ lordship over our life, He is able to take these contradictions and combine them creatively.

Drinking from new wells

"If anyone thirsts, let him come to Me and drink."—JOHN 7:37

274 Jesus Christ promises in this Bible verse that, when you connect with Him and become an authentic Christian, your faith will never suffer from thirst.

Your faith may falter and grow faint, but it shall never fail unless you refuse to replenish it with a refreshing drink from the Source, the Lord Jesus Christ.

One Sunday morning I was in a strange city. I was spiritually thirsty. I waited expectantly for my own television program to come on the air. I knew I could relax, enjoy the music, see familiar faces, and join in worship. I expected a blessing. But when the program came on and I began listening, I became self-critical. I thought, *Schuller, you can do better than that!* When the program was over, I was disappointed.

Another religious television program with which I was unfamiliar came on. The style of worship was completely opposite to mine. Yet I found myself lifted to God in a spiritually satisfying experience. God used the voice of an unknown minister to meet my spiritual need.

Still another religious television program followed, and again the voice and the personality were most dissimilar to my own. Within a few moments, two Bible verses were quoted that gave me the upward thrust my faith needed that morning.

I prayed, "God, what are You trying to tell me?" I waited and listened. Within my being this truth came as a message from my heavenly Father: "Schuller, you will never be alone; you will never be thirsty, *if you are willing to drink from new wells.*"

Thank You, Father. I now know I have a faith that will never die.

Perceiving the worlds around you

"The appearance . . . as it were, a wheel in the middle of a wheel."—EZEKIEL 1:16

It is important to be lifted by your faith to a level of self-reliance where you will be able to recognize, observe, and appreciate the varied worlds around you this very moment. **275**

Today's Bible text tells that the prophet Ezekiel looked up and saw wheels within wheels. We need only to read the newspaper to be aware of wheels within wheels and worlds within our world: the sports world, the entertainment world, the business world, the women's world.

New York City points up the worlds within the world. There are people on the East Side of New York who never get to the West Side!

Do you know how many worlds are around you?

Do you dare to explore, to become an adventurer, to take a trip to a foreign country, or to even get into a taxi and check out your own neighborhood? It takes a lot of faith to choose to become perceptive!

Dare to step out of your own small world to see how the other side lives.

At the same time begin a wonderful ministry of Christian charity, leaving behind a witness to another world—somebody cared enough to pay a visit!

That's what Jesus did when He left one world—heaven—and came to another—earth. Jesus knows a lot more heaven and earth than you or I. He specifically came to earth to tell us about the world called heaven. Someday you will want to go there, too. Have the faith to step into that world by affirming Christ today.

Adapting yourself to the unfamiliar

"May the Lord make you increase and abound in love to one another and to all."—1 THESSALONIANS 3:12

276 It is a natural experience for everyone to suffer from an inferiority complex during certain times or circumstances of life. Our goal is to have an adequate supply of faith in ourselves and in our ability to meet any situation in life. Each of us may feel very secure in our own home or community, but when we suddenly are put into unfamiliar surroundings, we can easily become frightened.

Faith is adapting yourself to the unfamiliar, even when the cultural environment is dramatically different—clothes, language, skin color, food. Faith says you are adaptable!

It is remarkable to see how the Christian faith bridges cultural gaps. Long before international jet-setters arrived on the scene, missionaries crossed oceans to step ashore on strange continents. They had the faith to leap into an unfamiliar and sometimes hostile culture. Through the eyes of our Lord, they saw deeper than the skin. They looked upon every person as a precious, priceless immortal soul, redeemable by God.

If we ever become afraid and threatened by the unfamiliar, we can be sure we are facing an area of life where our faith is proving inadequate. It simply means this is an opportunity to grow!

Christ Jesus, thank You for helping me to see every person as a soul for whom You died on the cross. Give me the faith today to adapt myself to the unfamiliar, so that I can be Your hands and Your heart, loving them. Amen.

Relating respectfully to "foreigners"

"One God and Father of all, who is above all,
and through all, and in you all."—EPHESIANS 4:6

Faith is relating respectfully to those whose skin is a different color, whose eyes are shaped differently, and whose language and dress are different. Faith respects all people, for
God's family transcends race, language, and culture. In Christ
there is no east or west.

277

How do you relate to "foreigners" with whom you make
contact—such foreigners as a foreign idea; contrary ideology;
or an unheard-of concept? Are you so set in your ways that
you refuse to listen to peculiar ideas?

Faith believes you grow intellectually when you understand
and respect someone else's position.

Possibility-thinking people are people who achieve enough
emotional maturity to view objectively foreign:

- persons
- ideas
- races
- foods
- dress
- music
- religion
- language

They are secure enough in their belief system to listen to a
contrary presentation without becoming frightened or furi-
ous.

It takes a lot of faith to relate.

Dear God, give me enough security in my faith to relate to
all people without being disrespectful, unkind, or frightened
by what may seem foreign. I thank You that through faith I
have confidence to communicate Your love with those who
don't share our faith. I thank You that I belong to Your family,
where there are no boundaries and no foreigners. In You we
are all one. By the way, Lord, I'm enjoying our relationship on
this walk of faith. Thank You for planning it that way. Amen.

Discriminating against prejudices!

"[Love] does not rejoice in iniquity, but rejoices in the truth!"—1 CORINTHIANS 13:6

278 Think of this: People who are prejudiced display a lack of faith. Somehow they cannot believe that persons of another faith, race, or ethnic group really are as good as they are. Prejudice, such as racism, provokes enormous hatred. And what is hate? It is the fruit of fear. Angry people are persons who feel threatened. And people who are insecure or easily threatened are people who lack faith in themselves and others.

You are really walking the walk of faith, when you discriminate against prejudice. Discrimination can be a positive mental attitude when it focuses on the elimination of negatives from life.

Learn to sort the good from the bad,
the positives from the negatives,
the enobling from the shameful,
the excellent from the mediocre,
the right from wrong!
the beautiful from the ugly,
the kind acts from the unfair,
the Christ-like from the crude.

Discriminate against prejudice. This is the most intelligent choice, for prejudice ignores the pursuit of truth.

The person who walks the walk of faith will ultimately succeed, for he not only dares to face truth, he seeks truth.

God's promise is that faith will move mountains. So, as faith discriminates, eliminates, and eradicates presumptuous judgments of issues and individuals, it throws open the door for illumination of new insights and new truths. In the process, growth occurs, and you are on the way to moving mountains.

Disengaging yourself from destructive prejudices

"For there is no partiality with God."—ROMANS 2:11

Is any person really free from destructive prejudices? I don't **279** believe I am. I'm doing some real soul-searching as I write these words.

Prejudice is always destructive, for it blocks my capacity to understand another person's position. It keeps me imprisoned in a distortion of the truth.

Today, let us all honestly ask ourselves: Is there any active or latent racial prejudice in my life today? Am I guilty of religious prejudice? Am I prejudiced against those who are financially superior or inferior to me?

How can you be freed from the prison of prejudice? First of all, believe that God wants to build bridges—not throw up barriers! He is interested in creating a sense of family among us human beings on planet earth. A spirit of community must replace the spirit of conflict.

If I ask God to heal me of my prejudices, He will surely do it, "for there is no partiality with God." He does not see the differences that you and I see.

God does not see people as rich or poor. He does not see the color of our skin! He is not impressed with our academic credentials.

At the feet of God, we are all the same—sinners saved by grace, potential saints in the making!

God's saving grace alone can break the chains of prejudice that bind us.

Thank You, Father, that You are disengaging me now, releasing me this very moment, liberating me in this time of prayer from prejudices, known and unknown. Thank You, God. Amen.

FAITH IS . . .
Tearing down the walls

"The rich and poor have this in common, the
LORD is the maker of them all."—PROVERBS
22:2

280

"All my life I was told I couldn't do it," the letter read. She
went on, "My father was never successful. My mother was
poor. We never had money for anything other than the basic
necessities of bread and food. Even then, we only had a meal
with meat probably once a week.

" 'You've just got to remember that we're poor. We can't do
it. The answer is no. You just have to learn to accept your
place in life.' These were the responses I heard each time I
wanted to do something different or new.

"When I wanted to go to college, again my folks said to me,
'We don't have the money. Where do you think you're going to
get the money?' Then, a scolding voice, 'Get out and work. It's
time to buy your own clothes. College is for rich kids.'

"I kind of felt like I was herded into a negative box that was
put inside a small backyard where the walls were so high I was
never allowed to dream my dreams.

"Then I started listening to the 'Hour of Power.' I heard the
minister talk about possibility thinking.

"I heard him say that every human being has the same
right—to dream great dreams! I heard the minister say that
nobody has a money problem. It is always an idea problem. I
heard that possibility thinking teaches that we can get out of
our own prison of self-imposed limitations.

"I felt free for the first time in my life! I realized that God
made me just as good as the rich kids.

"Dr. Schuller," the letter went on, "I want you to know that I
got the faith five years ago, and today I got my college degree!
I'm going to become a school teacher and inspire kids in poor
communities to dream big! They can do anything they want
to do!"

Possibility-thinking faith tears down the walls! Impossibility thinking builds the walls.

Inquiring into scientific reality

"For You will light my lamp;/The LORD my God will enlighten my darkness."—PSALM 18:28

281

Of all of the prejudices that Christians need to attack, none is more important than the prejudice against scientific inquiry. On the other hand, scientific inquiry also requires discrimination against prejudice.

Unquestionably there are scientists who prejudge religious truth negatively and approach their scientific research with a presumption that there is no spiritual reality. In the process they flaunt truth in the name of brilliant analysis. What a contradiction!

It is to the credit of Christianity that we have great universities. Scientific inquiry has found tremendous support from the Christian religion. Our compassion for suffering souls has motivated Christians to support research into the cures for many major diseases.

Great universities like Princeton, Harvard, Yale, Stanford, and the University of Southern California—to name a few— are universities that were started by Christians committed to the pursuit of truth.

Science and religion should not be viewed in an adversarial relationship.

> **Science and religion are Siamese twins; opposite sides of the same coin—the coin of truth.**

True religion is a pursuit of truth, for real truth liberates. So positive religion educates, and education sets persons free from ignorance, superstition, and prejudice.

It takes strong faith to pursue knowledge! Insecure people fear free inquiry.

People of faith never fear truth! No wonder so many brilliant scientists are also positive believers.

Liberating people

"If you abide in My word, you are My disciples
indeed. And you shall know the truth, and the
truth shall make you free."—JOHN 8:31

282 Jesus was not interested in slaves, but in servants. He did
not attempt to build an empire so that He could become master over slaves. Rather, His idea was to become an inspiring Lord
who can motivate people to develop their possibilities. In the
process we become helpful servants, not oppressed slaves.

If religion enslaves people, one can challenge the morality
of that faith! One of the legitimate criticisms that is leveled
against a great deal of institutional religion in all of the major
faiths—Christianity, Judaism, Islam, Hinduism, Buddhism—
is that it indoctrinates. Religion, under the management of
insecure leaders or insecure theological positions, can indoctrinate people until they are no longer capable of hearing or
understanding any viewpoint other than what was crammed
into their minds.

> **True Christianity seeks not to indoctrinate, but to ed-
> ucate. For when we indoctrinate, we enslave; but when
> we educate, we liberate.**

In all of our enthusiasm, let us be guided by this noble
ethic:

> **The dignity of every person is a nonnegotiable value.**

Any time we fail to use our efforts to liberate people, we
violate their right to the kind of dignity that only comes
through freedom.

What, after all, is the purpose of truth, but to set us free?
That was the teaching of the Founder of our faith, Jesus
Christ.

Help me, O God, my Father, so to live that I shall not op-
press people, but liberate them. Amen.

FAITH IS . . .

Gazing into the eyes of a stranger

"By this all will know that you are My
disciples, if you have love for one another."—
JOHN 13:35

Love starts with a look. Faith uses the power of a gaze to **283** establish creative communication and redemptive relationships.

**Communication is looking into somebody's eyes with
the goal of establishing a friendship.**

I remember when I visited the primitive people of the high-
lands of New Guinea. Our tiny plane landed on a small clear-
ing in the jungle, where we were transported first by Jeep and
then on foot through the tall tropical forest. My missionary
guide said to me, "You cannot see them but they are all
around us. They are watching us. Just keep smiling! Keep your
hands stretched out with your palms open so they will know
you can be trusted. They will look at your eyes! And they can
tell if you are afraid."

Suddenly, the woods opened and out leaped a naked,
painted "savage." His eyes searched mine suspiciously. But I
returned the gaze confidently, smiling all the while, praying
hard. Then with a wave of his spear, he summoned the others
to greet me. Our communication was almost entirely limited
to looks, so I sincerely prayed that God's love would shine
through my eyes.

Faith is gazing at a stranger with the love of Christ shining
through your smile.

What jungle do you need to enter today?

Hold your head high and dare to look everyone in the eye,
all the while sparkling with the reflection of Christ's love
within you.

Countering the negative with a positive

"Love suffers long and is kind."—1
CORINTHIANS 13:4

284 You? A negative reactionary? Me, too? Yes, by nature every human being is a negative reactionary.

The natural response to a negative situation is a negative reaction.

When someone is angry at us, we get angry at him.

When someone insults us, we insult him back.

When a threat comes our way, we are defensive.

When we are afraid, we become hateful.

This human tendency to negative reaction is infectious throughout the human family.

What we are witnessing in society today—nationally and internationally—is a negative chain reaction! So our society has become violence prone!

We all worry about a nuclear war, the chain reaction, and the nuclear fallout. But we should also worry about a danger that is present now! It is the *negative* chain reaction of *negative* thinking and the *negative* emotional fallout that is bombarding the human family. I call this widespread infection of negativity *sin!*

In the Christian religion there is a doctrine that teaches that every person is conceived and born in sin. Does this mean that every newborn baby is "sinful?" If by *sin* we mean "something negative or evil *that we do*," the answer must be no. A newborn baby is innocent of any wrong*doing*. But if by *sin* we mean "a negative condition," or something that I *am* then the answer is "yes." For every child is born nontrusting, *a negative reactionary in the making.*

But when we are born again, we are converted from doubt to faith! Jesus turns us from negative reactionaries to positive reactionaries!

Through the love of Christ within us, we are able to react to negative stimuli with positive responses.

FAITH IS . . .
Bridging the gap

"And you shall be called the Repairer of the Breach, the Restorer of Streets to Dwell In."— ISAIAH 58:12

People who live by faith bridge the gaps. They trust others **285** enough to believe that reconciliation can take place between two alienated persons. People with faith are by their very nature looking for the best outcome. Therefore, they see redemption, not condemnation, as the positive solution to be pursued.

No wonder the early believers were called "Repairer of the Breach" and "Restorer of Streets to Dwell In."

On the morning that I was ordained to the Christian ministry, I read my Bible and I claimed today's text as the theme for my ministry. I made a commitment never to make public critical, judgmental statements about other Christians or their ministries. This can only create chasms, generate divisions, nurture conflict, and invite suspicion among good people.

> **The person who is really living by faith does not criticize or condemn. Instead, he constructs a bridge of understanding and an avenue where interchange of opinions can be pursued.**

Remember, God has promised you prosperity if you walk the walk of faith! Here, then, is one of the real blessings: You feel good and your self-esteem is nourished when you devote your energies to building bridges between peoples in the world.

The next time you see a bridge, think of what it symbolizes! Two divided areas are joined by one bridge! You can be a bridge between conflicting persons. You can be the reconciling influence between groups that suspect each other and distrust each other.

You can become the solution! God will bless you for believing that!

Respecting persons after you know them

"Honor all people. Love the brotherhood. Fear
God. Honor the king."—1 PETER 2:17

286   Wow! Talk about a challenge. Is it possible to know and
respect *all* people? That would take a mountain of faith!

Is it possible to honor crude and cruel persons who destroy
life and love? Yes. We do not condone their behavior, but we
recognize that they are still souls for whom Christ died on the
cross. And we can still pause to pray, "God have mercy on
their souls."

On a far more practical level, the challenge you and I have is
to respect the people with whom we live, work, and closely
relate. Can we respect them after we've seen them at their
worst? Can we honor them as beautiful human beings even
after their weaknesses have been grossly exposed? The answer
must be a resounding YES.

How can our faith perform this miracle? Quite simply. Our
faith reminds us that we too are imperfect human beings.

> **Our faith reminds us that God loves us even though
> He knows us better than anybody else! And if God
> loves in spite of what we are, He will give us the grace
> to pass that charitable spirit along!**

I thank You today, O God my Father, for honoring me even
after I have disappointed You, for treating me like a noble person even after I have been guilty of disgraceful behavior in
Your sight. Help me now to treat my fellow human beings
with no less respect than You have shown me.

Thank You, Father, for this faith. It's working miracles.
Amen.

Hugging inlaws

"... love one another fervently with a pure heart."—1 PETER 1:22

The anthropologists have long noted that human beings tend to gravitate to their own kind. **287**

Human societies tend to be suspicious of ethnic groups that are racially, religiously, or culturally different.

It takes a great deal of faith to build a level of trust and affection with persons who have been outsiders but who suddenly move into your social circle.

An inlaw can be one who has become a part of your family through marriage. You did not choose the person to be included in your family reunions, but you have no choice.

But an inlaw can be anyone who enters, without invitation, your circle of relationships.

An inlaw may be someone who works in the same company as you; or it may be another member of your club, church, or community. You cannot avoid some of these people—like them or not. What do you do?

There will always be the uninvited people who step inside your circle. To resent or to resist them will set off a cycle of negative vibrations that inevitably will be counter-productive to your welfare.

By contrast, you can learn something from them. If you embrace an inlaw with a positive attitude, you will see and appreciate his value as a special person God has created.

In the process, inlaws become beautiful friends, enriching your life. You will be blessed because you are walking the walk of faith.

Forgiving yourself and others

"Though I have all faith, so I could remove mountains, but have not love, I am nothing."—1 CORINTHIANS 13:2

288

It's exciting in our walk of faith to see how God is able to do fantastic things through imperfect people when they receive forgiveness from God. Today let's take another step of faith—that step of forgiving ourselves. For many people who call themselves believers find it difficult to forgive *themselves* for their sins and shortcomings. The act of forgiveness is an affirmation of faith that your sins are forgiven! Your mistakes are being handled by the grace of God.

When you forgive yourself, you declare that you believe that you are still a wonderful and a worthwhile person.

When you forgive yourself, you tell the world—beginning with the God who made you—that you have not lost faith in your ability to make a distinctive contribution by sharing beauty and love with those around you.

The act of forgiveness is also an affirmation that we must forgive others. When you forgive someone who has offended you, you declare that you believe that there is so much good in them that you must forgive them, even as you desire more than anything else that God forgive you. In the process of forgiving you exercise faith and love!

Forgiveness is the sublime act of faith. Unless I forgive I do not love.

Affirmations: Today I shall forgive myself and in the process love what God loves . . . myself.

Today I shall forgive someone who has offended me, believing that faith can move this mountain.

I am walking the walk of faith today, for I am experiencing love.

Questioning respectfully

"Be of the same mind toward one another. Do not set your mind on high things, but associate with the humble. Do not be wise in your own opinion."—ROMANS 12:16

289

This Bible verse gives a clue to the secret of dynamic success in business, religion, and interpersonal relationships: learning to question respectfully. Switch from the accusatory approach to the inquisitive approach.

You demonstrate great respect toward your colleague, friend, colaborer, or family when you ask questions rather than level charges.

Because of training, conditioning, and human nature, most people impulsively react negatively when they spot an activity that appears to be offensive. They immediately pass judgment, express disagreement, and thereby promptly provoke an argument.

Faith does not react in such an irresponsible and unstudied way.

Rather, faith motivates us to use the interrogative approach!

We need to ask questions—questions that do not intimidate, but sincerely try to understand: "Am I understanding you correctly?" "Can you help me understand the reason you have done this?"

Questioning respectfully is faith in action.

Learn the art of positive communication.

Learn to develop the skill of asking questions that are success oriented—questions that will buy time, questions that will disarm an adversary, questions that will protect you from polarization.

Father, forgive me for passing judgment irresponsibly when I should have been questioning wisely, for accusing unjustly when I should have been inquiring sincerely. Forgive me for preaching sermons when I should have been listening. Amen.

Anticipating the best

"For Your lovingkindness is before my eyes."—
PSALM 26:3

290 My wife and I recently attended a religious conference in Europe. After checking into a London hotel, we discovered that one of our bags was missing. Expecting the worst, I telephoned the unclaimed baggage office. A pleasant voice answered, "Lost and Found. May I help you?"

The enthusiasm of the sincere offer to help caught me off guard. I was shocked by the helpful spirit. After I gave him the number and description of the missing bag, he asked me, "Do you live in Los Angeles?" I affirmed that I live near there.

"Oh, I go to California quite often. It's such a beautiful place," he answered.

I said, "Then you must have seen the Crystal Cathedral."

He said, "Of course! It's beautiful!"

His pleasant manners and happy conversation were unexpected blessings—and scoldings at the same time. I suddenly felt tremendous guilt for my subtle negative attitude. I had anticipated the worst when I should have believed that the best would happen.

> **Faith calls us to believe in the best. If you believe the best will happen and it doesn't, you lose nothing! For you have the joy of anticipating something wonderful! The happiness that comes through positive anticipation pays out dividends instantaneously. Each smile, every happy heartbeat, every elegant thought is an immediate reward.**

Lord, forgive me for being negative. Pardon me, Father, for not believing that I will be helped properly, cheerfully, and efficiently. Help me to have enough faith to believe that the best will happen, for You have only good planned for us. Thank You, Father. Amen.

Loving the unlovable

"Beloved, let us love one another, for love is of
God; and everyone who loves is born of God
and knows God. He who does not love does not
know God, for God is love."—1 JOHN 4:7–8

What do you do when your roommate or coworker is un- **291**
likable, and unlovable? Then remember who you are!

You are a person of faith! Believe that it is possible to see
some good in the most unlovable person. Practice possibility
thinking and believe that it's possible that the unsolicited
companion may turn out to be a friend in need.

Remember also that the walk of faith is meant to be a
growth experience. You are not an only child. You are part of a
family. God does not intend to treat you like a solitary child.
He intends to put you in positions where you experience
working and living with uncomfortable personalities.

What can you learn in these awkward circumstances? Patience? Yes. The ability to be charming? Perhaps. There is
something else to learn.

> **There is something beautiful in every person. If you
> can't see it or find it or feel it then you have a problem.**

For somehow you are lacking the sensitivity or skill to
motivate, inspire, or mold him into the kind of person in
whom some goodness glows.

The walk of faith does not permit you to be crude, rude, and
abusive to the unlovely person. You cannot stoop to that lower
level. Instead be calm and demonstrate an enormous amount
of faith that things will work out somehow.

Make me into the kind of a person who loves the unlovable,
O God. And when my patience reaches an end, then I'll get
out of your way. For it is *not impossible* for You to love the
unlovable person. Love them through me if you want to. Take
over and do the job that's too big for me. Thank You, Father.
Amen.

FAITH IS . . .
Pleasing God

"Without faith it is impossible to please
Him. . . ."—HEBREWS 11:6

292   In this text we see that faith ultimately is a nonnegotiable
human value. By that I mean

**It is impossible to have satisfying interpersonal rela-
tionships with others or with God without faith.**

God is not pleased until we walk the walk of faith. If I give
Him all the money I have but do not trust Him, He remains
displeased.

It's the same way in all of our personal relationships. If I
give attractive gifts of immense value to my wife but do not
trust her, our marriage will never last. Relationships can never
grow and thrive without mutual trust. Oftentimes I meet sincere but negative Christians who are pious and proud of pleasing God, but who fail to aid in constructive contributions
such as:

- launching positive helpful programs in their church or
  community.
- promoting projects to build a better society.
- joining in ventures proven to support the great causes that
  could build a better and more beautiful world.

The bottom line of pleasing God is right here:

**No holiness of life, no extreme generosity of giving of
oneself and substance, can compensate for the failure
to demonstrate great faith in God's promises and
power. When God calls, respond in faith!**

Today there is something God wants you to do. Respond in
faith; For without faith, you will never please Him, nor will
you be happy with yourself. Life leads to pleasure and happiness for God and for His people who trust Him enough to
respond in faith to His call.

Centering yourself in God's love

"All things are possible for You. Take this cup
away from Me; nevertheless, not what I will,
but what you will."—MARK 14:36

The whole purpose behind the walk of faith is that through **293**
personal commitment and self-development, you are able to
fulfill the plan that God has for your life! Therefore, the central aspect of your walk of faith must be to center your life on
the will of God. Remember, God's will for your life is always
born and bathed in divine Love!

To walk the walk of faith is to be the love of God in human
form and function.

> **You are truly successful when you are a healthy channel through whom God's living love can flow like fresh water to thirsty souls.**

How can you keep from being distracted from this one goal?

Obviously, persons who have an objective for personal
achievement are already spared from distraction. The athlete
in training, the scholar pursuing an academic degree, the professional climbing up the ladder, all have their eye on a goal
that consumes their complete dedication and commitment.

As you walk the walk of faith, picture today in your mind a
bull's-eye target—the kind of target used for dart games or
archery contests. Now let the center dot of the target be the
focus of your whole panorama of life—the love of God. Focus
your faith on this target.

That's what Jesus Christ did in the Garden of Gethsemane.
He easily could have been distracted from paying the price of
the cross. Like Jesus, you need to keep your eye on the number
one purpose of life—to be the love of God to a hurting
world.

O God, I center my faith on Your love today. I concentrate
on the faith and face of Christ. I ask You to give me His face;
and may it turn me into a beautiful human being, enabling me
to accomplish great things for You. Amen.

Finding a need and filling it

"Though I bestow all my goods to feed the poor
. . . but have not love, it profits me nothing."—
1 CORINTHIANS 13:3

294 We begin to understand now, why the promise that God attaches to faith is the promise of success.

Faith is love in action.

Love is finding a need and filling it;
I believe I can help someone in need.
Love is finding a hurt and healing it;
I believe I can comfort someone in pain.
Love is finding a problem and solving it;
I think I can come up with solutions.
Love is feeling someone's grief and consoling them;
I believe I can soothe the troubled mind.
Love is seeing the chasm and bridging it;
I believe I can be a reconciling, unifying spirit!

Real love is my deciding to make your problem, my problem.

In that definition of love, I do not give help to people in order to exploit them. I love them simply because when someone hurts, I hurt. When love is nonmanipulative, nonjudgmental, nonself-serving, then it's real love.

Have you noticed? That kind of love is nothing less than faith in action!

It takes a lot of faith to love. The fear of having your love rejected, the anxiety of "getting involved," the worry about not being appreciated, are only a few of the negative thoughts that keep people from loving people. Did you notice? All of the above excuses by the noncaring persons really are reflections of a lack of faith!

Insecure people dare not care! They feel too empty of love to give it and too unworthy to accept it. So they become truly incapable of giving or receiving love until they develop a powerful inner faith.

Channeling Christ's love

"I am the vine, you are the branches. He who
abides in Me, and I in him, bears much fruit;
for without Me you can do nothing."—JOHN
15:5

Faith allows you to open up and be yourself! It is connecting **295**
yourself, with spiritual integrity, in a relationship with Jesus
Christ. When that happens you can work wonders in helping
other people. Happiness, self-esteem, and self-worth will be
natural byproducts!

What is a Christian anyway? A Christian is a mind through
which Christ thinks, a heart through which Christ loves, an
eye through which Christ looks, a face through which Christ
smiles and encourages people, a hand through which Christ
touches, and a voice through which Christ offers hope. Can I
be a Christian?

You can do it if you are willing to be a conduit.

Recently a friend shared with me, "Your possibility thinking really helps me. I was having real problems with my son.
One day I was out in my garden. When I looked at the water
pipe, I thought to myself, *Christ wants me to be a conduit. He
wants to flow through me. I simply have to let Him do it.*

"Then," she said, "the phrase hit me: '*I can do it* if I will be a
con-du-it.'"

That's what a branch is to a tree—a conduit for the sap to
flow upward to bear fruit.

That's what an electrical wire is—a conduit for energy to
flow from the source to the place of need. That's what you and
I are in this life—conduits for Christ carrying love. Through
us, Christ can turn on lights in dark minds!

FAITH IS . . .
Touching someone you don't know

" 'Which of these . . . was neighbor to him who
fell among the thieves?' . . . 'He who showed
mercy on him.' Then Jesus said . . . 'Go and do
likewise.' "—LUKE 10:36–37

296   Today's Bible text is from the story of the Good Samaritan.
A man was attacked by thieves, was wounded and left half
dead. A priest and a Levite saw him and passed by. A Samaritan had compassion on him, bandaged his wounds, and
helped him. Jesus asked his disciples, "Which of these . . . was
neighbor to him who fell among the thieves?" They answered,
"He who showed mercy on him." Then Jesus said, "Go and do
likewise."

Here's where the walk of faith becomes exciting! Living out
Christian love is intensely personal and practical as we reach
out and touch someone. It's always risky to touch the life of a
stranger. It takes courage to risk "getting involved!"

It takes faith to touch somebody you don't know.

In the story of the Good Samaritan, our Lord's challenge
was directed not only toward physical poverty, but also toward
the emotional starvation that destroys human lives today in
all societies of the world.

What hunger for love, acceptance, and understanding exists
in the hearts of people around you today?

There is tremendous healing power in a touch. A psychiatrist told me confidentially, "About all I can do for many of my
patients is to give them a look, a word, and a touch. It's amazing how the *touching* becomes such a healing!"

In a world where many people hurt, there is no excuse for
our not touching with healing love. If we don't have the courage to touch them, who will?

Our first motive should be a desire to get involved! When
God sent Jesus Christ into this world, to His cross, He reached
down and touched us at our worst to save and to heal us! We
should be willing to do no less than Christ has done for us.

Bailing out a friend

"But there is a friend who sticks closer than a brother."—PROVERBS 18:24

There are very successful bail bond businesses which bail total strangers out of jail. By contrast, many people find it amazingly difficult to lend money to a friend.

297

My own father advised me, rightly or wrongly, "Loan money to an acquaintance, but never to a dear friend. If he is a friend, *give* him the money!

"When you loan a friend money, you expect him to pay you back. If he can't, your friendship will be strained. You'll not only lose the money, but a friend as well."

For Christ, "bailing out a friend" meant dying for you and me on the cross.

In ways that God understands better than any of us, Jesus atoned for our sins. He died upon the cross of Calvary to save us from all of our sins and guilts. Can you imagine what faith that took? He ran the risk of giving everything He had—including His life—to save His friends, who might not appreciate it!

Faith is "bailing out a friend." It is defending your friends behind their backs when they are being criticized, only to find out later they were probably guilty! Yes, it is risky. It takes faith to bail out a friend!

However, if you make a mistake, you're making it on the side of faith! If you sin, let it be on the side of love. If you err, let it be on the side of mercy. And that's always the wisest decision for one who is trying to live the life of Christ today!

FAITH IS . . .
Soliciting help for a great cause

". . . comfort the fainthearted, uphold the weak,
be patient with all."—1 THESSALONIANS 5:14

298   Don't you marvel at the person who has the courage to go
out and ring doorbells, sell tickets to a charity, or ask for volunteers?

What if someone asks you today to volunteer to solicit help
for a great cause or to give witness to your faith? Is your faith
ready to face these tests? Or would you rather cop out and
offer a contribution in money or the excuse, "I really don't
have the talent to testify to people about what the Lord has
done."

Welcome every challenge that appears to be something impossible for you to perform. If every vital Christian was willing to be a solicitor in positive, enthusiastic, and energetic
terms for Jesus Christ, we could see this world being converted to a society dominated by the love of God in short
order.

**God calls us to be responsive to His calling. It's God's
responsibility to enable us to be effective.**

The next time the church or community organization asks
for volunteers, speak up! Give it a try. Believe that you can be
effective!

I'm asking you today to be a solicitor for a great cause. The
cause? The Christian religion! Plan to invite someone to attend church with you this coming Sunday. Plan to invite
others to participate with you in exposure to the sources and
forces of positive good that are available. You can be somebody's answer to prayer. You can be the saving influence in
turning a life around! Simply be willing to solicit in the name
of Christ and lead some soul to the faith that has saved you.

Priming the pump

"Whoever drinks of the water that I shall give him will never thirst. But . . . will become in him a fountain of water springing up into everlasting life."—JOHN 4:14

At a remote road stop in the desert stood a deserted gasoline station. Alongside was a well with an old-fashioned pump.

299

A traveler, dying of thirst, stumbled into the outpost. He ran to the well, and there he saw a cup filled with water! But under the cup was a note.

Dear Traveler:

There's loads of water deep down in this well. Use this cup to prime the pump. Then drink all you want from the bottom of the well. When you've had all you want, fill the cup again for the next person who comes thirsting down the road.

Whatever you do, *don't drink from this cup* or there'll be no water to prime the pump—ever again.

The thirsty traveler read the note and looked at the cup of water. Unable to heed the warning, he brought the cup to his lips. Then he hesitated for a moment, and, in a sublime act of faith, followed the instructions.

He poured the water down the dry pump, worked the handle as fast as he could, and suddenly out of the mouth of the pump poured forth cold water from the depths.

Delighted, he drank. When he'd had all he could enjoy, he filled the cup and left it on the well with the note.

You prime the pump when you spend your last ounce of energy on the hope that your energy will be renewed.

Invest seed money. Call it venture capital. Because someone, somewhere helped you get started, pray that your success will help someone else down the road of faith.

With that kind of faith, and that kind of attitude, you'll never run dry!

Filling someone else's cup

> "For I was hungry and you gave Me food; I was thirsty and you gave Me drink. . . . inasmuch as you did it to one of the least of these . . . you did it to Me."—MATTHEW 25:35,40

300

What will keep you going and growing?

What can protect you from the perils of success?

What force can keep motivating you all the days of your life?

Where can you tap into a power source that will sustain and feed an unending compulsion to creativity and productivity?

I know of only one answer.

Focus on human need rather than on selfish pleasures.

Look at lost souls rather than on selfish comfort.

When the farmer sees hungry people devouring with relish the fruit of his labor, he knows that unless he gets back to work to produce a new crop, the next year there will be hungry people and starving children. That is his motivation for continued productivity!

"Why don't you retire?" I said to my financially secure farmer brother. "People still have to eat!" he answered. He is still at it.

Faith is filling someone else's cup. Self-serving and self-seeking is ultimately self-defeating. That's a fundamental principle of life.

Commitment to the service of others is the satisfying lifestyle. It is the only pathway to spiritual prosperity.

> **The walk of faith leaves you no choice but to focus on filling someone else's cup. In the process you are spared from the haunting hollowness of life that only God can satisfy.**

O God, as long as I live help me to look for someone who is hungry for encouragement. Help me to fill that cup! Amen.

Casting your bread upon the waters

"Cast your bread upon the waters,/For you will find it after many days."—ECCLESIASTES 11:1–2

Possibility thinkers are people who look for the impossible! **301** That's the age-old principle we deal with today.

It's this paradox:

It's impossible to give anything away. It always comes back to you.

- Give love and love will return.
- Show affection and people will be inclined to respond in a kind way.
- Be cold and frigid and people will give you a chilly reception.

When he drops an offering in the collection plate at church, the impossibility thinker says, "There it goes. I'll never see it again." Wrong! The money comes back to you faster than you'd ever imagine, from sources least expected. I'm speaking from the vantage point of practicing this principle for over forty years. It has not failed me yet!

It's impossible to throw bread on the waters—it does return. Try standing at the ocean's edge and throwing something in. The retreating wave will carry it out to sea, but the next wave will move it back until it's deposited again on the shore.

Naturally, it takes courage to make that first move. But, after all, what are your choices? Possibility thinkers are not controlled by fear, but by faith!

Affirmation: Today I shall make the commitment to walk the walk of faith because I'm going to throw some bread on the waters. "There it goes! It's going to be fun seeing how God gives back what I try to give away."

FAITH IS . . .
Lighting one candle

"You are the light of the world. . . . let your
light so shine before men, that they may see
your good works and glorify your Father in
heaven."—MATTHEW 5:14, 16

302   "Better to light a candle, than curse the darkness" was a
favorite quotation of Eleanor Roosevelt's.

You can't save the whole starving world from famine, but
you *can* save one child's life by feeding him.

You can't reverse immoral trends that threaten to take society down a cesspool of spiritual self-destruction, but you *can*
lead one person to God.

**You can choose today to be part of the solution, not
part of the problem.**

You can choose to be part of the uplifting force, rather than
contributing to the downward movement.

You can choose to be a dreamer, rather than a despairer.
Dreamers of great dreams create the real uplifting movements
in society and in the world. More often than not their dreams
materialize! But even when their dreams do not reach frui-
tion, they make a contribution in their day. They lift people
above despair and bring laughter, love, and joy to human lives.
And because of their dream, they are creative, constructive,
and helpful human beings.

Affirmation:

I will light a candle today rather than curse the darkness.

I will feed a child today.

I will lead someone to God today.

I will give someone the gift of hope today.

Dear Lord, I am deciding today to be part of the solution,
not part of the problem. I will light one candle. I will be Your
light in my home, at work, and in Your world. Keep shining
through me. Amen.

FAITH IS . . .
Applauding the positive projects

"Do not withhold good from those to whom it is due,/When it is in the power of your hand to do so."—PROVERBS 3:27

- Have you wondered what good you can do with your life?
- Do you sometimes feel that you really aren't doing anything significant?
- Are you tempted to look at others with their accomplishments and rate yourself as not too effective?
- Do you ever think, *I'm just a little person?*

Now hear this:

You become as great as the projects you support.

The little people are the negative-thinking critics of positive-thinking persons who try to do something great. You lift yourself or lower yourself, depending upon which side you take.

Remember that you are walking the walk of faith!

Applaud positive people who try to accomplish positive projects. Encourage them. Speak well of them. Defend them behind their backs. They need all the help they can get! They'll never be able to succeed without the support of a lot of good people.

Vote for the brave ones! Share in their victories! Participate in the joys of their success!

You can be sure you'll never enjoy the enthusiasm that comes through success until you connect yourself with dynamic causes.

Affirmation: Today I will applaud the people who are attempting the impossible and who need my encouragement and support.

When you come to the end of your life, you'll know that you participated as a partner in a good work. You'll be as big as the person or cause you support!

303

Adjusting your attitude toward the community

"Do not forget to entertain strangers, for by so
doing some have unwittingly entertained
angels."—HEBREWS 13:2

304   You are ready now to see how this mountain-moving faith
inspires you to "entertain strangers," who might be angels in
disguise.

Your faith is challenged as you adjust your attitudes toward
the community. As you support positive projects, you will become a part of the creative community of people who work
with you and for you. How do you criticize those who fail to
perform up to your expectations of them?

(1) Praise and thank them for all the good they have already
done.

(2) Then ask questions. Formulate respectful questions that
will reveal why they have done what they have done, and why
they have failed to do what you had expected them to do.

(3) Give them the opportunity to explain their position
without losing their self-esteem. "I'm sure you had a good reason. Would you mind explaining it to me?"

You will probably discover that in the pursuit of their assignment they have uncovered problems or opportunities that
you are unaware of.

Where do you need to do some adjusting today?

As a parent, do you need to adjust your attitude toward your
children today?

As a child, do you need to adjust your attitude toward your
parents today?

As mates, do you need to adjust your attitude toward your
husband or wife?

They are angels God has sent your way.

Faith is adjusting your attitude toward your community.

**Faith believes you are entertaining angels oftentimes
posing as strangers.**

Winning friends and influencing people

"A friend loves at all times."—PROVERBS 17:17

You are really blossoming! The walk of faith is transforming **305**
you. You are winning friends and influencing people! That
means that you can be a successful evangelist, missionary, or
communicator. You're succeeding in your social life because
Christ has turned you into a person who cares about others.
We succeed when we find a hurt and heal it. And everybody
who is hurting is searching for someone who is able to help
and who really cares.

You can be *the* person in their life!
T—the
  H—hearing
    E—ear
You can be The Hearing Ear!

Where can hurting people go to find a listening ear? Is this
one of the reasons why local bars are so popular? Is the bar-
tender the only one who has a listening ear?

Anybody can be a somebody to someone!

Christ is calling you to live His life through you today. Are
you willing to become a listening ear, a bearer of others' burdens? With your silence and assurance, you can encourage
others to *bare* their souls to you. Then you can *bear* their
burdens with them!

You begin the process of becoming a creative communicator with a look—your eyes meet their eyes; a word—you respond with a kind hello; a touch—your hand touches their
shoulder.

You are on your way.

Faith is winning friends and influencing people—"I will be
an effective channel for Jesus Christ." God bless you.

Socializing with a purpose

"Here am I! Send me."—ISAIAH 6:8

306   It takes a lot of courage for many people to socialize in circles that they consider above their own class. But you have worked on releasing yourself from your prejudices. You have learned to adjust your attitude to strangers. The walk of faith has given you the self-assurance to win friends. Now you are ready for the new adventures you can experience if you feel free and self-assured in any social circle.

You can do it!

Here's the secret. It starts in a prayer of faith which I use often. It has never failed me.

Lord, show me the person to whom You want to speak through my life today.

Begin each day with that prayer.

Be open and sensitive to every opportunity to communicate with another person. It may be the salesperson in the store, a solicitor at the door or on the telephone, or a hostess at a social event.

Move through society with a mission. Socialize—with a high and holy purpose.

Every day there is some person to whom God wants to speak through your life.

Remember, it's God's responsibility to do the talking; you simply have to be available. He may want you to silently respond with a kind look, or to listen with a caring ear. He only needs an honest love that you will emit and transmit from your soul!

Live with this prayer.

Try it every day for thirty days. That's faith in action.

Mending the broken fences

"How often shall my brother sin against me,
and I forgive him. . . . Jesus said to him, . . . "up
to seventy times seven."—MATTHEW 18:21-22

I was born and grew up on an Iowa farm. What did we do **307**
when we were not planting seeds or harvesting the crops? We
were mending fences constantly!

As you know, the carefully surveyed borders on the Iowa
farmlands are always marked by fences to keep cattle con-
fined to each farmer's property. Broken fences are seriously
viewed and promptly mended, for broken fences soon rupture
relationships between good neighbors. Therefore the wise
farmer accepts the fact that fence mending is an important
part of farming.

Faith *expects* that fences will need to be mended! It assumes that relationships will be strained, perhaps ruptured. It
doesn't discard the friendship because of a deep disagreement.
That is simply a fence that needs to be mended.

You don't sell a farm because the fences keep breaking
down. You don't sell a car because the tires keep wearing out.
You don't discard a marriage because you keep having dis-
agreements. You don't throw out clothes when they're dirty.

Yesterday, an architect friend of mine said to me, "We've
been married thirty-six years. My wife and I cook together, eat
together, play tennis together, make love together, and disagree together." How his eyes twinkled!

**Mending broken fences—repairing broken relation-
ships—is God's specialty.**

How often He comes back to us to forgive us. When the
disciples asked Jesus, "How often shall my brother sin against
me, and I forgive him . . . seven times?" (Matt. 18:21). Jesus
answered, "I do not say to you, up to seven times, but up to
seventy times seven." (Matt. 18:22). That's how faith works—
mending broken fences!

Explaining your position diplomatically

"The Spirit of the Lord GOD is upon Me,/
Because the LORD has anointed Me to preach
good tidings."—ISAIAH 61:1

308   You are now ready on the walk of faith to be a diplomat for God. Your faith has matured to the level that you express your convictions with confidence and kindness. You dare to disagree agreeably—that's diplomacy!

What are the distinguishing marks of a diplomat? The first mark of the diplomat is that he is always *friendly*. This respectful attitude is a must in diplomatic relationships, for it allows your adversary to accept your frank disagreement without becoming hostile to you.

The second characteristic of the Christian diplomat is that he seeks to be *fair* in all communication and relationships. When someone holds a different viewpoint, be fair in your judgment of him, even though you cannot agree.

The third characteristic is to learn how to be *frank*. Dare to say such things as, "I see it from a different perspective," or "I want to agree with you, but in good conscience I really can't."

Fourth, and finally, the diplomat is *firm*. Resist pressures to violate your values.

Faith is explaining your position through *friendliness*, *fairness*, *frankness*, and *firmness*.

Today you have become, through faith, a successful diplomat for Jesus Christ. Congratulations! You have really matured in your faith.

You have learned the four principles for effective communication. They will work in all of your interpresonal relationships. You will no longer be manipulated and intimidated. You will be positively, politely, diplomatically aggressive. You sense a tremendous feeling of liberation in and by the power of your Lord.

FAITH IS . . .
Communicating effectively

"Therefore we are ambassadors for Christ."—2
CORINTHIANS 5:20

Let's think some more about how you and I can be success- **309**
ful communicators. Faith changes our attitudes toward people; and when our attitudes are positive, effective communication is already established! Inner thoughts soon show
through our communication, verbally or nonverbally. Depending on our attitudes we will be either restrained or recep-
tive to the first sensitive word, smile, look, or touch.

When we walk the walk of faith, our self-esteem gives us
the self-confidence to mix and mingle in any circle with confidence.

> **Our Lord allows us to be ambassadors. He wants us to
> be His official messengers, instruments through
> whom His attentive caring can be communicated.**

How can we be effective communicators or ambassadors?
My wife is a beautiful illustration of how this works. Arvella
was a beautiful farmer's daughter from Iowa. Years later she
found herself sitting at the head tables with famous people.
*How can I possibly carry on a conversation and be an inter-
esting dinner companion to them?* she asked herself. She
knew nothing about their background, other than that they
were famous and powerful.

In her quiet time the Lord gave her this wise counsel: The
next time she found herself in an elevated social setting, she
spoke little, asked questions, and sincerely listened. When the
evening was finished, the gentleman with whom we had dinner turned to me and said, "What a wonderful wife you have.
She is such a wonderful conversationalist."

We all can be good conversationalists if we will love the
person next to us enough just to listen.

Today I shall be an ambassador for my Lord. I shall begin by
making sure my attitude is positive. Thank You, God. Amen.

Cleaning up our environment

"For God did not call us to uncleanliness, but
in holiness."—1 THESSALONIANS 4:7

310 "Why bother to pick it up?" I overheard one person say to
someone who picked up a piece of litter. "Somebody is going
to drop something in the next ten minutes anyway!" Every
homemaker has said: "I no sooner get the house clean than it's
dirty again."

What are the options? Certainly we can't let dirt build up
and live in filth. We can't let it go from bad to worse!

I was inspired by the story of a citizen who bought a small
portable sandblasting machine to use on his neighborhood's
cinderblock walls that had been defaced with obscenities and
pornographic graffiti.

"Why bother?" he was asked. "They'll just mess it up
again!"

His answer was, "For the same reason I take a bath every
night!" His positive approach became infectious. Today it's a
clean neighborhood.

> **Service offers an immediate payoff—the instanta-
> neous gratification that comes when you know you
> have done something right!**

Affirmation: Today I will ask myself, "How can I help clean
up my environment? After all, I have to live in it!"

Lord, help me to begin with the environment of my mind.
Help me to clean up the litter of negative thoughts, and recurring sinful impulses. Thank You, Father, for cleaning up the
same old graffiti again and again! You never give up on me. Is
it because You've chosen to live within me?

Quilting the scraps

"Then [Ruth] went and gleaned in the field after
the reapers. . . . So Boaz took Ruth and she
became his wife . . . and she bore a son."—
RUTH 2:3; 4:13

Our Lord didn't believe in waste; possibility thinkers don't **311**
believe in waste. One company's waste product is another
company's opportunity!

Faith is quilting the scraps! It creates beauty from throwa-
ways.

In America's early days frontier people could not afford to
throw anything away. Empty tin cans were cut and flattened
to be used for patching holes in the grain wagons. All clothing
was homemade. Scraps were carefully kept to be sewn together in a multicolored collage and stuffed with cotton to
create a quilt. To break the boredom of sewing, it was not
uncommon to have quilting parties. ("Possibilitizing" creates
a party out of a boring chore.)

We hear a great deal today about the shortage of energy.
There is no shortage of anything—unless it's possibility
thinking!

Our real problem is waste. We waste money, we waste food,
we waste energy, and we waste ideas.

One day my wife agreed to pick me up at noon at a specific
location. She was fifteen minutes late, and during that time I
composed one of these devotionals, recording it on a little tape
recorder. I couldn't afford to waste those fiffteen minutes. I
quilted the scraps of time until it all came together to make
this book.

Look for possibilities in wastebaskets.

Remember how Ruth went gleaning in fields after the harvest was over. Faithfully she gathered the scraps. Read how
she was blessed in the lineage of our Lord.

FAITH IS . . .
Pyramiding your success

> "He who had received five talents . . . brought
> five other talents . . . His Lord said to him,
> 'Well done . . . I will make you ruler over many
> things.' For to everyone who has, more will be
> given."—MATTHEW 25:20–21

312 Here is a principle that will help you understand why successful people usually succeed more than ever. It's called the pyramid principle. When you're walking this walk of faith, take a little and invest it with all the faith you've got! The little divides and multiplies. Carefully invest the new earnings and the returns multiply again.

A person begins the walk of faith by risking what he has, expecting to multiply it. As you keep investing, you pyramid your success.

Read today's text again. Doesn't it mean that if you choose to play it safe by storing all your assets in a vault to protect them from theft or loss, you are sure to lose them all? Of course! It's just a matter of time before inflation alone will consume the uninvested dollar.

If you try to keep what little you have, you will lose it.

The only way to keep what you have is to keep moving ahead. Faith is pyramiding your success.

When I started the Crystal Cathedral congregation, I began with one member—my wife. It was hard work to gather up the first hundred members. After several years we had a thousand members. Then, the growth really skyrocketed. Why? Because by that time the one thousand members all were inviting their friends to come to church! The pyramid principle began to work!

If you're willing to start with one solid step, take a second, then expand slowly but effectively, you can build your pyramid of success, too! That's exercising the power of your faith! You are on the right road. Stick with it!

Thank You, God, for challenging me to keep moving ahead, step by step, setting the goals higher. Amen.

Painting yourself into a corner

"A desire accomplished is sweet to the soul."—
PROVERBS 13:19

I've painted myself into a corner many times. Foolish? Not **313** really. "A desire accomplished is sweet to the soul." That means we all need the good feeling that comes when we have accomplished a project we've dreamed about. When we make commitments to deliver—before we know how we are going to produce—then we paint ourselves into a corner. In the process we put ourselves under pressure to achieve. Every possibility-thinking person does this—often!

Perhaps you have sent out the invitations to the party. You have invited people to an open house. You have volunteered to host the next meeting at your house. You have agreed to serve as chairman of the committee. What are you doing?

You're painting yourself into a corner! Then how do you get out of the corner? Here is where faith comes in. Extraordinary resources of thought and energy automatically come to your rescue. You never knew you had it in you to finish the job, to accomplish your desire.

I have been a jogger for nearly fifteen years. One morning I decided I would run over four miles. I didn't feel like it, so I deliberately ran two miles from my home. Once I had done that I had passed the point of no return. Now there was no way I could quit. I had painted myself into a corner. The decision was made for me. I simply turned around, running and puffing back home, adding up to four miles!

> **Do you dare to paint yourself into a corner? It works every time! You discover resources within you you never knew you had.**

Splitting the diamond

". . . which have been given to us exceedingly great and precious promises."—2 PETER 1:4

314   I have had the exciting opportunity of seeing the most beautiful diamonds in the world—the crown jewels of the czars of Russia in the Hermitage Museum in the Soviet Union, and the collection of imperial gems of Persia in a bank in Teheran—but the largest and most beautiful diamonds are in the crown jewels in the Tower of London in England.

The largest diamond ever found is in that collection. When it was discovered, it was almost the size of two chicken eggs. It was determined that the gem would have to be split in order to bring out the potential beauty within. Studies were made. Then came the decisive moment when the blow would have to fall. There was the risk that the stone would be permanently ruined. Today the masterful results are there for you to see. Two diamonds—each nearly the size of a chicken egg— dazzle the eye.

Faith takes you to the point of no return, where there is no looking back. Win or lose, the decision must be made.

When Hannibal crossed the Rubicon on his massive military journey to conquer Rome, he watched until the last of his troops was safely across the river. Then he ordered the bridges burned! Hence the phrase, "burning bridges behind you." He wanted no opportunity for his troops to retreat. It was his way of exacting total commitment to a venture that had to succeed. It is no wonder that he won!

Are you facing such a moment today? Make sure that your move is a positive one!

Strike a blow that will deepen your commitment to your God-given goal. Run the risk of a loss. There is no success without taking a chance!

FAITH IS . . .
Giving before receiving

"Give, and it shall be given to you: good
measure, pressed down, shaken together, and
running over . . . For with the same measure
that you use, it will be measured back to
you."—LUKE 6:38

It is easy to see why people who take the walk of faith live **315**
joyous and prosperous lives. Faith gives before it receives.
Flash a smile and people are friendly to you. But act shy, and
worried about rejection, and the sparkle of magnetic charm
will be frozen under the mask of apprehension. If you wait for
others to smile first, your walk of faith will be disappointing!
Give and you shall receive. The farmer knows this. He plants
the seed, giving it away, before he can expect a harvest.

**Life's satisfying experiences rush to the person who
gives before there is any guarantee of return.**

The successful entrepreneur understands this principle. He
prepares to spend "front money" for promotional literature
and preliminary architectural drawings, before he has any assurance of support for the project. He is walking the walk of
faith.

Do I want my life to be filled with singing and sunshine?
Then I need enough faith to give it out before I can expect to
take it in. What gifts can I give to God today? A positive lift to
encourage someone who is down? A happy word to someone
who needs a new drink from the fountain of joy? I'll take the
walk of faith today and step out to give of myself to someone
else.

But what if nothing comes back and I lose what I've given?
Well! I have already received something—the assurance that I
am walking the walk of faith! I'll win some; I'll lose some. But
of this I am sure: Life will start drying up; my youthful personality will become wrinkled and arthritic; and a slow, insidious decay will infect my heart, when I cautiously wait to give
until I receive. So long as I give before I receive, I remain vital
and truly alive!

Pledging support

"God loves a cheerful giver."—2 CORINTHIANS 9:7

316 I have a great deal of admiration for people who pledge financial support to worthy causes. They sign pledge cards and make commitments before they are positive they can deliver the money on schedule. Oddly enough, commitment usually opens the way to possibility!

> **Commitments are keys that unlock doors to great opportunities.**

Faith is trusting God to enable you to do what He asks.

It's exciting to me on life's walk to make pledges long before I have any idea how they can be fulfilled. Invariably doors open that I don't expect; my prosperity is at a higher level than I anticipate.

I truly believe God knows what's going on! And He is pleased by the signatures of courageous people that appear on financial pledges for His work.

- If you have the faith—God's got the power!
- If you make the commitment—God opens the way!
- If you make the pledge—God gives you the winning edge!

The next time you hear somebody ask for help, think twice before you say no. Doing so may be failing God's test of your faith!

Pledge your support. Pass the test.

And see how He will promote you to a higher level.

Do you have the vision to imagine something that seems just beyond your reach? How can you get hold of it? Does it seem so close, yet so far? Are you on the sidewalk looking into the store window? And the door is locked? Life's dreams are all there—but not for you? Wrong! Make the commitment! That's the key to unlock the possibility!

FAITH IS . . .
Tithing your income

"Bring all the tithes into the storehouse. . . ./
And prove me now in this, . . ./If I will
not. . . ./pour out for you such blessing/That
there will not be room enough to receive it."—
MALACHI 3:10

In the Old Testament God commanded His people to im- **317**
mediately set aside a tenth of their income to be returned to
the work of the Lord. This is called tithing. They were told
they could keep nine-tenths of the harvest, but the first one-
tenth was to be given back to God for His good work. Understandably there were those who felt they couldn't possible live
on nine-tenths. They felt they needed the entire harvest.

I'll never forget how scary it was when I first started tithing.
I didn't think I could possibly feed my family on the balance
of my small fixed salary. Then I was forced to be honest and
face the challenge God put directly before me. "Prove Me,"
were His words. He was saying, "Schuller, I dare you to practice your faith. Either you believe in Me, or you don't. You are
either living by faith, or you have surrendered to doubt."

If I list the most important decisions in my life, I have to say
my most important decision was to give my life to Jesus
Christ and to His service in ministry.

My second greatest decision was to marry Arvella. The
third most important and positive decision was to take 10
percent off the top of every salary check I received, and give it
back to God.

A tithe is not a debt we owe, it is a fertile seed we sow.

I dare you to start tithing today! You will find another reason why God blesses the men and women of great faith!

Plant the seed—and the harvest will astound you! For
tithing will make a believer out of you! God will have a measurable opportunity to prove to you life's most important lesson: nothing is ever achieved until somebody has believed!
Yes, tithing made a possibility thinker out of me! It transformed my life, my destiny! Try it!

FAITH IS . . .
Merging to make miracles

"Whoever desires to become great among you
shall be your servant. And whoever of you
desires to be the first shall be slave of all."—
MARK 10:43–44

318 It takes two to make a miracle. When a believing human
being merges his will with God's powers, miracles happen.
Miracles require faith—and faith is often spelled w-o-r-k.

There is a great misconception today that faith is simply a
matter of asking God to perform a miracle, sitting back, and
waiting for it to happen. Don't be misled! Prosperous, wealthy
Christian people don't become great by manipulating, perhaps
dishonestly, to get to the top of the ladder. They work for it
after they've prayed through their plans!

Jesus Himself encourages the pursuit of greatness. But our
Lord makes it clear that the pathway to success is the path of
service.

If you want to be great—be prepared to be a servant.

This works in the business world, too. In a free economy,
people buy only the products and services that meet their
needs. The professional person who becomes ego-involved instead of human-service-oriented, soon finds himself in trouble.

Great things happen when we follow our prayer with hard
work. Work means serving; and serving involves thinking
about others' needs and meeting them at their level.

Today, ask yourself: Have I been sitting back just waiting for
God to pour out blessings in my life without making an effort
myself? Am I willing to merge with God to make a miracle? I
believe it will happen as I become a servant.

Wading into deeper water

"When you pass through the waters,/I will be with you;/And through the rivers,/they shall not overflow you. . . . Thus says the LORD,/who makes a way in the sea/And a path through the mighty waters."—ISAIAH 43:2, 16

Miracles happen when you practice the faith of deep water. **319**
Your first acts of faith were like approaching the water on the beach with a timid toe, suspecting an unpleasant chill. You continue to move cautiously, deeper and deeper into the water. Soon the water reaches your waist, then your chest. Now your arms reach out to fan and skim the surface. You are leaving the solid bottom. By faith you swim to the deeper waters.

Faith always calls you forward. It never allows you to settle back and be satisfied. Faith compels you to wade deeper, go the extra distance.

Faith keeps you from giving up. Faiths calls you again, echoing and reechoing that solitary word, "More!"

It takes faith to wade into deep waters—especially when you don't know where the bottom is.

You do not know what the future holds, but you know who holds the future.

God is your Captain, and He knows the waters well. He keeps calling you onward and forward. God is committed to leading us always onward to new life. God knows that something dies within us when we are so safe and secure we no longer need daring and courageous faith. He is not satisfied if He sees you become stagnant. For stagnation quickly leads to swamps.

God, give me the courage to swim in the strong stream, to wade into the deeper water, to move into an area where it will be impossible to succeed without Your help! Only then will I know I live by faith. Thank You, Lord. Amen.

Striking water in the desert

*". . . waters shall burst forth in the wilderness,/
And streams in the desert."—ISAIAH 35:6*

320   The shepherd walks with his sheep even today, across blazing desert sands until he comes to a rock. There at the foot of Mount Sinai, he will do what Moses did. Moses satisfied his thirst by striking the rock in the desert. And water gushed out of the rock.

Unbelievable? Impossible? The truth is it still happens today. My son-in-law, Paul David Dunn, observed this himself when he traveled with a Bedouin to Sinai. The rocks in Sinai are granite, but have soft, porous limestone veins running through them. These limestone veins trap and hold rainfall in the rainy season. The water seeps down through invisible arteries inside the rocks collecting like little natural cisterns.

The Bedouin's staff only has to crack the side of a dry rock for water to gush out!

Faith is striking the rock that will gush with water to save the thirsty traveler.

You strike rock when you maintain and hold an unswerving positive attitude toward your predicament.

Strike the rocky experiences of life with faith and good will emerge.

Dear Father in heaven, thank You for causing deserts to spring forth with refreshing water . . .

for turning mountains into gold mines . . .

for turning upsetting experiences into unbelievable blessings.

Thank You, Father, for giving me the faith to dig for wells in the desert. Amen.

Walking on the water

> "Peter . . . walked on the water. . . . But . . . he
> was afraid; and beginning to sink he cried out,
> 'Lord, save me!' . . . Jesus . . . caught him, and
> said to him, 'O you of little faith, why did you
> doubt?'"—MATTHEW 14:29–31

By now I'm sure you understand that the walk of faith is **321** really a call to walk on water!

What happened? Was Peter suddenly defying the law of gravity? Is there some law known only to God that can override this law? The entire miraculous event is meant to teach this principle: we have to move ahead even when it seems impossible!

> **Until you attempt the impossible—until you're willing to walk on the water—you're not walking the path of faith.**

Every mountain has its peak. Every river has its deepest point. Every trouble has a life span. Every recession has its low point. Tough times turn around when you do—when you turn from doubt to faith.

God knows the altitude of the Alps and the depths of the seas. He will not call you beyond His ability to see you safely to the other side. As a father urges a creeping infant to take those first faltering steps, attempting awesome impossibilities; so God always calls you beyond your abilities.

It may seem that God is calling you to do the impossible. It may seem that God is telling you to defy the law of gravity.

It may seem that God is telling you to walk on water. Believe! For the walk of faith says, "It's possible."

O God, I want Your blessing on my life. I need Your divine blessing in my heart and mind and soul. And I know You will not give it to me until I give myself to You and take those first fearful steps. I'm trusting You, Father, as I move forward in faith. Amen.

Hypnotizing yourself positively

"Call to Me, and I will answer you, and show you great and mighty things, which you do not know."—JEREMIAH 33:3

322 Christian medical practitioners have come to appreciate this Bible verse, as they utilize the God-given powers of "depth relaxation," or hypnosis. Mrs. Schuller gave birth to our fourth child, Carol, with the help of a medical doctor who specialized in hypnosis, or depth relaxation. Her first three children came after long, painful experiences in childbirth. When she became pregnant with our fourth, a Christian friend, Robert Zimmerman, now a practicing psychiatrist in New York City, recommended the hypnosis approach. After several months of conditioning, she became suggestible and responsive to the positive thoughts the doctor was applying to her mind, such as:

You and God are partners in the act of creation. Relax and let God take over.

Part of the preparation included pinpricks. The doctor said, "I'm going to take a piece of metal and touch your skin. You will feel the cells move as they separate, allowing the metal to enter their domain."

The process was slow, but very effective. "It is not pain unless you call it pain. It is the fear of being hurt." Positive thought after positive thought was poured into her mind. When Carol was delivered, Arvella was transcended above pain. She was overwhelmed by an unforgettable experience of the presence of God. She was living in another dimension. She was using the power of faith that God has created within all of us! It is available to you.

How do you go about tapping this transcendent power of faith? Begin by deprogramming yourself from all that is negative . . . now allow positive thought after positive thought after positive thought to pour into your mind.

Transcending the present plane

"For indeed, the kingdom of God is within you."—LUKE 17:21

"Great dreams and great dreamers are never fulfilled—they are always transcended." Alfred North Whitehead said it. It's really true. The pyramiding principle and the laminating principle, which we studied earlier, are examples on the materialistic plane. On a spiritual level, faith does give us the power to transcend our present plane. It is possible to lose all awareness of the physical body when we are totally immersed in thought. A good illustration is fear. Many times people have been cut and bleeding but never noticed it until they felt the wetness of flowing blood.

323

In a different way, when I'm in the process of writing, I become so absorbed in thought that I become like the absent-minded professor, completely unaware of activities happening around me.

There are several "planes" of scientific reality. Many remain undiscovered. We think in terms of first, second, and third dimensions (length, height, and breadth). How about a fourth? And a fifth? What powers does a mind possess? What are the limits of the powers within you?

"The kingdom of God is within you," Jesus said. What are the ultimate dimensions implicit in this statement?

Miracles do happen!

Cases have been documented where cancer has spread throughout the body—and then the cancer miraculously disappeared. What forces are operating? What mysteries are at work? Considering all of the unknown realities that do exist in the known and the unknown universe, it is audacious, arrogant, and stupid to deny the possibility of a wonderful God working in all of us! Yes,

Faith says it is possible to transcend time and space!

Swimming upstream

"Now this is the confidence that we have in Him, that if we ask anything according to His will, He hears us."—1 JOHN 5:14

324 It doesn't take much faith to float down a river: "Even a dead fish can float downstream." But it takes a lot of faith to row upstream or swim against the current. Making a new mold, starting a new trend, forming a fresh fashion, resisting the popular wave, does require faith. It takes a great deal of self-reliance and self-assurance to break out of the mold and break new ground.

Watch the people who are rowing upstream. Chances are, they're not doing it to be popular or to follow the herd. They must believe in what they are doing, because they are bound to be criticized.

> **What does it take to row upstream? It takes a belief in your own brilliance, the confidence that you are absolutely as smart as any others who are succeeding!**

Come alive.
- Preserve your God-given invitation to rugged individuality.
- Discover your uniqueness.
- Maintain your separate identity.
- Resist the temptation to become a sheep that simply runs blindly with the flock.

Who knows how far you can go and what new discoveries you'll make when you decide to become an explorer? Do your own thing, and start rowing upstream.

Make sure of one thing: be led by God. When He calls, grab the oars and jump into the boat.

Confessing openly your inner convictions

"For there is nothing covered that will not be revealed, nor hidden that will not be known."— LUKE 12:2

"Dare to say no," Charles Spurgeon once advised young **325** seminarians, adding, "It can be worth more to you than a knowledge of all the foreign languages."

It takes courage to say no. That's why the development of your faith is all-important. Until your faith is strong enough for you to verbalize your inner convictions, you will cease to be a moral influence for goodness and righteousness in our society.

A wise man made this observation years ago: "All that is required for evil to conquer is for good people to do nothing."

Adolf Hitler rose to power because good people lacked courage to confess their convictions and protest the evil of his ways.

> **Powerful negative forces in our world must be offset by the strong voices of men and women with inner convictions and the faith to speak up!**

By now your faith is becoming strong enough to turn you from a person who has been easily intimidated to a person who is quickly motivated to a leadership position! Jesus said, "You are the salt of the earth; but if the salt loses its flavor, . . . it is then good for nothing . . . You are the light of the world. . . ."

Congratulations! I applaud you! Sure it takes a lot of faith! But you've got it. Now use it.

Teaching someone to think

"Do not neglect the gift that is in you."—
2 TIMOTHY 4:14

326   Does anybody have more faith in human nature than professional educators—who teach others to *think*?

You liberate people when you educate them. You dare to trust them with the freedom to make their own decisions. There have been periods in church history when the religious establishment discouraged people from reading the Bible for fear they might come up with interpretations that would conflict with the official theological position. Insecure people indoctrinate. Secure people educate.

More than one dictator has hesitated to wipe out illiteracy for fear of the power of the printed page. However, when Mao Tse-tung conquered China, he decided to indoctrinate the people in order to unify the country. This meant he had to wipe out illiteracy.

Until the advent of communism, 90 percent of the Chinese people were illiterate. Fourteen thousand characters made up the alphabet, and only a few people could read. By dictatorial fiat, Mao Tse-tung substituted a new and simplified alphabet for the ancient Chinese characters. This opened the possibility of teaching the peasants to read.

Christians saw this as a great opportunity to teach the Bible to millions of Chinese who had never been able to read. Bibles were printed in the new alphabet, and today the good news is penetrating the villages of China.

Imagine how much faith God has in you! He gave you the ability to think! He put you in a position where you have learned to read. He has given you incredible liberties. He trusts you!

O God, thank You for letting me go! I welcome my freedom to think and to believe. I will not disappoint You, Father. I will keep the faith. Amen.

FAITH IS . . .
Seasoning life around you

> "Salt is good, but if the salt loses its flavor, how will you season it? Have salt in yourselves, and have peace with one another."—MARK 9:50

Christ says it so clearly. He expects His disciples and followers who walk the walk of faith to be the salt in the society.

327

What precisely does this mean? Let me illustrate: Can you imagine how bland food is without salt? That's precisely what happens in an institution—whether it's a club, church, or legislative body—without new ideas and creative opportunities.

A community, state, country, or life becomes very matter-of-fact until a possibility thinker steps in. When he dreams great dreams, he seasons life. He creates
- beauty where there was drabness.
- excellence where there was mediocrity.
- excitement where there were only ho-hum attitudes.

Watch out, world, wherever there is a possibility thinker, life is never going to be the same again!

When possibilities begin to bounce around and big ideas produce big projects, a sleepy little town starts awakening! This is the exciting challenge!

Put some energy and enthusiasm in the lives of people around you!

Dynamic leaders who season the world with fulfilling plans can liven things up in a hurry!

Dear God, may I never lose my saltiness.

May I never stop dreaming dreams that can put excitement in my life. May I never surrender to the great "yawn," the boredom that comes through impossibility thinking.

Today, I am going to get things moving! I will be the seasoning in the feast of life. Thank You, Lord. Amen.

FAITH IS . . .
Inching ahead

"If you have faith as a mustard seed, you will say to this mountain, 'move . . .' and nothing will be impossible for you."—MATTHEW 17:20

328 One of the elements that makes faith powerful is its requirement to believe in the might of the miniature. A tiny seed—but what a mighty plant can emerge!

A small thought passing through the mind inconspicuously, without fanfare, can be easily overlooked. There are latent possibilities in the small thought, the little act, and the commonplace functions of life. I telephoned two friends today. One was hospitalized. I encouraged him and prayed a positive prayer for him. When I finished, his voice was broken with emotion as he thanked me. It was such a small thought. It took only a minute.

The other call was to an attorney friend who is experiencing business difficulties. I assured him that whatever happens I recognize him as a person of unquestionable integrity. By reassuring him of my respect, I gave him a lift! Again, it was such a little thing to do.

A telephone call, a positive reinforcement—these encouraging words to a troubled person can make the difference between life and death! A simple act of thoughtfulness may appear to be such a little thing. But it can turn the mood from depression to hope, and in so doing move a mighty mountain!

Today, move a mountain with a little thought. Pick up a telephone, write a letter, or make a hospital call; simply be positive and optimistic. Build the spirits of someone who needs a lift!

Thank You, God, that I have been given the gift of encouraging people around me! I'll make every day beautiful by some small act of love and kindness. Amen.

Steering a steady course

". . . and He [Jesus] steadfastly set His face to go
to Jerusalem."—LUKE 9:51

When you are a believer in yourself and your dream, you **329**
become believable to others. Stay steady on the course, never
taking your eye off your ultimate objective.

**You may compromise your position or accommodate
your strategies, but never take your eye off the ultimate goal.**

Do not be rattled by setbacks. Don't allow panic to grip you
when projections fall short and cash flow produces a crunch,
for faith steers a steady course.

My friend who is a pilot once told me about the time when
he was making a bombing dive over enemy waters during
World War II. "I was just at the end of my descent and ready to
level off when I was hit." He said, "Instantly I recalled what
was drilled into us at pilot school. 'When you are in real trouble, don't do a thing! Just *think!*' So I never touched the controls. My first impulse was to grab the controls, but at that
precise moment that was the worst thing to do. The controls
were already set. And my plane leveled off. Had I touched the
controls, I would have nose-dived into the bay!"*

When you take a potentially fatal hit, just *think!* And *think
positively!* You'll make it.

You know, Jesus Christ steered a steady course. He announced that He was going to be our Savior. He predicted that
it would mean death on a cross. He never backed away from
His cross. He "steadfastly set His face" to pursue His God-
given goal.

---

*Robert H. Schuller, *Tough Times Never Last, But Tough People Do* (Nashville:
Thomas Nelson, 1983), pp. 101–103.

Soldiering the battle

"Take up the whole armor of God, . . . having girded your waist with truth, having put on the breastplate of righteousness, . . . above all, taking the shield of faith . . . the helmet of salvation and the sword of the Spirit . . ."—
EPHESIANS 6:13–17

330   Why does this walk of faith involve so many difficulties?

If God loves me, why do I have so many troubles? If God is so good, why does the road have to be so rough?

It's important to remember that the walk of faith is designed to serve God's cause in His kingdom.

We are invited to be soldiers in God's army—not tourists on an around-the-world trip.

I have written some of these pages in Europe, where, as a tourist, I stayed in fine hotels, slept in beds between white sheets, and ate from tables with white linen!

My brother covered the same territory a few decades back when he served the American Armed Forces as a medical litter-bearer during World War II. It was his job to run to the front lines, pick up the wounded and the dying, and race them back for emergency treatment.

My brother traveled as a soldier. I traveled as a tourist.

At no point does the Bible invite us to go on a worldwide luxury tour with Jesus Christ as our guide.

Rather we are commissioned to be God's soldiers in a rough battle to conquer the enemy and liberate the land for the glory and the good of the human family!

Affirmation: Faith is soldiering for battle. I can expect tough times. Therefore, I will put on the helmet of salvation and the shield of faith. I shall carry the sword of the spirit. I shall wear the breastplate of righteousness! I expect to win!

Thank You, Father for reminding me today that I am called to be a soldier, not a tourist. Thank You for setting my faith straight again today. Amen.

Undergoing to be an overcomer

"This is the victory that has overcome the
world—our faith."—1 JOHN 5:4

331

Anybody who is going anywhere is going to be undergoing
something! And anybody can be an overcomer if he has
enough faith. Endurable optimism is what gives you the
power to succeed. To put it another way: the undergoers become overcomers! Let me teach you a prayer today that I believe will give you the extra faith to be victorious and to
overcome.

Almighty God, You know what I am undergoing. Help me
to overcome. Don't let me become a pessimist. Preserve my
optimistic outlook. I may lose many things, Father, but let me
never lose my faith.

- Lord, You were the Undergoer who became the Over-
  comer!
- You died on the cross;
- You rose on Easter.

Today hundreds of millions of people around the world
know You, love You, respect You, admire You, draw inspiration and life from You!

You promise to be my Friend. You promise that if I keep
believing I will win. You promise: "This is the victory that has
overcome the world—our faith." Give me the courage to overcome the negative feelings that may depress my spirit, deflate
my hopes, and defuse my enthusiasm.

> **My faith tells me that I have Your power within me
> now, because You are standing beside me, encouraging
> me all the way with Your promise, "Victory will be
> yours, My friend."**

Thank You, Jesus Christ. Amen.

FAITH IS . . .
Following through—anyway

"Love . . . bears all things."—1 CORINTHIANS
13:7

332 Love and faith are two faces of a single coin. Can there be love without faith? Can there be faith without love? Read today's text this way: "Faith bears all things." What do you do when you trust someone, and they let you down? Faith follows through on your part of the bargain—anyway. Did someone leave you stranded, not sharing part of the burden? Faith carries on—without them!

When you made a commitment in happier times you never expected that the scene would shift into such a negative situation. Now that the tide has turned, what do you do? Do you use the present difficulty as an excuse to get out, or does your strong sense of honesty and integrity compel you to live by the commitment you made in good faith?

Faith is the positive attitude that if you are faithful to the contract you will be able to hold your head high. You will be a believable and trustworthy person.

Such perserverance sustained and strengthened by your integrity will win you a reputation that will command great support the next time you prepare to move into new possibilities.

Our Lord Jesus Christ gave a great illustration of this. He experienced the agony of hell on the cross. Even though His heavenly Father was silent, Jesus kept the faith! He went on about His positive work of redemption. Faith keeps on believing through the difficult times in a God who is still kind, compassionate, and good. That's precisely when you need God most!

Laughing up a storm

> "A merry heart does good, like medicine,/But a
> broken spirit dries the bones."—PROVERBS 17:22

To the best of our knowledge, the human being is the only **333** creature that has the capacity for humor.

Humor after all is impossible without faith.

People who lack faith are easily irritated and agitated! Uptight and touchy, they are easily provoked to anger and are slow to see amusement in life's negative experiences.

Only a self-confident, self-assured person has enough faith to laugh at himself and his critics.

Yes, humor is one of the most beautiful reflections of faith in a human being. Positive-thinking believers become the kind of people who smile through their tears and laugh despite tragedy.

Humor, as we now know, is part of the healing process. It's now well accepted that humor releases endorphines, chemicals in the brain that are stimulated by positive emotions. We have always known thoughts stimulate the body glands to produce secretions. Researchers at UCLA Medical School have proven that the brain is, in effect, a gland that produces chemical secretions when stimulated by the positive emotion of humor.

Is it irreverent to welcome comedy in the middle of tragedy? Not at all! It is God's design to relax the tension of grief. Humor in times of horrific hurt will contribute to the healing and comfort so desperately needed in the tortured community.

Affirm today: I will resolve to bring laughter to life. I can always purchase some balloons, blow them up, and watch children laugh as I release the balloons to sail off or float down to the little hands of a child!

Today, I'll prove to the world I'm a believer—I'll laugh a lot!

Today, I will laugh up a storm—in the middle of one.

Compromising on trivialities

"Turn away my eyes from looking at worthless things,/And revive me in Your way."—PSALM 119:37

334 Walking along the beach in Hawaii, I noticed two native Hawaiians in the shallow surf. They held a little screen between them, which they were shaking back and forth. I walked over to them and inquired, "What are you looking for?" They named a little ocean creature that I had never heard of.

I watched them pick a little beetle off the screen and put it in a can with several others. Then they casually discarded several attractive seashells.

"You threw away some pretty shells!" I exclaimed.

They looked at me incredulously, but answered respectfully, "You can't catch fish with shells. With these little beetles, we catch big fish, food for our family!"

Faith is the fine art of compromising wisely. Shells are *trivial*—they are pretty but not life-supporting. Fish is *basic*—it is food to sustain health and strength.

There is always the present danger of being distracted from the basics by being attracted to the trivial.

You have to turn this business of compromising into a fine art.

Faith compromises the alluring, veneer values in favor of the intrinsic values.

Thank You, Father. You are guiding me and giving me Your wisdom.

I won't make the mistake of losing a dollar by trying to save a dime.

I will not sacrifice my marriage for some cheap relationship.

I will not give up my godly faith for some passing pleasure.

I make this commitment now—to give up the trivial in favor of the really valuable.

Help me, Lord. Amen.

FAITH IS . . .
Knowing it can be done!

"I can do all things through Christ who strengthens me."—PHILIPPIANS 4:13

Faith is an inner conviction.

It is an unshakeable assurance.

It is the profound "knowing" that comes before reality confirms it.

Faith is a sense of destiny: "It's possible." "It's going to happen."

Faith is knowing that you can do it.

The person who walks the walk of faith knows he can solve his problem!

He *knows* that he can detach himself from that awful habit.

He *knows* he can extricate himself from his negative enslavements.

The person who walks the walk of faith faces his projects, affirming:

I *know* I can do it—*if* God will help me. And I'm sure God wants to help me!

I know I can do it *when* I'm totally dedicated to Him, which I really am!

I know I can do it *after* everything is in readiness. And I am trusting God to help me get my act together!

I know I can do it *only* with the help of my Lord. He is my best friend. He wants me to succeed.

I can do all things *through* Christ who strengthens me! I know it's possible after all.

Deep down in your heart, you know it will work out. An unquenchable confidence keeps fueling your feelings that you're going to make it.

Again and again the person who succeeds did so because he or she didn't know it was impossible!

Renting with option to buy

"My people will dwell in a peaceful habitation,/
In secure dwellings, and in quiet resting
places."—ISAIAH 32:18

336 It is not uncommon to sense tension in residential communities between homeowners and people who rent nearby apartments and houses. It is assumed—not always correctly—that people who are buying a home and investing in real estate have a far greater vested interest in the community institutions: local government, public schools, and social services.

Now, for people who would love to buy but can't afford to, the sellers of new homes in California have established a practice of allowing people to rent their homes with an option to buy.

Remember? There are degrees of faith! There are those with faith so strong they simply plunge into the purchase agreement, as it were. They put up a heavy chunk of earnest money, which they are prepared to forfeit if the transaction is not executed. They are willing to risk thousands of dollars to secure their purchase position in the market.

But what about those sincere people with faith that toddles on childish feet! God gives them the chance to build their faith. He makes it easier for them to take the first faltering steps, encouraging them to try. Let them simply rent the house but apply the rental fees to the purchase price, if they will make a firm commitment within a reasonable period of time. We should not criticize those with feeble faith but rather applaud them for their first steps of faith, however faltering they may be!

At least people who want to believe put themselves in a position where they can maneuver themselves into a stronger corner and step up at a later date. They're getting their foot in the door.

If you don't have the faith to make the total commitment, at least take that first step.

Analyzing the obstructions

> "If any of you lacks wisdom, let him ask of
> God, who gives to all liberally and without
> reproach. . . . But let him ask in faith . . . for he
> who doubts is like a wave in the sea driven and
> tossed by the wind."—JAMES 1:5–6

I had an experience last week that illustrates today's theme **337**
dramatically. I made a trip to Fort Wayne, Indiana, for a special
speaking engagement. My schedule was really tight. The
plane landed only thirty-five minutes before I had to walk into
the black-tie event. I was rushed downtown to the coliseum,
then backstage to a dressing room where a rented tuxedo was
waiting for me. "You have only ten minutes, Dr. Schuller. The
governor is waiting for you. So hurry." These were my instructions.

I tried on the coat. Perfect fit. I then slipped on the trousers.
Perfect fit. I checked the shoes, socks, cummerbund, black tie.
Everything was there. I slipped on the white shirt. The neck
was perfect, the sleeve length was perfect, but it was a tapered
shirt. Much more tapered than I. At that point, there was a
knock on the door. "Are you ready, Dr. Schuller?" I said, "Not
quite!" A button at my wasit—now, I'm not exaggerating—
was ten inches from the hole. I took one look at that shirt and
noticed it had a seam on both sides. I had only two seconds to
solve my problem. I ripped the shirt seams open, creating so
much space that I closed the buttons neatly. I pulled the cummerbund on and then the coat. Naturally I kept the coat but-
toned, and during the entire speech I never waved my arms.

Of course, at the end of the evening I told my friend to send
me a bill for the shirt. It's amazing how easily we can be intimidated or manipulated by material things. They can take
control and take charge unless you and I have the faith to
analyze the obstruction and begin to take action.

Daring to fail

"He [God] will not allow your foot to be
moved,/He who keeps you will not slumber.
. . . The Lord shall preserve your going out and
your coming in . . . forevermore."—PSALM
121:3,8

338   For over thirty years as a pastor, I have counseled untold
hundreds of persons face-to-face, and tens of thousands by
mail. Beyond a shadow of a doubt, the vast majority of these
persons who profess to walk the walk of faith and who claim
they are living by faith, are, in fact, missing the mark.

Mountain-moving faith is something they have never truly
experienced. Why? Where did their faith get bogged down?

What hidden sandbar grounded the ship?

What rubble under the water snagged the hook?

What obstacle in the road blew out the tire?

What impurity in the fuel caused the engine to fail?

What infectious germ entered the body of faith to produce a
debilitating sickness?

In one single phrase, the problem can be easily summed up:
"fear of failure."

I determine to succeed in the walk of faith by making one
simple decision, one powerful affirmation:

I will dare to fail.

I will not be afraid of failure, for God has promised that He
will be my help. He will not allow me to stumble or fall.

He will plant my feet firmly one step at a time. And with
each upward step, I shall climb without a fall!

Then I shall pause and turn around.

I'll be shocked at how high I have climbed, and how successful I have been!

Great goals are never reached until you decide to dare to
fail!

Advertising your abilities

"Let your light so shine before men, that they
may see your good works and glorify your
Father in heaven."—MATTHEW 5:16

Yes! Let the world know you believe—in yourself! "You **339**
mean toot my own horn?" you ask.

I answer, "Yes, unless you can find someone else to blow it
better."

"Isn't that dangerous self-congratulation?" you ask.

I answer, "Depends on how you do it. Just don't be a shrinking violet."

When you advertise your ability, you are bragging—about
the goodness and greatness of God in your life! Tell the world
what God can do! Let everybody know the difference faith
makes in your life! Share with people how you've been able to
conquer problems through walking the walk of faith.

Expose, without modesty, in word and in deed, the good
things God has done in your life. Let your light shine!

Don't be afraid to sell yourself!

After all, who created you?

After all, who redeemed you from evil and failure and sin?

After all, who gave you your abilities and talents?

After all, who gave you the motivation that drives you upward and forward!

After all, who gave you the integrity and enthusiasm that
makes you the kind of worker the average employer would
love to hire? It is, of course, God and His Son, Jesus Christ.

When you advertise your abilities, you are bearing witness
to the power of faith in your life!

Get on with it. Advertise—today—without fear. Don't
worry about becoming proud or arrogant. The easiest job in
the world for God is to humble a human being.

> **God's biggest job is to keep you believing, minute by
> minute and day by day, how good you really are once
> His Spirit has moved into your life!**

Hammering the nails

"As for me, You uphold me in my integrity,/And set me before Your face forever."—PSALM 41:12

340   Faith—like a driven nail—aims at connecting separated elements, binding them into a stronger, more effective union.

The process of faith, too, is not unlike the hammering of the nail. Carefully select the right nail for the right job. Select the correct length. Too short, and it will fail to hold. (Do I have enough faith? Is it too weak? Do I need more patience?)

Too long—and it will go all the way through, doing more harm than good. (Am I being too patient? Neglecting treatment? Avoiding the painful and inevitable extraction? Hurting myself and others by delaying the costly decision?)

Faith is making the move, now. It is hammering the nail once I have selected the right one!

I take that nail and hold it cautiously, steadily, between two fingers. I raise the hammer. I tap the nail gently. I repeat the tapping. A bit harder. The nail stands on its own now, precariously, but steady and unmoving. The next tap of the hammer is crucial. I don't want to dislodge it, and send it flying. I need to drive it a bit deeper. Another whack. A hard one now! It's halfway in the wood. I can't even wiggle it. Now I can drive it full force. It is almost all the way in. I can just get the claws under it to extract it if I want to. I don't ever want it to come out! A final all-out blow. There, the head of the nail is below the surface of the wood. I can see the indented print of the hammer head. It will never come out!

That's the process of building a strong faith!

Each new adventure with God is another blow driving your faith deeper.

Each moment you spend in positive prayer makes your faith more solid.

Each positive affirmation of faith contributes to the self-confidence and power God gives you as you move forward on your walk of faith.

Standing up to be counted

"He who walks with integrity/walks
securely."—PROVERBS 10:9

The challenge to "stand up and be counted" comes to every **341** person more often than he might choose.

Faith becomes the force that puts us on our feet!

Fear might keep us sitting on the sidelines.

Worry about possible conflict we may encounter through sharing our commitment might seal our lips.

The fear of offending someone when standing firm on our convictions, might urge us to maintain neutrality.

But faith commands integrity, and integrity forces us to confront the issue.

Ultimately your character and mine will be evaluated by our integrity.

Have we been honest, reliable, and responsible? Faith, more than any other single factor, causes us to develop and to maintain a character branded with the hallmark of integrity!

The faith that calls for integrity will actually be strengthened in the process.

> **Internal peace of mind comes to a person who *knows* that he did the right things.**

Consider the anxiety-prone, over-cautious person. He is so security minded that he doesn't want to take sides! He lacks the courage to stand up for his own convictions. Does he secure his position when he loses his integrity? Does he become a braver, more self-confident person through this duplicity? Is this the strategy for personal security?

On the contrary, by remaining evasive he loses the respect and the support of his most powerful and important friends. In the process one actually loses the base of his security!

How wise was the writer of Proverbs when he wrote these words: "He who walks with integrity/walks securely."

Embracing God's grace

> "For by grace you have been saved through faith, and that not of yourselves; it is the gift of God, not of works, lest anyone should boast."—
> EPHESIANS 2:8

342 What's the best gift that faith can deliver to your life?
It is the gift of salvation from sin.

It is the peace of mind that comes from knowing that Christ died for your sins on the cross.

It is the serenity of spirit that comes over you when you know God has pardoned you.

It is the mental health you experience when old guilt is gone.

How can you earn this salvation?

You can't. A gift is something you can only accept. If you earn it then it becomes a salary—not a gift!

You are pardoned, forgiven, and saved by the grace of God. And what is grace? It is God's love in action for those who don't deserve it.

Grace is the most beautiful word in the English language. Nothing is more valuable than a gift that is given when you don't deserve it—

- love before you've earned it.
- credit when it is not justified.

The hardest task in the world is for an honorable person to accept something he has not earned. This explains why people are extremely reticent and resistant to accepting the gospel of Jesus Christ, salvation by the grace of God.

Today make one of the greatest leaps of faith that is possible! Embrace God's grace. Accept His understanding and forgiveness. Trust Him not only to cleanse you of sin and negativity but to inspire you to treat other persons the same way.

You suddenly realize that you are *forgiven not through the good works you do, but to do good works!*

FAITH IS . . .
Glorifying God with great victories

"Now to Him who is able to do exceedingly
abundantly above all that we ask or think,
according to the power that works in us, to
Him be glory. . . . Amen."—EPHESIANS 3:20–21

Does possibility thinking sound arrogant? Can this walk of **343**
faith become a vain venture? Is there the danger that you're
really glorifying yourself? Are you in it for yourself more than
for your Lord?

The answers to all of these questions are abundantly clear.

God is glorified by the great victories of His people.

And what is victory? Any God-given idea that, with His
help, has turned into an actual achievement!

If God started the project with an idea planted in your brain,
and God stimulated the success by motivating you to plunge
ahead and run the risk of failure and criticism, and if God will
finally see you through to an ultimate success, who really is
glorified? Both you and your Lord. God wants you to be honored. He wants you to experience a wonderful sense of humble pride in accomplishment! After all, you are His child.

All parents love to see their children enjoy a proud accomplishment. But who really gets the credit? Of course the glory
goes to our Lord! You do not need to piously announce in
every breath, "I'm doing this for the glory of God." The
achievements of those who believe carry with them the un-
mistakable label that God has been at work.

How then can you best glorify God? By committing yourself to the great ideas God has entrusted to your stewardship,
which He expects you to return to Him as human achievements worthy of being offered as gifts on the altar of my God.

O God, I will attempt to glorify You, not simply through
pious prayer, but through great achievements! Amen.

Pressing the wrinkles

> "O God, You have taught me from my youth;
> . . . /Now also when I am old and gray-headed,
> O God, do not forsake me,/Until I declare Your
> strength to this generation."—PSALM 71:17–18

344 "Oh, I don't think I should wear this dress, it'll get too wrinkled," I heard my wife say.

"Of course it will," I reminded her, "but you can press out the wrinkles."

Faith is wearing a suit—even if it does wrinkle! It's taking the shiny car out—even if it is raining. It's deciding to live the Christian life—even if I can't live it perfectly and sinlessly.

Faith believes that cars can be washed again; sins can be forgiven one more time; mistakes can be corrected. Or they can turn us into wiser, wealthier, or more wonderful persons; and wrinkles can be pressed out!

Faith presses out the negative wrinkles! You have to do that all the time.

Do you see the universal principle here? Every time you forgive others and give them another chance, you press out a negative wrinkle.

We do it in our marriage too, don't we? "I'm sorry I hurt you." That's pressing out a negative wrinkle.

But faith also presses *in* the *positive* wrinkles. Since some wrinkles can't be pressed out like wrinkles around the eyes, then it's very important how you choose the wrinkles! I know people who live positively, year after year. By the time they become old and gray they have what I call "twinkle wrinkles."

No wonder they're more beautiful the older they get! The "twinkle wrinkles" are actually attractive lines pressed into their face by a lifetime of positive thinking.

All the while a positive mental attitude presses out the wrinkles and lines left by life's troubles, trials, and tribulations.

Meditation: Imagine your mind like a wrinkled garment. Imagine your faith as a steam iron erasing the wrinkles! Imagine the hand of Jesus on the iron! Amen.

FAITH IS . . .
Sculpting your spirit

"Let this mind be in you which was also in
Christ Jesus."—PHILIPPIANS 2:5

"I don't like the looks of that man," Abraham Lincoln is **345**
reported to have said to an aide.

"A person can't help what he looks like, Mr. President," the
aide replied.

"Oh, yes, he can," Mr. Lincoln answered.

Negative-thinking people develop faces that become hard,
or hostile, or unfriendly. Skepticism sketches scars on the face
of a cynic, creating wrinkles that carve deeply into the face. It
bears repeating again and again: beauty is mind deep.

Each thought, like a drop of water on a marble statue, will
leave an effect, however indelible or invisible it may appear,
on the shape and sculpture of your soul. Today, resolve that by
the grace of Jesus Christ, you can and will become a beautiful
human being. Here's an affirmation beauty treatment:

• I shall believe in a God of goodness and generosity. This
will reflect a hopeful sparkle in my eye.

• I shall believe the best about people.

• I shall have peaceful attitudes toward my fellow human
beings; which will cast a beauty across my face.

• I shall never become a mean-looking person!

• I shall believe that hardship and pain, trouble and sickness
will all shape my appearance with a look of kindness and
compassion. For I believe God will bless my sufferings. This
belief will shape my face into a serene and sweet-looking face.
People will meet me and leave remarking how beautiful I
looked. I shall walk upright, shoulders back, chin high, well-
postured, proclaiming to the world that I am self-confident,
for I am walking with Jesus Christ. He is my Savior; He is my
guide; He is my inspirer. He is my *number-one encourager*. I
am living and walking with Him day by day. I am becoming
more and more conformed to His likeness. I am becoming
beautiful. Thank You, Lord.

FAITH IS . . .
Grandfathering my hopes

> "The mercy of the LORD is from everlasting to everlasting . . ./And His righteousness to children's children . . ./And to those who remember His commandments to do them."—
> PSALM 103:17–18

346 There was a time when the word *grandfather* was known only as a noun. Today in governmental circles it has become a verb. Politicians use the word *grandfather* to mean passing off liabilities that we incur today to future generations. This is a negative use of the word. I want to use it positively.

Remember the gas in the tank that you probably won't use? If you don't use it yourself, you can grandfather it. Somebody who comes down the road can benefit from it.

Faith believes that when you take positive action, great good will result. You may not personally benefit from it, but somebody will.

I'll never forget the tornado that raged across our Iowa farm home destroying all of the nine buildings, most of the livestock, and virtually all of our personal possessions. Not the least of the damage was to the orchard. Yet my arthritic, crippled father, cane in hand, walked through the demolished orchard and said, "We'll plant an apple tree here," as he left a scratch in the tortured ground. Then he made another X in the scarred earth and said, "We'll plant another apple tree here."

I looked at him and said, "But, Dad, you're an old man. Do you expect to live to eat the fruit of these trees?"

To my surprise he retorted swiftly, "The fruit I eat is from trees somebody else planted! I have to plant trees for others who will follow me."

Grandfathering! What a beautiful philosophy of life! Today I want to think of investments that will outlast and outlive me! Can I plant a tree? Can I share a treasured recipe? In some way, I can pass on the knowledge of my walk of faith to my grandchildren yet unborn.

Surrendering to love

"There is no fear in love; but perfect love casts out fear."—1 JOHN 4:18

On the walk of faith, faith is the most important value in human life—except for its Siamese twin, love. The two cannot be severed through any form of spiritual surgery without killing both. **347**

One thing is certain: When you surrender to love, you can't be making a big mistake.

When you are in doubt, do the most loving thing.

If you ever face a situation where faith and love are in adversarial positions, let love win out. Faith will follow.

> **Faith has enough trust in mercy that it can dare to surrender to love! Love without faith is weakness. Faith without love is dangerous.**

It is well to remember this when you face times when you are compelled to ask yourself:

- Is this the time for me to step down and retire?
- Should I stop fighting this cancer?
- Should I continue to battle for my viewpoint? Or is there a time and place when I should surrender?
- Are there times when giving in might actually be a greater move of faith than stubbornly hanging in there?

As a pastor, I once offered this prayer for one of my people, and I share it again today for your benefit.

Lord, give me the guidance to know when to hold on and when to let go, and the grace to make the right decision with dignity. Amen.

Singing a new song

"Oh, sing to the LORD a new song. . . .
Proclaim the good news of His salvation from
day to day. . . . His wonders among all
peoples."—PSALM 96:1–3

348 There are four levels of prayer. The first level of prayer is *petition*. Go to God and ask Him for help.

The second level of prayer is *intercession*. Don't ask for anything for yourself; instead, pray for someone else who really needs God's help.

The third level of prayer is *praise*. Go to God and thank Him for all the blessings you enjoy today.

The fourth level of prayer is "two-way" prayer. Simply go to God and ask Him questions; then let Him answer. "Dear God, is there anything that I should praise You for today? Is there any reason why I should be thankful?" Now *listen!* Listen for God's answer, "Yes, be thankful that I am here. Be thankful that you are alive, and can talk to Me!"

After suffering heart failure and undergoing major surgery, Jerry Lewis said, "Every morning I know that I am a winner, for I have survived! Everybody who wakes up in the morning is a success!"

You can choose today to sing a song in discordant melodies of gloom and doom. That's an old song; it's a worn-out record.

Try singing a new song!

God is alive. Sing a song of praise to Him. He has spared you from more problems, pains, and perils than you will ever know! Start singing!

Dear God, I am a believer. I'm going to sing a new song today. My mood is changing. That's a miracle! It's going to be a great day, Lord! Thank You for turning me around. Amen.

Retiring from retirement

"Take heed to the ministry which you have
received in the Lord, that you may fulfill it."—
COLOSSIANS 4:17

"I'm retiring from retirement—too risky," the bright, twin- **349**
kling senior citizen chuckled. Then he became very serious. "I
really mean it. This business of retirement is downright dangerous. It is putting strains on my marriage. I'm so bored. I'm
grumbling too much. I'm turning into a crotchety old man,
and I'm not going to let that happen."

"What do you plan to do?" I asked.

"I've decided to drive a cab!" I was amused and amazed,
since he has a professional degree and an impressive resumé.
"I've been a passenger in cabs all over the world," he explained, "and I've observed that taxicab drivers are in the
unique position of being able to talk to people. I expect to be
able to share my faith in my country and in our system of
politics and economics, and to say a good word for Jesus
Christ!"

Faith is *fulfilling* your calling, not retiring from it. What
calling must you fulfill today?

Let's step out of retirement today and do the ministry that
Christ has entrusted to us.

- Today I will be an encourager to someone who is discouraged.
- I will give someone a sincere compliment today.
- I shall believe that my positive faith will help someone
  become a believer in themselves and in God.

I feel the presence of Christ within me. It's a wonderful feeling, letting a beautiful God live within me and love people
through me. Wow. There is a good work waiting for me to do
today! I'm getting out of retirement and into the stream of life
again.

Looking forward with hope

"Hope in God;/For I shall yet praise Him, The help of my countenance and my God."—PSALM 43:5

350 Are you really walking the walk of faith? Ask yourself these questions: Am I looking ahead with hope or am I looking back with disappointment? Do I tend to count my strike-outs or do I tend to count the hits?

If you keep score of your mistakes, setbacks, and disappointments you undermine your faith as surely as a raging, flooded stream undermines the foundations of a building.

Charles Spurgeon, the famous English clergyman, once faced a great disappointment. He went to visit a farmer who was a devoted elder in his church. The farmer said, "Pastor, what is that cow doing?"

Spurgeon looked and answered, "Well, she's looking over the wall."

The farmer said, "Yes, she is looking *over* the wall because she can't see *through* it."

In the walk of faith there will be times when you face walls that you can't see through. But you can look over them! When you look *beyond*, *around*, and *over* the obstacles, fanciful or factual, an amazing thing happens: You visualize yourself with the obstacle behind you! When you can imagine success, then an inner energy is generated that can best be described in one short word: *"Hope"*!

Hope is the difference between ultimate success or failure; between life or death.

> **I choose to live and succeed by continuing to look forward with hope.**

In the process I know that I am exercising the mountain-moving faith which God promises to bless!

Spotting the hidden potential

"Love . . . believes all things."—1 CORINTHIANS
13:7

Have you noticed how some people spot opportunities **351**
while they are still opportunities, and others never recognize
opportunities until they have become accomplishments?

> **Possibility thinking is the mental process that intu-
> itively sifts and spots opportunities while they are still
> fresh and potentially viable.**

"Love believes all things." So possibility thinkers have the
capacity to believe in *all things*, which means that:

- You see opportunities in obstacles.
- You believe that a stumbling block can become a stepping
  stone.
- You believe that frustrations can become meaningful
  forces to guide you along the right path.
- You believe that God uses both the good and bad experiences to mold, motivate, and educate you.

More than once in my life, when facing an enormous setback, I have prayed aloud to God, "Now, Lord—it's going to be
very interesting to see what you will make out of this mess!"
Believe me, He has always surprised me with His creativity!

The Lord does not lack the imagination to build something
beautiful out of that which has been broken.

The heavenly Father is no failure! His goals are to turn you
and me into wonderful people. Through sunlight and storm
He is sculpting your soul. You need only to keep on believing
that something beautiful is going to emerge out of all of this.
Choose to believe in this wonderful, sovereign, sensitive
God—today!

FAITH IS . . .
Living without insurance

"Heaven and earth will pass away, but My words will by no means pass away."—LUKE 21:33

352 The most valued possessions of life cannot be covered by insurance! The challenge of faith is to live life abundantly and adventurously—even without insurance!

Who can insure you against cancer?

against car and plane crashes?

against loss of a loved one?

against an untimely death?

against painful divorce or personal relationships?

Yes, careful observance of natural laws of providence can reduce risks in these categories.

Yes, dynamic philosophy of life can minimize the chances of pain in the human heart.

But the reality is this: Life without risk is impossible. So there is no alternative to faith! Faith is our only option!

In *Alice in Wonderland*, the white knight, as he prepared for a journey, anticipated all the possible problems that could befall him. To withstand attacks from lions, he covered his horse with sheets of steel. To protect his horse from alligators, the knight attached knives to the legs of his horse. By the time the horse and rider were protected against all of the fantasized dangers, the horse collapsed under the weight!

As you walk the walk of faith you live without insurance, but your faith is your assurance.

Christians trust God's Word, and God's promises of eternal life! They are convinced that heaven and earth may pass away, but the words of God will never pass away!

Thank You, God, that You are calling me to march forward. You beckon me to holy adventures in the journey of life. Thank You for the insurance I do have: the insurance of Your promise that You will never leave me nor forsake me. Thank You, God. Amen.

FAITH IS . . .
Abandoning all fears

"Who shall separate us from the love of Christ?
Shall tribulation, or distress, or persecution, or
famine, or nakedness, or peril, or sword? . . . In
all these things we are more than conquerors
through Him who loved us."—ROMANS 8:35, 37

I admit I was once a chain smoker, indulging in what I now **353**
know to be a very physically destructive and hence a negative
and sinful habit. But addiction to cigarette smoking was a difficult habit to break. It was fear of lung cancer that finally
caused me to quit. But it was a positive desire to live more
than a fear of dying that made me break the habit.

How does faith conquer all fears? A psychiatrist once said,
"The fear of death is the mother of all fears." If you conquer
the fear of dying, you really conquer all other fears as well.

How does faith conquer the fear of death? Faith believes
there is a God who made this world and is alive today. He
came to this world in the form of a human being—Jesus
Christ. Jesus died on a cross to save you and me from our sins.
Through Him, we have forgiveness of sins and a solid assurance of pardon, which removes all guilt and all fear of judgment.

I know that if I die tonight, I need not fear divine judgment;
for Jesus Christ will be my lawyer to represent me before the
Great Judge. He will plead my case, and I shall be admitted to
the presence of the Eternal One with joy and gladness!

Have you accepted Jesus as your Friend, your Savior?

> **Jesus Christ, I accept You now as my Savior. I open my
> mind and life for Your refreshing love to flow in me
> and through me. I rejoice with tears of gladness in the
> salvation which You give me now. I need fear nothing
> anymore!**

Enduring all the way

"Love . . . endures all things."—1 CORINTHIANS 13:7

354 Faith can be compared to a battery. Some people have faith with a short life span, while others have super staying power.

Staying power is what you need today. Your faith will become so strong that you will have the power of endurance adequate for whatever your life encounters.

God gives endurance to match encounters.

My dear friend, the late Corrie ten Boom, often told the story of how she expressed her anxieties to her father when she was a child. "Daddy, I wish I had the faith to face tragedies with a cheerful spirit."

Her father answered her: "Corrie, the Lord will give you the faith when you need it! Just keep trusting Him."

Then he went on to explain, "Corrie, when I send you to the store, I don't give you the money to carry in your pockets while you are playing. I give you the money when you are ready to go to the market."

Corrie learned the lesson well. Years later she was arrested by the Nazis and placed in a concentration camp. She found that she had unbelievable faith to face the worst possible human tragedies without collapsing internally.

Have you really committed your life 100 percent to Jesus Christ? Have you accepted Him as your Living Friend? Your person Savior? Your ultimate authority? Your private Lord? If so, I guarantee that God will not allow you to be deprived of your most needed resource at the most critical time. He will provide faith when you need it the most, and you will endure to the end!

Compromising before quitting

"Love . . . hopes all things."—1 CORINTHIANS
13:7

Faith produces success *when it is strong enough to compro-* **355**
mise before quitting.

Compromise can be kingly! It takes an inwardly secure person to back down, back off, settle for less, and still make a go of it.

Retreating is sometimes the wisest way to advance. Compromise today; make up for it tomorrow. Give a little now. Regain it—and more—down the road.

Mao Tse Tung used this principle of success very cleverly. "One step back, two steps forward." It was a major element in his success. It is a clever device that has been used by other Communist powers worldwide.

"I'm going to blow my brains out, Reverend." The man was desperate. Life was too much for him to handle.

"Before you quit on living," I urged, "why don't you quit doubting and give faith a chance."

He was a proud man who wanted to run his life without any interference from an almighty God. But the result was alcoholism and now attempted suicide.

"Why don't you compromise a bit?" I asked. "Why don't you give in to God? He's there. You've just been too stubborn to give yourself a chance to become a believer!" The good news is this man compromised—before quitting. He turned his life over to God and became a believer.

Compromise is the gateway to the great way.

What compromise do you need to make today? If you're facing tough times, don't quit. Compromise!

FAITH IS . . .

Bowing out gracefully

"Lord, now You are letting Your servant depart in peace . . . for my eyes have seen Your salvation."—LUKE 2:29–30

356 One of the beautiful old men in the Bible is Simeon. Talk about faith. He dared to pray that he might live to see the birth of the Messiah. The day finally came when Joseph and Mary brought their newborn baby boy to be circumcised. With a deep conviction that came from God, Simeon knew this baby was the Promised One. This Jesus would be the fulfillment of the Old Testament prophesies.

Simeon's prayer was answered. And so he added a charming affirmation: "Lord, now You are letting Your servant depart in peace."

What more could we hope for as we come to the end of the year? The time comes to close the book, to turn in the report, to offer your resignation, or to accept retirement from the company.

It takes a lot of faith to climb a mountain! But it takes just as much faith to climb down.

Can your walk of faith carry you through your golden years, down the sunset trail, to the very end, with joy in your spirit? Yes, it is possible with Christ as your guide.

Jesus knew how to bow out gracefully. After paying the price, making the sacrifice, and shedding His redemptive life's blood on the cross, He left His earthly life with the words, "It is finished" (John 19:30). He had completed the job He was sent to do.

> **Simeon's words are a promise to all who never yield to the temptation to wrestle their destiny out of the hands of the sovereign and merciful God. You and I, like Simeon, will come to the end of life with pride behind us, love around us, and hope ahead of us. That is bowing out gracefully.**

Facing death unafraid

"For God so loved the world that He gave His only begotten Son, that whoever believes in Him should not perish but have everlasting life."—JOHN 3:16

Can you handle the prospect of thinking about your own **357** death? Does your mortality depress you or frighten you? Then deal with this fear forthrightly and deal with it now. For the fear of death is the mother of all other fears.

Once you have destroyed the fear of death, you have slain the ultimate dragon that would devour your soul of its peace and the power that comes from a peaceful mind.

What is death anyway? It is a transition. Every person lives three lives. The first life is nine months long. Then we die. Yes, birth is a process of dying to a world we've known for nine months. But it's also the process of being born.

When we live our second life, the soul is prepared within the womb of the body to be born out of this body into eternity! And eternity is life where consciousness surpasses the consciousness of this earthly plane in the same way that consciousness in my life today transcends my consciousness while I was still in my mother's womb!

So death is a transition. Death does not have to be anything to fear. The only thing to fear is hell. And God offers to every person the promise of heaven if we will only accept His Son, Christ Jesus, to be our guide across the chasm between time and eternity.

> **Why am I so sure that when I die I will step, not into a thunderstorm, but into the sunlight? Because Jesus Christ is my Savior and my Friend.**

Today I ask you to take the greatest leap of faith confronting the prospect of your death. Accept God's promise of salvation.

Immortalizing yourself—forever

"I am the resurrection and the life. He who believes in Me, though he may die, he shall live."—JOHN 11:25

358   Human beings of all ages and all cultures have gone to all lengths to try to achieve immortality.

For instance, I recently visited an apartment building where there was a bronze plaque in the entrance bearing the title: First President of the Homeowners Association.

Don't misunderstand me. The desire to want to be immortal should not be condemned! For when a person says, "I don't care if anybody remembers me," more often than not he or she suffers from a negative self-image. It is normal, natural, and basically healthy for a person to want to be immortalized.

The inclination to achieve immortality is honorable. The universal instinctive hunger for immortality is God—implanted! Respect and respond to this human hunger. The problem is, how do we go about achieving immortality?

Our faith holds the perfect pathway to immortality.

It tells us that we shall achieve immortality in the imperishableness of this human soul. Go back and read John 3:16. Reread again and again the Bible verse of today.

We are told that if we believe in Jesus Christ, though we may die, we shall live!

I believe that! Because I believe that Jesus Christ arose from the dead. He is alive today. He has experienced the transition from mortality to immortality! And He wants to bestow that same incomparable treasure to you, today!

Thank You, God, for giving me the gift of immortality! I accept Your promise of eternal life. I know You will keep Your promises. Amen.

FAITH IS . . .
Parting company hopefully

"Go therefore and make disciples of all the nations. . . ; and lo, I am with you always."—
MATTHEW 28:19–20

Negative thinking is so widespread in our society that our entire vocabulary is permeated with negative-thinking clichés.

359

Today, replace a negative-thinking farewell phrase with a positive send-off!

This past year I've been trying to change a very popular phrase that appears harmless enough, but in reality is far too negative. It is the parting comment, "Take care!"

Can you imagine the mental climate that is created when tens of millions of people repeat over and over again, many times a day, the words "Take care"?

After all, the subconscious mind doesn't make judgments. Rather, it accepts the recorded negative directive as an order to be fulfilled! Little by little, those words subtly take over our thinking.

Programmed to be cautious, and avoid risk, we reticently approach the next opportunity subconsciously programmed for *caution*, rather than *courage*.

Here is the truth:

People who take care never go anywhere.

When positive-thinking people part company, they *don't* say, "Take care"; they say, "Take a chance and take charge!"

Can you imagine God's saying to Christ before He was sent from heaven to earth on His saving mission, "Take care, My Son"?

Can you imagine God's saying to you as you catch His dream, "Take care, My child"?

Our Lord's final farewell was not a cautious, tender good-by. It was a courageous challenge to go into all the world and make disciples "of all the nations," and then a promise, "I am with you always."

Impressing others

"Let all that you do be done with love."—
1 CORINTHIANS 16:14

360 A quarrelsome, crotchety woman made an awful scene on a city bus. As she stepped off the bus, she threw a parting insult to the driver. Just before he closed the door, he called out to her, "Lady, you left something behind!"

She stopped abruptly on the sidewalk, turned around, and asked, "Oh, what?"

"A very bad impression!" the driver said, as he closed the door.

Longfellow's words impressed me when I was a little boy in school.

> *Lives of good men all remind us*
> *that we can make our lives sublime*
> *and in departing leave behind us*
> *footprints on the sands of time.*

What the world needs today is a good impression of the human family. What unbelieving people need is a good impression of Christians! What negative-thinking people need is a good impression of positive thinkers.

Faith puts our life on a path that guarantees us we can leave a good impression behind! And that is important. In the process we inspire others to live life on a loftier level!

That means that you and I have a fantastic opportunity today to be cheerful, optimistic, encouraging, hopeful, thoughtful, and beautiful human beings! In the process we'll leave a wonderful impression behind. Let's be wonderful walking advertisements for Jesus Christ!

And people will admit, "If that is what Christianity is, I want it!"

Preparing to live to be one hundred

"Indeed, You have made my days as handbreadths,/And my age is as nothing before You."—PSALM 39:5

If you are walking the walk of faith, you should be planning to live to one hundred years of age! I am! I'm planning and hoping to live to be one hundred. Then what? Then I'll write a book entitled *How to Set Your Goals When You Are One Hundred Years Old.*

361

At the time of the writing of this book, there are over thirty thousand centenarians in America.

Meanwhile, good physical exercise, proper nutrition, vitamins, a wise diet, coupled with the power of positive faith—to say nothing of continued medical developments—all add up to the very real possibility that you may live to be one hundred!

"I don't want to live that long," one negative thinker said to me. "And spend the last 5-10-or 15 years feeble, senile, and a burden on others."

"Shame on you!" I scolded. "Think possibilities! You can—if you live, eat, exercise, pray and think right. Be peppy, bright, keen, until the end. My grandfather was—and he lived into his ninety-seventh year! Don't cheat yourself on years of life—or life in those years!"

Not being prepared to live to be one hundred is to be controlled by a lack of faith!

Doubt tells you that you are getting old and you ought to give up and simply die. If you are eighty years old, get excited about your future. When you are one hundred years old you'll look back and say, "I wish I had realized how young I was when I was eighty years of age. If only I had known I had a fifth of a century still ahead of me!"

If you are walking the walk of faith today, you will indeed prepare yourself to live to be one hundred! What goals do you have today? What good do you still want to accomplish? Imagine yourself being alive, awake, active, alert, and enthusiastic until the end—and your faith will make it so!

FAITH IS . . .
Renewing your strength

"Those who wait on the LORD shall renew their strength;/They shall mount up with wings like eagles."—ISAIAH 40:31

362   Are you bored? Tired of life? Do you feel burned out? Today's walk of faith gives four steps to renew your strength and fly high naturally through God-given dreams that generate energy, excitement, and enthusiasm. The steps are:

1. Don't **sigh.** If today is difficult, don't feel sorry for yourself, sighing, "Why me?" Sighing only saps strength. Rather, ask the right question: "Why not me?" Why do you think you should be exempt from the trying human experiences that challenge you to be tough and courageous?

2. Do **try.** Yes, you can make it anyway! You are loaded with mental powers! You can go anywhere from where you are today, when you T-R-Y!

T—*Trust God.* He will give you an idea that will appear absolutely impossible. That's probably a sure sign that it comes from Him.

R—*Reach out to Him.* He will give guidance to you and to others for support.

Y—*Yield your life to God's Holy Spirit.* He will give you the power to move surely and successfully.

3. Do **buy.** Buy the idea that you can be a successful person just as well as anybody else. Don't let this challenge pass you by. Grab it. Pay the price. Look for no shortcuts. Seek no easy solutions to your problems.

4. You will **FLY!** You will be renewed. You can mount up with wings like an eagle. You will fly high over disappointments that normally ground you. Faith is flying high—God's way—with dreams, not drugs.

This is God's minute. Pause to pray. Open your mind. Ask Him for a dream. He will renew your strength.

Decide to do something positive today, and you will mount up on wings of faith!

FAITH IS . . .
Shielding, fielding, and wielding!

" 'Surely God is in you,/And there is no other;/
There is no other God.' "—ISAIAH 45:14

What triumphant power there is in faith! Look what a **363**
tough-minded faith you have!

1. Faith provides *shielding power.* Shield your mind from
the negative thoughts by affirming:

• I have broken free from the tyranny of past mistakes, sins,
and errors.

• I no longer react to great ideas with the "impossibility
complex."

• I am in love with myself, with life, with the Lord, and
with other human beings.

• I find that this perfect love casts out all fear.

2. Faith provides *fielding power.* Now use this faith-power
to field the opportunities around you. Affirm:

• I gather the opportunities. When I was a child, I had
dreams of finding lots of nickles and dimes on the ground or
in the grass. That childhood dream has become a reality!

• I search for opportunities to grow, to study, to develop possibilities all around me!

3. Faith provides *wielding power.* Wow! How wonderful
this possibility-thinking faith works! You are *shielded* from
the negative thoughts that tell you it won't work. Immediately you begin to *field* the opportunities, and now you
wield leadership.

Take command!

Set goals!

4. Faith provides *yielding power.* Faith gives you the freedom to take control. Affirm:

• I will *not yield* to any negative persons the right to make
the decisions that affect my future.

• I yield my life to the lordship of Jesus Christ, the greatest
possibility thinker of all time!

• I am abiding in Him, and He is abiding in me. Today, I
stand stronger and taller than I did when I first stepped foot on
this walk of faith!

FAITH IS . . .
Starting—and then starting over and over again

"Love never fails"—1 CORINTHIANS 13:8

364   Yes, faith gives you the power to conquer your biggest problem: getting started!

The hardest part of any project is beginning. The gravitational pull of negative emotions is a powerful force to keep us from launching out.

Did you remember this lesson in our earlier writings? *The person who starts can never be a total failure.* At least he succeeded in overcoming his inertia. He did not fail to try!

Faith gets you started because it assures you that this is the one battle you cannot lose. Starting is winning now! Your job today is to get started, today—at least—you will be a success! For you will win over the fear of beginning!

Which means you have conquered your fear of trying. You have overcome your fear of failing. You have exercised initiative and have taken leadership over your own destiny. You have broken free from mental chains that have bound you. You have snapped the handcuffs that the enemy of negative thinking has clamped around you. So getting started guarantees you success *today!* Will you succeed every day?

And when you don't succeed? Then what do you do? You start over again! My first book, "Move Ahead with Possibility Thinking" was rejected by several publishers, but I didn't lose faith! Finally, it was picked up, and my writing career was launched.

It's exciting to think of this thrilling freedom that is yours! You have the freedom to start over again right after you have had a failure! Have you had a failure in your educational program? In personal relationships? In your walk with the Lord? Have you slipped and stumbled on this path of faith! Faith simply tells us that we can start—and start over again!

That's why we can declare: Faith never fails!

FAITH IS . . .
Admiring what works

"Now thanks be to God who always leads us in triumph in Christ."—2 CORINTHIANS 2:14

I saw a fantastic saying on a bumper sticker: "If it works, **365** don't fix it." Yes, if it works, don't tamper with it. Don't re-organize a successful operation just to "make your own mark." Don't reject a great tradition just because you want "something new." Be sure of this—if anything lived long enough to become a tradition there must be something good in it. Does it work? If so *mind it, don't mend it.* For you might do more meddling than mending.

There is always the danger that our ego will get involved. We will be tempted to redesign a workable plan to fit our style only to find out it doesn't work as well.

Admire good ideas that work—even if you didn't think of it first. Don't be too proud to imitate somebody who is doing a better job than you are. After all it has been said that imitation is the most sincere compliment you can give.

- Hitch your wagon to a star.
- Follow a leader.
- Listen to the winner.

Faith is admiring what works. This gives you the clue as to how faith liberates you from ego involvement in your judgment of other persons, projects, procedures, and positions. Faith saves you from rejecting ideas simply because *you* didn't think of them!

> **People who walk the walk of faith never suffer from a lack of inner spiritual resources. They have enough faith to look honestly at what's happening, to admire what works.**

Compliment the achiever—even if he's your competitor. You will be walking the walk of faith on a higher elevation than most people ever dream of reaching.

Leaping into the unknown

"So he, leaping up, stood and walked and
entered the temple with them—walking,
leaping, and praising God."—ACTS 3:8

366   Faith is often called a "leap." How appropriate! How else
could you possibly move from one point to another when
there is no direct link?

How do you cross over a crevice when there is no bridge?
Faith is leaping across gaps that exist between
> the known and the unknown
> the proven and the unproven
> the actual and the possible
> the grasp and the reach
> the "I've got it" and the "I want it"
> the knowledge and the mystery
> the material reality and the spiritual reality
> the truth exposed and the truth undiscovered
> the goals achieved and the goals still pursued
> youth and maturity
> sickness and health
> sin and forgivenness
> life and death
> time and eternity.

Yes, there is always a chasm between today and tomorrow. I
cannot be sure I can cope with tomorrow. But by a running
leap I will jump into tomorrow with expectancy! There is always a chasm between my present achievements and my unfulfilled hopes and dreams. By faith I make the leap—and
grow!

There is always a chasm between where I'm at and where
I'm going—by faith I make the leap forward!

What lies ahead? Tomorrow? Next week? Next month?
Next year? Beyond this life?

I believe in faith! I believe in believers! I believe in God! I
believe in Jesus Christ! I believe in tomorrow! I'm going to
take the leap of faith!